LIVES
THROUGH
THE
YEARS

LIVES THROUGH THE YEARS

*Styles of Life
and Successful Aging*

Richard H. Williams
Claudine G. Wirths

❧❀❧

FOREWORD BY TALCOTT PARSONS

Atherton Press
New York
1965

FOREWORD

❦

TALCOTT PARSONS
Harvard University

Lives Through the Years is clearly one of the most important contributions to the growing social science literature on the process of aging in American society. The subject has, of course, gained enhanced importance through the changing age-structure of the population; now some 9 per cent are over the mystic line of sixty-five and the proportion has, in spite of great increases in birth rates in the last twenty-five years, more than doubled in the course of the present century.

However its onset may be determined, as for example by occupational retirement, the final phase of the life cycle must acquire a special significance, since an increasing proportion of the population experience it, and do so in relatively good health. It is, furthermore, a period of considerable duration for a large majority, one may say, of cases.

The study reported in this volume is a continuation of that reported in the book *Growing Old* by Cumming and Henry. These authors put forward the important conception that *disengagement* was a central feature of the aging process in its social aspects. The present study develops a highly important set of refinements of the original version of this conception, in both empirical and theoretical respects. These refinements concern timing, which in terms of chronological age seems to be widely variable, distinctions among the modes of involvement *from* which disengagement takes place, and the possible range of attitudes which different people take, and styles of management they adopt, of the disengagement process. Disengagement then becomes not so much an empirical generalization as a theoretical focus for the analysis of the "action" problem of aging. This, documented as it is by a large body of case material which is also thoroughly analyzed in generalized terms, represents an important scientific advance.

One particularly appealing aspect of it is the leads this treatment gives toward defining possibilities of positive as well as negative changes in role and status which are correlated with the late phase of the life cycle. This is in line with the view that, for those who survive well into it, this terminal phase should have, within the American value system and social structure, a *consummatory* significance. It should be a period both of attaining new goals in the context of social relationships, and of receiving a new kind and level of rewards. There is, of course, the group which has looked forward from an early period to retirement and the enjoyment of its freedoms as a goal; for them the problem is relatively simple. But the conception that through flexibility it is not only possible, but relatively common, to develop alternatives to the main preoccupations of the "middle" years which are consistent with a continuing "style," and the way such possibilities are documented, is an important contribution to this problem.

The whole subject of aging is, of course, inseparable from that of the meaning of death in a society. The "aged" are, in the nature of the case, in a terminal phase of their lives, and must be oriented to that fact. It is particularly interesting and important that the authors find relatively little preoccupation with impending death, and still less evidence of "fear" of death. Fears, so far as they concern the individual himself and not his loved ones or impersonal causes with which his life has been bound up, center on disability rather than death. This clearly includes both capacity to continue to the end in what have become for the requisite age period the valued and appropriate activities, and unwillingness to "become a burden" to others. These findings seem to me to be important evidence for the view that American society is relatively realistic in its orientation to death. The well-known "denial" hypothesis would seem to imply a far greater underlying anxiety than the authors have found evidence for.

ACKNOWLEDGMENTS

The entire Kansas City Study of Adult Life has been a collaborative venture between the National Institute of Mental Health and the Committee on Human Development of The University of Chicago. The design and early phases of the study were developed jointly by the senior author, Professor William E. Henry, and Professor Martin Loeb, now Professor of Social Work at the University of Wisconsin. During the course of the study, the senior author has consulted primarily with Professor Henry, Professor Robert J. Havighurst, Professor Bernice Neugarten, and during the early phases of the study with Dr. Elaine Cumming, who was field director in Kansas City for a part of the study. The phase of the study reported in this book was developed independently by the senior author. However, he wishes to acknowledge the wise counsel and constructive criticism of Professors Henry, Havighurst, and Neugarten, and more recently, of Dr. Sheldon Tobin. Dr. Tobin has also furnished the authors with valuable statistical analyses to compare with their own analyses.

The authors also wish to express their appreciation to the many others who have participated in the Kansas City Study of Adult Life as a whole, and to the panel of respondents who cooperated with the study over a five-year period. Finally, they wish to note with thanks the services of Lucille Moore, whose work went far beyond the preparation of the manuscript.

CONTENTS

✦❀❀✦

TABLES AND CHARTS

Tables

Charts

LIVES
THROUGH
THE
YEARS

ONE

❧

Background
and Nature
of the Study

The social sciences have much to gain by the intensive study of individual lives over time. The present study, which is a part of the much larger Kansas City Study of Adult Life, is based on a close examination of the lives of one hundred sixty-eight elderly men and women interviewed and observed over a five and one-half year period. The data regarding this period have been supplemented by life history material, whenever available, in an effort to provide both longitudinal and retrospective views of every case.

This extended case study approach toward analyzing human behavior has been largely neglected since the early 1920's. William I. Thomas and Florian Znaniecki's *The Polish Peasant in Europe and America*[1] provided a good example of its use at that time. More recently, interest has revived somewhat with the production of such books as *The Study of Lives*, edited by Robert W. White,[2] *Schizophrenic Women*, by Harold Sampson, Sheldon L. Messinger, and Robert D. Towne,[3] and *The Work Careers of Mental Patients: Eight Portraits*, by Ozzie Simmons.[4] The latter two books were also based on col-

[1] William I. Thomas and Florian Znaniecki, *The Polish Peasant in Europe and America*, 5 volumes (Chicago: University of Chicago Press, 1918–1920).

[2] Robert W. White (ed.), *The Study of Lives* (New York: Atherton Press, 1963).

[3] Harold Sampson, Sheldon L. Messinger, and Robert D. Towne, *Schizophrenic Women: Sudies in Marital Crisis* (New York: Atherton Press, 1964).

[4] Ozzie G. Simmons, *The Work Careers of Mental Patients: Eight Portraits* (New York: John Wiley & Sons, 1965).

1

laborative studies with the National Institute of Mental Health, in which the senior author of the present study had some participation.

During the course of this work, two key concepts have emerged and been refined. One is a new concept of successful aging, which is derived primarily from the theory of action as developed by Talcott Parsons. The other, which emerged empirically from the research data, is the concept of styles of life. Six styles of life have been identified and discussed in this study.

The senior author first outlined this latter concept in "Styles of Life and Successful Aging" in Volume I of *Processes of Aging*.[5] That study was based on twenty cases, with six rounds of interviewing over a three and one-half year period. Both authors prepared "Styles of Life and Successful Aging, II" for presentation at the International Congress of Gerontology in Copenhagen, Denmark, in August of 1963. That step in the study was based on sixty-three cases that had had the life history interview by the clinical psychologist, and interviews with significant others. The present study is based on one hundred sixty-eight cases, or all panel members who were left to complete round seven of the regular interviews, and hence, who had been studied over a five and one-half year period (a four and one-half year period for respondents in their seventies and eighties).

CONCEPTS, MEASUREMENTS, AND THEORIES OF SUCCESSFUL AGING

Five main frames of reference, central to the Kansas City Study, have been used in addition to one we developed independently. Each one can be converted into a view of successful, or optimal, aging:

1. *Social life space.* From the beginning of the Kansas City Study, there has been considerable interest in, and data gathered concerning the structural properties of, the social life space of the respondents and their modes of interaction within it.[6] The measurements developed are

[5] Richard H. Williams, "Styles of Life and Successful Aging," in Richard H. Williams, Clark Tibbitts, and Wilma Donahue (eds.), *Processes of Aging*, Vol. I (New York: Atherton Press, 1963), pp. 335–371; and Richard H. Williams and Claudine G. Wirths, "Styles of Life and Successful Aging, II," presented at the International Gerontological Research Seminar, Markaryd, Sweden, August 1963.

[6] Richard H. Williams, "Changing Status, Roles and Relationships," in Clark Tibbitts (ed.), *Handbook of Social Gerontology* (Chicago: University of Chicago Press, 1960), pp. 261–297; and Richard H. Williams and Martin B. Loeb, "The Adult Social Life Space and Successful Aging," presented at the annual meeting of the Gerontological Society, Chicago, 1956.

the scores for activity in eleven roles—worker, family (parent, grand-parent, kin, spouse, and homemaker), and community (club member, citizen, friend, neighbor, church member—indices of the number of people with whom the respondent interacts, and scales relating to use of leisure time. These data may be used in relation to a view of successful aging which holds that the basic values for older people are values found for all age groups which stress maintaining a rather large life space and being very active in it. Life space, as defined by Kurt Lewin, is: "The entire set of phenomena constituting the world of actuality for a person or group of persons."[7] To age successfully, in this sense, precaution should be taken against shrinkage of the life space, and substitute activities and relationships should be found when necessary.

2. *Disengagement.* The theory of disengagement holds that intrinsic to aging is a process of mutual severing of ties between the individual and the social system in which he lives, reduced normative control by his social system, and reduced obligations to it.[8] The process may have its main impetus from within the individual in relation to his personality and ego needs, or from parts or all of his social system. Its forms can differ by sex, class, and culture. It can occur in different segments of a person's system of action, and at different rates in different segments. The same measures mentioned above may be used in relation to disengagement, especially when they are taken over time. More psychological measures may also be used, such as ego energy and ego style.[9] This theory can be converted to a view of successful, or optimal, aging by holding that to age successfully, a person must be prepared to cope with disengagement and, hence, maintain a better balance in relation to an ultimately inevitable process.

[7] H. B. English and Ava Champney English, *A Comprehensive Dictionary of Psychological and Psycho-analytical* Terms (New York: Longmans, Green and Co., 1958).

[8] The most formal statement of the theory of disengagement is given by Ernest Damianopolous, in Elaine Cumming and William E. Henry, *Growing Old* (New York: Basic Books, 1961), Chapter XII, pp. 210–218. It has been further elaborated by William E. Henry in "The Theory of Intrinsic Disengagement," presented at the International Gerontological Research Seminar, Markaryd, Sweden, August 1963, and by Elaine Cumming in "Further Thoughts on the Theory of Disengagement," *International Social Science Journal, 15,* 3, 1963, 377–393.

[9] Robert J. Havighurst, Bernice L. Neugarten, and Sheldon S. Tobin, "Disengagement and Patterns of Aging," presented at the International Gerontological Research Seminar, Markaryd, Sweden, August 1963.

3. *Life satisfaction.* Robert J. Havighurst and his colleagues have developed a concept and measurements of life satisfaction in direct relation to a view of successful aging. "The basic definition of successful aging was: a person is aging successfully if he feels satisfied with his present and past life."[10] Scales were developed and applied to the panel at two times, together with an index of change. For present purposes we wish to emphasize that life satisfaction need not be viewed as a theory of successful aging. It is possible to look at life satisfaction as a measured attribute of a given subject, as we shall do, and then see its relation to degree of successful aging as defined in some other way.

4. *Personality type.* Several approaches to personality type have been used in the total study. William E. Henry, in *Growing Old,* delineated five types for men (focused active mastery, achievement doubt, adaptive retreat, fixed conformity, and ego defect), and five types for women (externalized personal mastery, internalized passive mastery, externalized domination, internalized rigidity, and externalized ego defect).[11] These types were derived from an analysis of TAT protocols, with an emphasis on affect control. William Crotty made judgments relating essentially to degree of maturity, based on intensive life history interviews. David L. Gutmann developed four types: active mastery, passive mastery, constricted, and magical mastery (or defective). Havighurst, Bernice L. Neugarten, and Sheldon S. Tobin are currently using four types in their development of patterns—the integrated, unintegrated, armored-constricted, and passive dependent. In each case, a value judgment can be used to convert these concepts into a view of successful aging, whereby successful aging is associated with mature and integrated personalities; this was done explicitly in another study, by Suzanne Reichard, in terms of patterns of adjustment to aging.[12]

5. *Patterns of aging.* Havighurst, Neugarten, and Tobin have combined these frames of reference to derive patterns of aging. The derivation uses life satisfaction, social interaction, and personality type. If one placed a heavily weighted value judgment on any one of these three variables, one could derive three different theories of successful aging and compare them. Their present approach, however, appears to

[10] Robert J. Havighurst, "Successful Aging," in *Processes of Aging,* Vol. I, p. 305.

[11] Cumming and Henry, *Growing Old,* Chapter VI, pp. 106–127.

[12] Suzanne Reichard, Florine Livson, and Paul G. Petersen, *Aging and Personality: A Study of 87 Older Men* (New York: John Wiley & Sons, 1962).

place greatest weight in terms of value judgments on integration of personality, next greatest on life satisfaction, and least on amount of interaction. With this approach, four of their patterns represent relatively successful agers, three relatively unsuccessful, and one, "the disorganized," clearly unsuccessful.

CONCEPTUALIZATION DEVELOPED IN THE PRESENT STUDY

Social Systems of Individual Actors

Our interest in "social life space" has continued but has taken a different emphasis from the earlier formulations cited above. The term "social system" usually refers to a system of action of a plurality of actors, with no particular one as the primary focus. But the concept is also useful in relation to individual actors, and most appropriate in analyzing cases and life histories. As the senior author has stated elsewhere:

> A given actor, such as a respondent in the panel, can be taken as the focal point and questioned about the dimensions and structure of his social life space, modes of interaction in it, attitudinal set toward it, satisfaction or dissatisfaction he derives from it, and degree of its stability over time. This system should not be looked on or analyzed as a group qua group. Each actor in this system has his own social system. Ideally, data should be gathered from various points of the system and not solely from the individual actor, but they should be gathered with the point of view of the original actor as the focus. The researcher should get such data through interviews with significant others, direct observation, or instruments.[13]

This book is thus a study in microsociology, a somewhat neglected field.

The social system of the individual actor is a system of action, that is, behavior which is meaningful. Meaningful means oriented toward ends, goals, and values which, in turn, can be communicated to and usually shared in by others. Thus, it is composed of all the transactions of an individual in his social life space. We cannot attempt to describe the total concrete system. However, some parts of it are more salient than others, and, as a system, it has certain structural and functional properties which characterize large numbers of transactions over time.

[13] Williams, "Styles of Life and Successful Aging," p. 338.

Structural Properties

In the analyses which follow, we shall be concerned with three main sets of structural properties in the social systems of individual actors:

1. *Social position.* The actor's position in his social system is composed of the roles he plays in it, the status (esteem and prestige) he enjoys, the authority (legitimate exercise of power or influence) he has over others in the system, and his protected rights or the limits beyond which others cannot influence or interfere with his own actions. Two general characteristics of his position are the number of significant others with whom he interacts, and the amplitude of the system, that is, whether it is constricted and narrow, intermediate, or covers a broad range of interests and activities.

2. *Orientation to interaction.* Interactions may be functionally diffuse and related to living in general, as they tend to be in the family, or functionally specific and confined to a delimited purpose, as they tend to be in the business world. They may be affective and imply some emotional gratification, or emotionally neutral. Parsons has combined these two sets of orientations in what he has termed "the pattern variables."[14] Their application to the study of the aging process was first developed by Elaine Cumming and described as follows:

> 1. A diffuse-affective set toward interaction carries the expectation of potentially unlimited mutual obligation and affection, and the anticipated relational reward is unconditional acceptance, or *love.* The nuclear family is the ideal type.
>
> 2. A diffuse-neutral set toward interaction carries an expectation of potentially unlimited mutual obligation, but no expectation of mutual affection. The ideal type occurs in such goal-directed collectivity as a union, a charitable organization, or a fraternal order. The anticipated relational reward is *esteem,* and the tone is moral and evaluative.
>
> 3. The specific-affective set toward interaction carries the expectation of short-run gratification. The anticipated relational reward is *responsiveness* in the immediate situation. It occurs in any interaction undertaken purely for recreation; it can be called a hedonistic set.

[14] Talcott Parsons, *The Social System* (New York: The Free Press, 1958), p. 130.

4. The specific-neutral set toward interaction carries the expectation of adequate mutual performance toward a goal apart from the interaction itself; no emotional gratification is involved. The ideal type is work and the contractual world. The anticipated relational reward is *approval*.[15]

3. *Types of social relations.* Continuing interactions with other persons may be particularistic in the sense of involving obligations and norms focused on a particular "very special" person, such as husband or wife, or they may be universalistic, in the sense of involving obligations and norms applicable to all mankind or to broad categories of people, such as citizens or customers. They may contain many expressional or symbolic elements, or be confined to purely instrumental or intrinsic ones.

In general, particularistic relations tend also to be functionally diffuse and affective in orientation and to include various expressional elements, whereas universalistic relations tend to be functionally specific and emotionally neutral and to be largely confined to instrumental elements. Other combinations are possible, however, especially in relation to the diffuse-neutral and the specific-affective sets of orientations, which tend to fall in the middle of the universalism-particularism continuum and to contain an admixture of instrumental and expressional elements.

Functional Properties

The functional properties of these systems with which we shall be primarily concerned relate to certain characteristic uses of action energy. We are not implying any analogy with physics in using the term energy. We mean the capacity of acting. To act at all requires a basic minimum of physical or biological energy. A person who is in a coma cannot act. But, as the senior author has stated elsewhere, "one should also stress that within these limits set by biological conditions of action there are important sociopsychological (and normative) factors which act as highly important variables in the amount of energy and the level of performance which the actor will invest in a given course of action. Energy may be readily mobilized in a given direction or, on the other hand, it may be blocked off, bottled up, and immobilized by anxiety."[16]

[15] Elaine Cumming, Lois R. Dean, David S. Newell, and Isabel McCaffrey, "Disengagement—A Tentative Theory of Aging," *Sociometry, 23,* 1, 1960, 32–33.

[16] Richard H. Williams (ed.), *Human Factors in Military Operations* (Chevy Chase, Md.: Operations Research Office, 1954), p. 26.

One way to view "mental health" is the adequacy with which action energy can be mobilized and put to use in ways meaningful to the self and to others. It is not possible to make precise measurements of the uses of action energy since we do not have standard units for this purpose. We are convinced that they can be estimated and rated in scientifically useful ways, and, in fact, such estimates are made frequently in everyday life, with varying degrees of validity and reliability. That they can usually be made with a fair degree of accuracy is one source of the stability of the social system; otherwise, expectations about one's own courses of action and the actions of others would be constantly shattered.

The uses which we have found especially important in relation to the analysis of the processes of aging are:

1. *Anomie,* as applied to large-scale social systems, such as whole societies,[17] refers to one of three major ways in which they may become disorganized or break down. "It represents a breakdown of motivating factors. There is a general listlessness of behavior. The tension level is too low. Little is accomplished and that quite sloppily. In extreme cases it is likely to be accompanied by a significant rise in the rates of suicide, alcoholism, and drug addiction."[18] (The other two ways in which systems break down are schism, where parts of the system split off from the rest, and generalized conflict with the limited case as "the war of all against all," or a generalized struggle for power.) As applied to the social system of the individual actor, anomie has a similar connotation, with emphasis on low level of mobilization of energy, and some disorganization in the use of energy which is mobilized.

2. *Alienation* refers to two reciprocally related tendencies, a tendency not to accept and participate in the norms and values of others in the individual's social system, and a tendency to antagonize others so that they withdraw behind barriers. The individual is thus alienated from his system and alienates others in it from himself.

3. *Isolation* refers to the situation in which the system has become constricted due to alienation. It does not refer to the size of the system or the absolute amount of interaction as such. One of the cases in Chapter 4 interacted with very few persons, and with them minimally, yet he was not an isolate in the sense used here. Alienation and isolation in the social system of the individual are similar to schism in large-scale systems; the individual becomes split off from parts of or sometimes most of his system. An individual can have a rather high degree of alienation and yet manage not to be very isolated, and, vice

[17] Emile Durkheim, *La Suicide* (Paris: Alcan, 1896).
[18] Williams, *Human Factors in Military Operations,* p. 34.

versa, a small amount of alienation may produce a high degree of isolation, depending on the characteristics and needs of the significant others. Hence, these two variables are rated separately.

4. *Coping* refers to the degree to which the individual can mobilize his action energy to realize his ends and expectations. It is best judged in crises, when the situation contains threats or barriers, and new courses of action are required.

5. *Clarity and saliency of style* refer to the functional set of the action system of the individual. They refer to a judgment concerning the clarity of the style itself, and not to the clarity with which the judgment can be made. This concept will be discussed again briefly below, but it is best seen in the direct context of the case studies.

Respondents have been rated on a three-point scale in relation to each of the five characteristic modes of use of action energy. A rating of 1 places the person toward the "good" end of the continuum, and a 3 places him toward the "bad" end. Thus, with anomie, alienation, and isolation, a rating of 3 indicates a high degree of the characteristic in question, whereas with coping and stylishness, a rating of 1 indicates a high degree of the characteristic.

One Approach to a Definition of Successful Aging

We have reviewed four ways in which successful aging has been viewed in the Kansas City Study of Adult Life: as indicated by the amount of activity in which the individual engages, his ability to disengage, his satisfaction with life, and the maturity or integration of his personality. The concept of the social system of the individual actor can be used to derive two additional views of successful aging which, in turn, can be combined to form one approach, just as Havighurst, Neugarten, and Tobin have combined the other four views of successful aging in another, and complementary, approach. The results of the two approaches can certainly be compared in relation to the same panel, and possibly they can be combined, a consideration to which we shall return in the concluding chapter.

The first view is in terms of exchange of energy between the individual and the rest of his social system. How much output of energy does he contribute to the significant others in his system, and how much input of energy from others does it take to keep him going? If he is in balance in this respect, or there is a plus value on the output side, he is said to be autonomous. If it takes more input from others to maintain him than he gives to them, he is said to be dependent. There is a qualitative aspect of the autonomy-dependency continuum which we cannot overlook. If the energy which does flow out from the individual to his significant others is used to frustrate or injure them, and thus prevent them from optimal mobilization of their own energy, we count it on the minus side, toward dependency. One could distinguish dependency and destructiveness analytically, but for the present purposes we have found it more useful to think of the single continuum of autonomy-dependency to express the total balance of energy. To be autonomous, a person must contribute to the system in terms of the goals and values of the significant others. With destructiveness, the input goes up, because others are pouring back energy to combat it.

This continuum can be applied to all of the basic requirements of action systems, such as wealth, or command over scarce means, power, or the ability to make decisions and influence others, recognition by others, and affective response from them. We give more weight to affective response than to other requirements because we have observed it to be more crucial to the total balance in the individual system. For example, if the subject is in balance on affective response, even a high degree of economic dependency on others is much less damaging to the system than if he is not, and, conversely, if he is out of balance on affective response, his total system can be dependent, even though he is economically autonomous.

The second view relates to a judgment concerning the stability of the system, including, especially, the stability of its position in relation to autonomy-dependency. What is its probable future course? Will it persist, change its characteristics significantly, or collapse? Some people seem pretty well set in their mode of life and their balance with others, and are not likely to change short of some catastrophic change in their conditions. Others are not nearly so well set, and the probability of change is great. It is conceivable that a person could be "precarious" by this definition because he was dependent but on the verge of becoming autonomous. Such instances are, however, probably extremely rare in this age group.

We have defined successful aging in relation to a combination of two aspects of success. If the over-all relation of the individual to his social system is both autonomous and persistent, he is aging successfully. If it is autonomous but precarious, he is aging less successfully. If it is dependent and persistent in dependency, he is aging still less successfully, and if it is dependent and precarious, he is least successful, while still having a system. Completely unsuccessful aging, in these terms, means collapse of the system, which will result in his becoming a public charge, or in institutionalization, or suicide.

The four major categories just described give a continuum from highly successful aging to the almost completely unsuccessful. We have found that we can make judgments placing panel members in the four categories and on one of three levels in each category, with a high degree of reliability between the two raters, as indicated below. Thus, we have a twelve-point scale of successful aging. The relations between the categories and the most likely directions of shift in categories are indicated in Chart 1.

Chart 1. Relation Between Categories of Success. Most likely directions of shift in success categories: broken lines indicate weak possibility, solid lines indicate strong possibility.

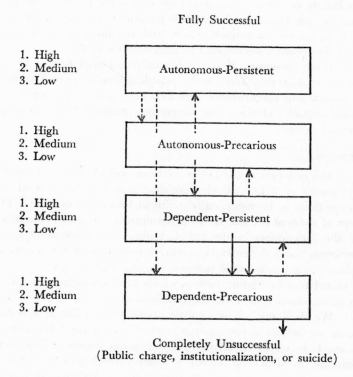

These judgments are made in relation to the individual's system of social action and must be clearly distinguished from two other types

of judgment. First, they are not judgments about the biological system
—health and probability of death—of the individual or of others in his
system. A person can be on his death bed and still be judged autonomous-persistent as far as his system of action is concerned, provided
he is not comatose. If he is comatose, he is not dependent-precarious
in our terms; he has simply ceased to act due to the biological conditions of his action system. On the other hand, a person's attitude
toward his health, and the way he uses the health which he has in his
transactions with others, are important. Similarly, if the most significant other of the respondent is his wife, and he is in a dependent
relationship to her, his system is more precarious if she is in a terminal
illness than if she is not.

Second, the judgments are made about the social system of the individual and not about the wider societies in which he lives, such as
his family or community. The family as a group could be quite precarious, yet the individual quite persistent, or vice versa, although
such instances are probably rare, and the broader systems generally
have significant influence on the individual's system.

These concepts are stated formally and analytically. We believe,
however, that they have some practical significance. The more dependency and precariousness are associated with the aging process, the
more resources of the wider society are demanded to deal with problems of aging.

Styles of Life

The concepts defined thus far have been developed formally from
the theory of action. Their empirical aspect is simply that we have
found them to be analytically useful in looking at our data. The concept of styles of life was developed empirically from the intensive study
of the individuals in the panel. Unlike the concepts of autonomy-
persistence and dependency-precariousness, style of life is not, as such,
related to a definition of successful aging. Rather, it has proved to be
a useful tool in finding factors which produce or influence successful
or unsuccessful aging as we have defined it.

We shall say relatively little about style of life at this time, because we believe it can emerge most clearly in the full context of the
cases. It is a general attribute of the social system of individuals, essentially the structural set of the system, which governs the areas and
degree of major investment and involvement. Style can be most readily
judged when the individual is faced with major decisions, and particularly if the decisions involve conflicts between two areas of life,

such as work and family. Each style has its characteristic structural properties, especially in relation to orientation to interaction and types of social relationships.

We have delineated six styles, as indicated in the titles of the next six chapters, and believe they are exhaustive of all styles, at least for this panel of respondents. At one point we considered adding a seventh style, called "Struggling Through Life With Maximum Frustration," but then we were convinced that this reflected a set of circumstances within which some of the respondents lived and that each of them did have one of the six basic styles.

We are also convinced that everyone develops a primary style, although some develop it strongly and some only weakly. We have, therefore, used the variable "clarity and saliency of style" as one of the characteristic modes of use of action energy, and have rated each respondent on a three-point scale in this respect. Styles in individual social systems are an important factor in meeting a basic requirement of all social systems, a reasonably stable framework of expectations about the behavior of others.

Each respondent has been given a "name," or descriptive designation. This procedure was used for two reasons. First, the designations are intended to convey the range of variations within a style, and various contents of the style. Second, we shall have frequent occasion to make references to cases already analyzed, for comparative purposes or special analyses. We have found it far easier to remember the nature of each case by descriptive title than by number. The writers do not know the actual names of the respondents, nor would they use them if they did.

The Reliability of the Judgments

The two authors each read the same twenty cases without discussing them in any way. On the basis of all the relevant evidence in each case, judgments were made concerning eight variables or characteristics in each case. The two judgments of each case were classed as being identical, near, or apart.

1. *Style.* Identical meant that the person was classed in the same style. Near meant that we both agreed that is was Familism, Couplehood, or Living Fully on the one hand, or World of Work, Living Alone, or Easing Through Life With Minimal Involvement, on the other hand. Apart meant crossing from one of these two general categories of style to the other.

2. *Success category.* Identical meant placed in the same success

category, near meant one category away, and apart meant two or three categories away.

3. *Success ranking.* Identical meant exactly the same rank within the twelve ranks, near meant one rank away, and apart meant two or more ranks away.

4. *Anomie.* This feature was rated 1 to 3, with near meaning one point apart.

5. *Alienation.* Same.

6. *Isolation.* Same.

7. *Coping.* Same.

8. *Clarity and saliency of style.* Same.

After we had compared our judgments on each of these eight variables and discussed the cases, we made our own global judgment concerning whether we had viewed the case in an identical way or in nearly the same way. (As it turned out, we considered that we were not far apart on any case.) The results are indicated in Tables 1 and 2.

Table 1.   Reliability Check: Results by Number of Cases

Variable	*Identical*	*Near*	*Apart*
Style	11	7	2
Success Category	13	6	1
Success Ranking	11	9	
Anomie	12	8	
Alienation	14	6	
Isolation	16	4	
Coping	14	6	
Saliency of Style	9	7	4
Global	15	5	

Table 2.   Significance of Agreement*

Variable	X^2	*P*
Style	24.04	P < .001
Success Category	18.73	P < .001
Success Ranking	79.11	P < .001
Anomie	8.80	.01 < P < .025
Alienation	13.45	.001 < P < .005
Isolation	20.20	P < .001
Coping	13.45	.001 < P < .005
Saliency of Style	1.25	Not significant

* The test of significance was made by Dr. Sam Greenhouse, Section on Theoretical Statistics and Mathematics, Biometrics Branch, NIMH.

It should be noted, in particular, that the three most important judgments in terms of the general theory being developed—style, success category, and success ranking—reached a level of significant agreement with $P < .001$.

The lack of significance of agreement in our judgments about clarity and saliency of style is largely attributable to a small amount of disagreement on style itself. Three of the four cases of judgments "apart" on clearness of style were due to this factor. Once this matter had been clarified by sharper definition, we immediately agreed on degree of clarity and saliency of style. This would have given us a distribution of twelve identical, seven near, and one apart, which would be significant at $P < .05$. The same factor affected three of the seven "near" judgments. When that was clarified, we had a distribution of fifteen identical, four near, and one apart, which is significant at $P < .001$. We were then confident that our judgments about clarity and saliency of style were reliable.

This process served not only to indicate the reliability of our judgments but, in the few cases where there was some apparent disagreement, also to clarify our differing conceptualizations and thereby eliminate the basis of the disagreement.

TWO

❧❦❧

World of Work

The centrality of the World of Work and the role of worker in American culture has been frequently mentioned. Similarly, retirement has frequently been claimed to be a central problem in the aging process, perhaps its most important crisis of transition. And yet, as a style of life, as judged by orientation, values, and the ways decisions were made, the World of Work appeared in only twenty-five of the cases in this panel, or less than one-sixth. When it did appear, it tended to appear very clearly; twenty-two of the twenty-five were rated 1 on degree of style, one was rated 2, and two were rated 3. As might be expected, more men than women had this style, but the degree of sex difference was rather surprising—twenty to five. Many of the women in this panel worked, but in only five cases did work become their style of life.

On the whole, panelists who had this style were aging rather successfully, but this is true of the panel as a whole. Six were rated autonomous-persistent 1, and fifteen of the twenty-five fell into the autonomous-persistent category. There was a somewhat greater tendency for persons with this style to be autonomous-precarious than for persons with other styles—seven, or almost one-quarter of them. None was dependent-persistent, a success category that appears antithetical to this style. Two were dependent-precarious and clearly unsuccessful.

NOTE: Case titles have been carefully selected to enable the reader to remember the cases easily whenever they are referred to in the book. The titles also suggest different nuances within the style of life and, in some cases, the orientation to action. Some titles have been taken from the respondents' own descriptions of themselves. No disrespect to anyone is intended by any title.

THE MOST SUCCESSFUL AGERS

The Contented Salesman

This sixty-year-old man was a wholesale traveling salesman. He was unmarried and lived with his eighty-seven-year-old mother and an eighty-two-year-old aunt, who did practically all of the household chores. He did some of the shopping, but disliked it. He had had a grammar school education, and was in social class 3.

In June of 1956, he enjoyed traveling and mentioned the main problem of old people as being lonely because they could not travel around. He commented that many people are considered old before they really are because of early retirement. He expected to retire in five years because of company policy and said he would like to open a small business on a lake in the Ozarks, where he could still work and enjoy his hobby of fishing. He was on the road half of the time. When in Kansas City, he used his home as his office, came home early, and did the little office work required. He was not a recluse and had many friends on the road. His brother and brother's family visited about once a week. He loafed on Saturdays or went to the Ozarks to visit friends and to fish. He belonged to four organizations, but was on the road so much that he rarely attended meetings.

In April of 1957, there were no changes in his mode of living. But in March of 1958, we found he had changed jobs at the age of sixty-two, although he was close to retirement and had worked with the same company for twenty-six years. He took a reduced retirement income and gambled on making good in another job, selling somewhat different equipment and selling only in Kansas City. He stated strongly that he disliked the idea of retirement, that it would be his own decision, and that he would continue to work as long as he was able. He seemed very satisfied.

In December of 1958, his aunt had died, but otherwise there were no changes. He seemed to miss traveling somewhat, but was quite happy and doing well in his new job. Work was mentioned as the most important thing in his life.

In August 1959, we found the situation unchanged. His ninety-year-old mother was still keeping house. He had always lived with his mother. He indicated that he was very satisfied with his way of life and would not change it. He was earning a salary, had a few investments, and some retirement income from his former job.

One of the questions used in this round of interviews read:

Mr. Jones worked for a large corporation. He was doing fairly well, had bought a nice home in the suburbs, and was able to give his family everything they wanted. At the end of the working day, Mr. Jones would look forward to an evening at home with his wife and family, tinkering in his workshop, or reading aloud in front of the fire. One day Mr. Jones' boss told him that he was in line for a major promotion. The new job would mean that Mr. Jones would run an entire department and would have much more salary. But the new job would keep him on the road a lot, sometimes for weeks at a time. Having given him the facts, Mr. Jones' boss asked for a decision. What did Mr. Jones say to his boss? Why?

We have found answers to this question to be rather consistently related to other clues concerning style of life. In this instance, the respondent said that Jones would take the job without any hesitation.

In February 1960, things were still the same. He again talked of how he had always liked his work. He would also like to own a resort on a lake. He liked being sixty-four, with the security he had achieved. If he had his life to live over, he said that he would get a little more education and would start a savings account earlier in life (so he could buy that resort on the lake). He would not marry "under the same circumstances." The meaning of this last statement became clear in an interview with the clinical psychologist in September of 1960. The best time of his life was in the early twenties when he was "sowing his wild oats." Then he became so involved with his work on the road that before he knew it, "it was too late to marry." Although he had lived with his mother all his life, he was never a "mother's boy" nor was he oriented to family. In fact, by this time he was expressing some irritation at the increased responsibility for his mother and would have liked to be freer. The psychologist found him to be a man whose values centered in honesty, integrity, and hard work.

In January 1962, things were still the same, although he had changed companies again, this time because the company had gone out of business. He was very proud of the fact that, when his former company sold out, he, at the age of a little over sixty-five, was one of three selected to go to the new company. He had found the new company very satisfactory. He was generally satisfied with life and said he "slept like a baby." By this time, he had lost interest in traveling. He did not see as many friends as when he had been on the road, but this did not bother him. He had given up swimming, but retained his hobbies of watching baseball and football games and of fishing.

This respondent is very clearly a pure case of the World of Work style. He also well illustrates that the style, as such, does not imply the "grim" world of work. For him it was a very pleasant world which he had always enjoyed and which he would continue to enjoy as long as he was physically able.

He was also one of the most successful agers within this style. His exchange of action energy with others—his mother, his few friends, and his customers—was relatively low, but clearly in balance, and in that sense he was fully autonomous. He could continue indefinitely in balance as far as his action system is concerned. He was easily rated 1 on all of his characteristic uses of action energy; there was no indication of anomie, alienation, or isolation. He coped extraordinarily well and developed a very clear style of life. He already showed some signs of disengagement without difficulty, and further disengagement would be no problem. He might well retire gradually and had managed to maneuver himself into a position where he could do so, since on his last job during the study he was working on a straight commission basis and did not face compulsory retirement.

Beyond the World of Work

This eighty-two-year-old man lived alone in a low-rent housing project. He grew up on a farm and thought of his childhood as the best time in his life. He remembered and admired his mother as a "true Christian," and said that he had been a good boy. He thought of his father as a rural man, active in civic affairs and the church. During his childhood and young adulthood he looked up to "honest people in high office" and to an uncle who became a prominent lawyer. However, he himself was unable to obtain an education and got into construction work, first on an unskilled basis; he later held various semiskilled and, probably, skilled jobs in this same field. It was a long life of hard work. He did not like retirement at first but had not been working for about ten years and was now used to it. At the beginning of the study he was living on social security and old-age assistance. He had four sons, one daughter, and nine grandchildren.

In July of 1958, his wife was in the hospital with cancer, and he visited her there as often as he could. A son had asked him to come to Florida to live with him, but he was not sure that he would. His day was spent in sitting around, watching TV, listening to the radio, and having a little company. He went to church on Sunday when possible.

His daughter visited him fairly regularly, and he saw the son in Florida a few times a year. He said he was satisfied with his children and saw his grandchildren a few times a month.

In November of that same year he said that he was fine. His wife had died, but he was "managing all right" for himself. In fact, he said very little about his wife and appeared at this time not to show grief reactions. During this period he did quite a bit of visiting. He spent two or three days a week with people in the southern part of town and had visits with his children and friends. He wanted to keep active, and that was why he did so much visiting. The children in the housing project visited him fairly frequently and called him "Grandpa." He liked conversation and liked to debate both sides of issues "for the fun of it." He gave visiting, TV, and keeping up with the news of the world as the most important things in his life now.

In June 1959, he did not seem to be going out or visiting quite as much. The church was too far away for him to attend. He was thinking of moving so that he could see his relatives every day. One friend had died, and one was very sick. He missed both of them; they had played cards together. He emphasized, again, that older people needed more to do and said that he was much more satisfied with life when he was working.

In November of that same year, he mentioned two points in his life when he had made decisions which he somewhat regretted. Back in the early 1900's he had had an opportunity to buy some property and accumulate wealth. However, his wife did not wish to move, and so he decided against it. Later on, he had had an opportunity with a construction firm which would have required a great deal of traveling. Again he turned that down because his wife was opposed to it. It was clear that he regretted both decisions, but he insisted that they were his own.

In February of 1961, we found him in essentially the same situation. He had not moved, although he was thinking, again, of spending part of the winter in Florida with his son. His daughter came in to clean the apartment every other week. He said his children and grandchildren were in and out often. He spent about one weekend a month staying overnight in one of his children's homes. He had been having some financial difficulties but had managed to pay all of his debts and now felt a little more secure. In fact, he was able to go to a ball game occasionally. He stated that he liked to go to state fairs, movies, and musicals when he could afford it. He said that he had "never been choosy" about friends and had made friends with all kinds of people. He had formerly been active in fraternal organizations and unions. He said that he was lonesome, but seldom blue. Now he stated that his wife's death was very hard on him and that he missed her terribly. Again he emphasized that he could manage all right and was still enjoying life.

It is clear that this man's style was the World of Work. However, it is equally clear that he did not achieve the clarity or saliency of style that we found in the preceding case, and we have rated him 3 on this variable. This case is a particularly good illustration of the point made in Chapter One—that this variable has to do with the clarity of the style itself, rather than the clarity with which the judgment can be made. In the present case there is some tendency in the background toward Living Fully as a style. He was proud of having made friends with people in all walks of life and from various backgrounds. He regretted decisions that he felt would, if made, have permitted him to live much more fully. He was very much of an activist and insisted that older people should keep busy. However, he never quite achieved Living Fully as a style. An activistic orientation in retirement fits the World of Work as a style.

There is no doubt that he was autonomous-persistent toward the top of the scale. He "paid his debts," an attitude which went beyond purely economic matters and symbolized his relationships with others in general. His characteristic modes of use of action energy were all very much in order and have been given a rating of 1. Although he was a strong activist, he was a person who was able to accept a considerable amount of disengagement, due in this instance largely to physical limitations. He is another good example of a satisfied successful ager.

A Dreary Life

This sixty-one-year-old woman was a semiskilled worker in a small industry. She was married and had two sons. Her husband was a self-employed skilled worker who drove around looking for work and found it somewhat sporadically. Unlike most of the people on this panel, she looked older than her age, and gave the interviewer a distinct impression of chronic hardship and tiredness. She lived with her husband in a very old and shabby bungalow in which the television set looked quite incongruous.

In November of 1956, she said she would prefer to live in a smaller town. She did not like the traffic or the streetcar system but she *had* to work and would necessarily stay in the city. She would prefer to live in a more friendly neighborhood. She considered people of sixty and over to be old, which was rather unusual for this panel, and she certainly considered herself, at sixty-one, to be old.

Her daily round was one of hard work, a very short evening with a half-hour of television, and bed at 9 P.M. She was indeed too tired to do anything else. She had been working at the same job, with essentially the same daily round, for the past ten years. She usually worked a half-day on Saturday and spent the other half-day doing housework. By the end of the week she was so tired that she dreaded Sunday. She could not make it to church, but listened to church services on the radio and said that religion "meant everything" to her. One son and his wife usually visited about once a week. The other son had gone to a distant city—she was not sure which—and she had not heard from him in several years. She saw a sister in Kansas City occasionally and sometimes wrote letters to another sister.

In March of 1957, there were no essential changes. The husband sat at the kitchen table in the background—weak, spent, and beaten. The respondent said that he had not been working steadily over the winter and that he had been ill but was somewhat better. For a time she had had to stay home with him. She was worried about money matters. They had been trying to sell the house without success. She did find time to do some reading and particularly liked to read the Bible and Christian magazines. She was watching television somewhat more than on the preceding rounds. They could not afford a telephone and she felt generally cut off from social relationships.

In August of 1957, she mentioned wishing to hear from her older son and not knowing why she had not. She was on a labor committee at work. She said she sometimes felt young and sometimes old, depending on how tired she was from work.

In November of 1958, we learned that her husband had been sick "off and on," whereas her own health was still fairly good. Her husband had also been in an accident and was taken to court, and all this had cost a lot of money. He was now not allowed to drive a car. We then learned that her husband's illness was a serious case of alcoholism. He had started drinking again the previous July. One result was that they had no company at all on Sunday any more, and she felt particularly lonely. She mentioned having four grandchildren, but she had not seen them in five years; they were the children of the son who had dropped out of the picture for her.

In July of 1959, the husband was still there but ill. He required a lot of care. However, she was following the same old round of work.

She did manage now to go to church, because they had finally sold the house and moved into a more central location. However, she would really have preferred to live in the suburbs where she could have a garden and chickens because she liked being outdoors, but she realized that this dream was impossible. She now saw her Kansas City son about once a month. She mentioned that her son and his family had lived with her for a time, but that this did not work out well because "no matter how much I did, it was never enough."

During this interview the husband kept complaining in the background about the interview and threatened to call the police. The respondent was quite embarrassed by this behavior and apologized at length to the interviewer.

We found another one of the story questions to be quite indicative of this respondent's attitudes. The question read:

> Mrs. Birch is an attractive widow of about fifty-five, who is living alone and whose husband has left her well off financially. She has met a man of independent means who wants her to marry him. Mrs. Birch is undecided. Her daughter, who has recently gotten married herself, disapproves of the whole thing. She says to her mother: "Are you sure it's a good idea? You're doing all right by yourself, aren't you?" What does Mrs. Birch decide? Why?

This respondent thought Mrs. Birch would not marry to avoid the risk of a chronically ill husband.

In February of 1960, her general mode of life had still not changed and she was, as usual, very tired. But by December 1961 she had stopped working. She was still very tired. However, she missed her work badly and hoped to get back to work the following spring. She missed the contacts at work. Although her work was dreary, it was the only source of satisfaction she had.

She described her husband as still being ill. The son now came over on Sundays for dinner. She, of course, saw more of her husband now that she was at home but said she did not feel close to him. She had heard from the missing son the preceding year, but only because he needed money. She would have very much liked to "neighbor," but she had lived there for two years and nobody had come to see her. It was interesting to note that her answers to some of the questions indicated that she still thought of herself as working, even though for the time being she was not.

We do not have a life history interview by the clinical psychologist with this respondent. However, through the seven rounds of interviews, considerable detail emerged concerning the course of her life. She had had a rather poor start in life, mainly because her mother was away in a mental hospital while she was growing up. She was rather afraid of her father and was alone a lot; the house was frequently cold (she lived all her life in Kansas City), and she did not have decent meals. However, in the last interview, she said she looked back at ages six, seven, and eight as being a carefree and happy time when people were good to her, particularly a neighbor who frequently took her into her home, fed her, cleaned her, and made her warm. She obtained her first job at age twelve, probably on a part-time basis. She managed to get some high school education, but had to leave before she finished and was very disappointed by this because she had wanted to be a teacher. She mentioned the ages of eighteen to twenty-one, even though working, as being the best years of her life, when she was freer. She married at about that time, and at the age of twenty-five she lost her first baby. She had another baby, but shortly thereafter was separated from her husband due to his drinking. She took the child and did paid housework. After a few years her husband promised to stop drinking and came back. She had steady work at that time, and the husband went back to drinking. When she was forty-five, her husband had another period of serious drinking. She left him for a couple of days but then came back. She said she had frequently been tempted to "get away from this trouble," but, for the most part, had "stuck with it."

This respondent was a particularly good example of successful aging combined with great unhappiness. She kept on pouring out her action energy, at work, for her husband, and as much as possible for her son, without getting much in return—least of all, satisfaction. Her only style of life was the World of Work, and this she achieved very clearly. There was not much else in her life except an unhappy marriage to an alcoholic. For her, life was hard work, and she frequently expressed her belief in the moral value of work. Thus, whether or not she was employed toward the end made little difference in her style of life.

There was no sign of alienation. Her value system was quite conformist, centering on religion and morality, including the moral value of work, and she did not tend to alienate others. Others were alienated from her world due to her husband's alcoholism. There were some signs of personal emotional disorganization, at least of deep dejection; if we had been rating life satisfaction, as such, we would have rated it 3, but in terms of anomie we rated her 2. She was quite isolated, was rated 3 on that variable, and was rated 2 on coping. She was placed in the high success category because of her action usage.

THE LESS SUCCESSFUL AGERS

No Hobby Except My Work

When this seventy-year-old clerk was first seen in 1958, she lived with her son, a professional man, her daughter-in-law, and her two teen-age grandchildren. She had been widowed for several years. She impressed the interviewer as being happy and having a lot of energy for her age. She had lived in Kansas City, in the same house, for more than forty years, and was very fond of Kansas City. The daughter-in-law worked part time. The respondent usually prepared dinner for the family, although the daughter-in-law helped somewhat. She made it very clear that the best part of the day for her was when she was working. She had worked in the same company for about fourteen years and expected to keep on working. She said, "I'm afraid I would be restless if I stopped." She also worked every other Saturday until noon. Sundays were spent in preparation for a big dinner, going for a drive in the car, and a small amount of visiting. She knew her neighbors only casually and did not visit with them. She was proud of the fact that her health was sufficiently good that she had been off work only three days in the last twenty years.

Like many other respondents in the panel, especially those in their seventies and eighties, she had grown up on a farm. While she was growing up she lived with her grandfather, grandmother, father, mother, and two siblings. She thought of her mother as the best woman she had ever known. This was true while she was growing up and also during her young adulthood. She did not marry until she was twenty-eight. Her father had been a good man, but she had felt closer to her mother. She thought of the ages between thirty-five and forty-five, which she referred to as her early married life, as being the best time in her life, when she was very active in church, PTA, and keeping house. Following this period, there was difficulty in the family, and she and her husband were separated for several years. They finally "patched things up," but he died shortly thereafter. At one point in the study, she mentioned sixty as the age she would most like to be, because she would have many years of work ahead of her, and at another point in the study she mentioned fifty, when she started working and enjoying life more and could come and go as she pleased.

In March 1959, she had been fairly well and had taken a trip to visit her sister in another state. She was especially annoyed that she had had to reduce her working hours because she had reached the limit prescribed by social security. She said she was sometimes lonely on weekends because she was "all caught up with work" and had nothing to do. However, in September 1959, she seemed to be working about as much as she had at the beginning of the study, from about 8:45 A.M. to 3:00 P.M. Her daily round looked just the same as it had at the beginning. In response to the story question about Jones, she said that he would accept the job, and added that his wife would probably be glad to get the husband out of the way. She was very proud of the fact that she could do as good a job at work as "the younger girls." The situation looked essentially the same in March of 1960. During that interview, she spoke very highly of her son as a studious, dependable, and moral person. In response to a question on the most important thing in life, she responded without hesitation, "My work!"—at the age of seventy-two, almost seventy-three.

In October of 1961, she said her health was fine and she was still working. Her son's wife had left him a few months before. Apparently it had been a rather unexpected move, and she commented that she had "never had anything in life hurt so." However, later on in the interview she said she was still on very good terms with her daughter-in-law. One of the grandchildren had gone away to school, and the other had married. She continued to live with her son, but they went rather separate ways. Although she was shocked by the break-up of her son's marriage, her mode of life was little affected by the change in household composition.

Her daily round was about the same as it had been at the beginning of the study. She cleaned the house "from top to bottom" on Saturdays. She emphasized that she did not enjoy the weekend and was always ready to go back to work on Monday. This interest in work was put even more strongly when she said she did not want to live much longer, at least not beyond the time when she could work. She mentioned the divorce of her son as the worst time since the last interview, and a trip to Colorado, Washington, D.C., New York City, and Niagara Falls as the best. As far as interests and activities apart from work were concerned, she said that she always read the paper, but thought that was about all. At the end of the study she commented, "I have no hobby except my work."

There was a very mild Familism in the background of this respondent, dimmed further by two marital separations, her own and her son's. She achieved the style of World of Work at age fifty, and it became her almost overwhelmingly predominant way of life. She had persisted in this style for nearly twenty-five years. Her style was strongly marked, and she has been rated 1 on its clarity.

Her success rating, in the middle level of the autonomous-precarious category, was made because she had few resources beyond work. Although she admired and approved of her son, their relationship was not close. She would probably do rather badly in relation to any problems of health. She showed no signs of anomie, but some signs of alienation and isolation. Coping, as far as her present mode of life was concerned, was rated 1. When no longer able to work, she would most probably fall temporarily into a dependent-precarious position, especially in relation to her son, and then might well have to be institutionalized or might possibly commit suicide. So little in life was meaningful to her, except work.

Grounded

This man spent his life so absorbed in his World of Work that he was never able to sense the real feelings of those around him, and their ultimate rejection of him was a bewildering experience.

This respondent was the oldest of six children born to a Missouri farmer. Schooling bored him, and at fifteen he ran away and joined the Army. He worked his way into the business world as soon as he left the Army, doing first one job and then another, usually parlaying what capital he had into part or total ownership of the "outfits" that employed him. Soon he began to operate on his own. He realized the need for more education, and actually picked up a year of college work. He married once, was divorced, married a second time and divorced, and in his thirties married for the third time.

By the time he was forty he was living in a midwestern state and doing a $40,000-a-year business. If this business failed, he felt he could always find another. Although he spent or gambled away much of his money, he still made more than enough to buy many satisfying (to him) material possessions.

At the time of the initial interview, he was living with his third wife. He had never had any children, nor did he ever express any wish for any. He was operating a company he had recently purchased. He and his wife lived in a pleasant home. He was the picture of a big, hard-driving, expansive and happy businessman, filled with plans for a new business in which he and his wife would share.

In July of 1957, the second contact was made. This time, the respondent had been quite ill. He had had a major stroke and was having to reorganize his entire work pattern. During his illness, he had been touched by the kindness shown him by his neighbors who, he had previously noted, meant nothing to him at all. In general, he tried to put on a hearty "good front," declared that things were "looking up," and said that some of his stocks were doing exceptionally well. His closest association, apart from his wife, was his invalid mother in a nearby city. He went to see her monthly. He also claimed to feel as close to his mother-in-law as to his own mother—which was probably true because of the shallowness of his affective relationships generally. When asked his plans for the future, he not only scoffed at retirement, but said he planned to open an additional business by 1962.

At the next interview, his physical condition was even worse. He was in the hospital more than he was home. However, he had been active enough to buy a new split-level home with a two-car garage and a color TV. He claimed to like best being with family (in this case, his wife), doing a good job at work, and visiting with family (mother, brother, and a sister). His marriage, he reported, had almost no unhappiness, and was more happy than most.

In the next few years his health grew steadily worse. He bought yet another new house, started another business, and begged his wife (who had gone to work) to stay home and be with him while he ran the business from his bed, but his years of failing to communicate left him without the necessary resources to influence her. It was evident to the interviewers that the wife was getting increasingly hostile to the respondent, even though he was blind to it and reported (as late as the next-to-the-last interview) that his chief pleasure was coming home to see his wife. This was why her rejection of him came as such a shock to the respondent, who reported at the final interview that his wife was divorcing him for his "property." He faced a bleak future in the hospital. He hated the routine and inactivity of hospital life. Pathetically, when asked to describe his most important traits at that time, he listed "hard worker, devoted husband, sensible about money."

After a year in the hospital, his friends (who were really only casual friends according to his earlier descriptions) had ceased to visit him. So when he felt the need for such contact, he would hire a cab, go into a city hotel, and call his friends to come and meet him there. One of his last important statements to the interviewer was, "My business was my whole life before I had my stroke. . . . If I had an ideal day now, I'd get in an airplane and ride just anywhere. I love flying."

Because work had been his whole life, his style, World of Work, was clear. His world of work had collapsed. His wife, the chief contact in his limited social system, had divorced him. He was all alone, ill, and friendless, thus in a precarious condition. But he still struggled to keep alive a spark of hope that he might get back to work, and he did not sit back passively when his isolation became intolerable. He put as much into his social system as he could and took little from it. Therefore, he was classified autonomous-precarious, at the bottom.

Psychologically this respondent appeared to use the defensive mechanism of denial quite extensively. However, an examination of the structural and functional properties of his social system clarifies the meaning of "denial" in his case. His transactions were very predominantly universalistic and instrumental, and his orientation was exclusively specific and neutral. When trouble struck and he badly needed the kind of support which could come only with particularistic and expressional relations, he was completely unprepared for the situation, and some anomie, alienation, and isolation resulted.

THE LEAST SUCCESSFUL AGERS

The Slipping Mask

This man, at age fifty-one, was a wholesale salesman who lived with his wife, eight-year-old son, and seventy-five-year-old mother-in-law in a rather nice, medium-sized house in a very attractive neighborhood. He was born in Kansas City. His wife worked part time as his secretary and assistant.

He was about six foot one, weighed perhaps two hundred twenty-five, and was still rather handsome, with iron gray hair. According to him, he lived on "one of the prettiest little blocks in Kansas City," and liked Kansas City "just fine."

He was often on the road selling, but when at home he spent the day calling on local customers. In the evenings he spent some time planning work for the next day and getting out orders, but what he really enjoyed was watching TV (mainly quiz and panel shows and sports) with the family. He also read magazines to relax before going to bed. His wife really ran the house, and he did very few of the necessary chores. On weekends he just relaxed; his wife and son went to church, but he rarely did. The relaxing was important because, he felt, he was getting to an age where he was going to have to take it easier.

He had a ready cliché when asked about religion. He said, "When that one great writer comes to write against your name, he writes not whether you won or lost. . . ." Then he added, "Because of my work, I can't attend church" (although he was home every weekend). He found the Masonic Lodge more satisfying, and he also attended one social club and one salesmen's club.

Eight months later he claimed things were fine and said he had taken off twenty-five pounds. But to the interviewer he looked unwell and a little shaky. Everything was about the same, he felt, except that he was getting out with the boy a little more now that the boy was older. He had a couple of in-laws that he saw regularly. He saw some of his neighbors as friends, but had recently asked that a house not be sold to a Jewish family because he preferred the neighborhood to be Gentile. He did not plan to retire—ever. He planned to cut down on territory as needed, but "die with his boots on." His wife did not plan to go back to work, other than to help him out.

Six months later he said he felt better than he had for years. He had had a break from selling on the road. In thinking back, he believed he had had more pep in his forties, but otherwise was pretty much the same. He did add that, as he had gotten older, he wanted friends in all age categories, whereas he used to prefer friends in his own age group. He noted, without comment, that the neighborhood was changing but wished he could see more neighbors. He did not consider himself elderly, but admitted he no longer kept up with the news as much as he formerly had (although he later denied this). Now he mainly enjoyed doing a good job at work and spending time with friends. He voted regularly when in town, and was neither a liberal nor a conservative.

At fifty-four, he was back to selling on the road, had aged noticeably, and had gained much weight. He was beginning to feel lonely fairly often—especially when on the road. He used to "run around"; now he just got a magazine, or TV, and stayed in his room. He had had a few less "breaks" than other people, he felt. The happiest time of his life was in his thirties, before he married, when he traveled around a lot. The worst time was the Depression when he could not support his mother properly, and she died during that time. He liked to be esteemed and approved and felt he was, but he seemed unhappy at his loss of ability to "have a big time" late into the night and get up and get going the next morning. In essence, all his answers betrayed growing uneasiness and growing tension over the future course of his life. He seemed really fearful of his success and needed to boast to build up his confidence.

Six months later, his wife had gone back to secretarial work full time to help out financially. She complained about having to do her husband's book work besides. She reported that when he was home he did nothing but sit or maybe visit with the neighbors. She said, "I think he drinks too much when he's out on the road, but I guess that is his recreation." Others reported things were far from good. One said he drank a lot, another said he did not get along well with his wife, and still another that his boy was "real spoiled."

The final interview found this man at fifty-six in a desperate state. He was preoccupied with his sex life, and he drank constantly throughout the interview. His health was deteriorating greatly, his son disapproved of him and his whole life, he had lost a favorite money-making line, and he and his wife were squabbling all the time. The mother-in-law had passed away, which relieved some pressures, but financially things were worse than before. The changing character of their neighborhood depressed him as he saw more and more of his neighbors move away.

This man was beginning to disintegrate and disengage rapidly in spite of his denials. Because he had never achieved good personal relationships, he moved swiftly toward anomie and alienation from family and friends when work and health began to fail. Isolation was in the offing. He had never really achieved any style but World of Work, and he was clearly dependent-precarious as his work suffered more and more from his personal disintegration. His wife was his mainstay, and she was threatening to leave him. Therefore, the future for him almost surely held a total collapse of his style and his personality. The kinds of fears that were crippling him were not likely to disappear but, rather, to get worse with age.

Nightingale With Clipped Wings

From the time she was a child, the fourth of six children in an upper-middle-class family, she dreamed of service to others. When she completed high school, she took hospital training and became a nurse. She nursed in various situations, but mostly liked to work with children as a school nurse. She continued to strive to do a better job, and when she was over fifty, went back to school and received her B.A. degree. If she had died with her cap on, she said, she would have had no regrets, although she sometimes mused wistfully to the interviewer over what it would have been like to have had children of her own. But, she said, "This wasn't the way my life was to be." She worked on and on until arthritis of the spine and a heart condition forced her to consider giving up her work and living at home with her brother and sister. Finally, she could fight retirement no longer.

The interviewers found her, at age seventy-seven, confined to a wheelchair and able to do only a few things as her share of the household tasks—primarily keeping household records. Her brother was still employed part time, and her sister kept house for all three. The respondent was bright and cheerful and reported that she saw both friends and neighbors, but mostly whiled away the hours by watching TV. She loved to have someone to talk to about her nursing days. Her work was still of primary importance to her.

Each succeeding interview found her growing more senile. The brother had now retired, and he and the sister were very annoyed by the respondent's loss of memory. They seemed to resent her inability to continue to function. The sister began to dominate the interviews, and the brother became openly contemptuous and verbally aggressive over the respondent's senility.

The final contact with the respondent was no better. She still retained her jolly, animated approach, an approach to life that had undoubtedly cheered the spirits of her many patients in her working days. But her mind had slipped into the past almost entirely. She reminisced about her old horse that she loved to ride as a child and about her nursing experiences. She could not walk, even with a cane, and was at the mercy of her siblings, but she did not complain.

Because of the state of her mind, and her inability to function, she was classed as dependent-precarious. The only thing she could give was her cheerful attitude, and those in her social life space wanted no part of it. She was not a total social isolate, and, in her mind, she led a gay and active life still, but actually she was in a state of disintegration and alienation and was unable to cope. Nevertheless, her style of life was World of Work, for she maintained her actual work as long as she was able, then continued an active role in the business affairs of the family, and when she could no longer function at this, she dwelt on her work in her musings.

ANALYSIS

The respondents described in this chapter, and others in this category described briefly in Appendix Two, all had a personal social system in which functionally specific and affectively neutral relations were dominant. But their degrees of commitment to the style and amounts of satisfaction obtained from it varied considerably, as did their modes of coping with this style in relation to aging, and their degrees of success in aging.

"The Contented Salesman" well illustrates that the World of Work does not necessarily imply killing oneself at work. This respondent could pace himself as he wished and enjoy "loafing," watching football and baseball games, and fishing. Yet, he needed a world of real work for life to be meaningful, greatly disliked the idea of retirement, and coped very well by maneuvering himself into a position, shortly before reaching age sixty-five, where he could retire gradually.

"Beyond the World of Work" makes an interesting contrast. Although his style also evolved in, and revolved about, work, his degree of commitment to the style and its saliency were much lower. He had left work behind with regrets, but not troublesome regrets, and had somewhat vaguely followed his not quite achieved secondary style of Living Fully. He had made many acquaintances in all walks of life, but one has the distinct impression that his relations with them, and even with his family, were never very deeply diffuse or affective. So he could fill his time with visiting and chatting.

Both men were successful agers, and both men were generally satisfied with their existing modes of life. But their modes of coping with aging were very different, due in large part to the different degrees of saliency of style. Had they reversed their modes of coping with aging so that "The Contented Salesman" retired and sat around chatting, and "Beyond the World of Work" tried to continue his work on a part-time basis, they probably would both have been quite unhappy, though still successful.

"A Dreary Life" contrasts sharply with these other two. The world of work can indeed be a dreary place. When it is dreary and also becomes a style, it is because the person's social system has developed in such a way that work is the only meaningful segment of life, and all other alternatives for style have been closed.

Yet work, in the sense of paid employment, can become essentially the only meaningful aspect of life, and still be far from dreary, as illustrated by "No Hobby Except My Work." Under these conditions, the success category is likely to be autonomous-precarious, due to lack of other resources for living. In fact, this lack of other resources, with its threat to the stability of the action system of the person, was vividly clear in all cases of less and least successful aging in this style. The World of Work as a style tends to go with an activist orientation to life. Disengagement is likely to be a more problematical issue and present coping difficulties. To age successfully with this style, one needs either to get in a position where one can pace oneself and retire gradually, or develop other resources for activism of a relatively specific and neutral sort.

"Nightingale With Clipped Wings" presents a good picture of a person with World of Work as a style, who aged successfully up to a point, but then reached a stage at which mental deterioration collapsed the action system and made successful aging no longer possible. She had made a good try at continuing her activist role into her retirement by becoming the keeper of the household records and by increasing her church activities, but as senility set in these activities were no longer possible. That she had, indeed, contributed to the household and at one point been definitely autonomous in her aging is partly attested to by the great irritation shown toward her by the brother and sister when she could no longer function in a useful manner. But her physical and mental deterioration had become so great that she was totally dependent. For this reason, this case differs from the other unsuccessful agers, such as "The Slipping Mask," whose action systems were dependent-precarious, although they were not senile.

"Grounded" had hovered between autonomous and dependent behavior for much of his life. It appears typical of some with this style of life that their chief contribution to those in their life space is a financial one because their relationships are primarily neutral. This respondent, for example, was so unaware of the dynamics of his home life that just a year before his wife divorced him he reported on what a fine, wonderful, happy home life he had, and how fine his wife was to him. It came as a great shock to him when she left him, although there had been ample evidence right along of serious annoyances on her part.

He was retired so forcibly and quickly by his physical health that he had little opportunity to adjust, but his mind still stayed in the World of Work and he continued to plan—most unrealistically—for future business opportunities he might work on. His activist nature was well shown in his approach to friends. If they did not come to see him at the hospital, he hired a taxi and went to see them. These were casual, chatting relationships, which was all he wanted. Deep affective needs still did not concern him. He would have been rated dependent-persistent except for his still hard-driving determination to get back into the World of Work again, even when it was painfully evident this could never be.

Such specific neutral people are married to their work in the most literal sense of this common saying. Their deepest needs seem met by the tight web of the work relationship. Another characteristic of people in the World of Work is also shown by "Grounded," namely his zeal and ceaseless efforts on behalf of his work. In describing another respondent of this type, one of the interviewers had this to say: "If indeed man expiates original sin through unremitting labor, then Mr. X is my candidate for the right hand of God." These people, for all their zeal, were not cold or unfriendly, but all human intercourse had to have productive purpose to be legitimate in their eyes.

In general, the World of Work is characterized by less amplitude and a narrower focus than the other styles, even Living Alone, and contrasts most sharply with Living Fully in this respect. Yet it can develop a sort of pseudoamplitude. One case in particular, "I Was Saved and Life Became Earnest," illustrates this point especially well. This sixty-year-old man was a minister, teacher, and lecturer. His lectures carried him to many parts of the country. In the early interviews it was uncertain whether World of Work or Living Fully was his style. Later on, and due in part to material from the clinical psychologist, it became clear that his religion was indeed work for him. It had a certain appearance of amplitude through all the travel and lectures, but it was all work. In fact, with all the pseudoamplitude, he gave the impression of feeling somewhat constricted. There was some vague Familism, but it was quite secondary and clearly not his style of life. As to success, he was autonomous-persistent, but toward the bottom. The autonomy was clear; he put a lot into his action system and was not an undue drain on anybody in it. The clinical psychologist may have been right about some underlying psychological disturbance, and he freely admitted to being nervous. These facets of his personality probably caused him some suffering and unhappiness, and thus affected his life satisfaction, but were not likely to affect his action system. Also, he would be able to continue his style of life and work on a basis of gradual diminution after formal retirement, a probability increased by the type of work he was in. But we would not bet on his stability as highly as we would on that of most of the panel in the autonomous-persistent category, and hence we placed him at the bottom of it. He might regress into some sort of emotional dependency after retirement.

The World of Work as a style has a special relation to sex. There were six men and two women among the most successful agers in the World of Work (autonomous-persistent 1), and this reflects the sex distribution for this style in general. However, it happens that the only very unhappy but successful (as defined here) person in this category was a woman. The other successful woman had serious problems of health which will be described in Chapter Nine. The two less successful women were rather unhappy, as was the one least successful. We believe that this distribution, although representing only five cases in all, is not accidental. It does not mean that working women are necessarily unhappy and dissatisfied. Most of the women in this panel who worked also achieved some other style. And many, although not all of them, were quite satisfied with life. The distribution, we have found, reflects the fact that, for this age group, in this culture, and at this time, the World of Work was a deviant style for women, and those who achieved it generally did so in connection with a life of adversity.

THREE

❧❦❧

Familism

Just as the centrality of the World of Work has been frequently emphasized in the literature of the social sciences and in popular writings, so has the decline of the family. It has certainly lost some of its functions and may have altered somewhat in structure with the lessening importance of kinship and extended family, although the extent of this latter change is a matter of some difference of opinion in current research. Yet, for fifty-five of the one hundred sixty-eight respondents in our panel, the style of life was Familism. Major decisions were made in relation to the family, the predominant values centered in the family, and the family was the most important area of life.

Thus, for this age and class range, in Kansas City, we are confident in saying that the changes in the functions and structure of the American family have not eliminated Familism as a style of life, and, in fact, it is still by far the most common style. We believe that, if similar intensive longitudinal case studies were made elsewhere, the findings might well be similar.

THE MOST SUCCESSFUL AGERS

Successful Disengagement

This retired semiskilled government employee was seventy at the beginning of the study. He lived with his wife and had grown children and several grandchildren. In early childhood he admired his father and mother equally, perhaps his father a little more. His father had been well-to-do, and the respondent had gone into business with him. He had had a rough time in the 1920's and the business had finally failed. It had been a big disappointment to him, since he had always wanted to be a businessman, even more so because it was difficult to get a job and provide for his family. After much effort he obtained a job with civil service status, which gave security for his family. One of his children had a prolonged illness, but the family was able to weather that storm, too. He mentioned his wife as a most admired person, wonderful, congenial, and pleasing; the only thing wrong, he indicated with a chuckle, was that she kept him working around the house.

He thoroughly enjoyed being retired and did not miss his work. He had worked hard and worried a lot, and liked being free of all that. He thought of himself as "more mellow, more settled, and less tempted." He had some desire to travel, but did not feel really up to it. His daily round involved a lot of sitting around and watching television. He did not go to church often, because there was no transportation, although he admitted he had never gone often in the past. He liked fishing, but again there was a transportation problem. He loved his children and grandchildren and enjoyed *short* visits from them. He gave familistic answers on the story questions. Jones sacrificed higher pay to be with his family, and Mrs. Birch married because "no woman wants to live alone." Interviews with his children indicated that they were familistic too. One neighbor said she felt toward him as a daughter to a father. He had lived in the same house for more than twenty years, knew several neighbors, considered a few of them as friends, but did very little visiting. He did not read much and played solitaire. He did not like the noise and confusion of baby-sitting. He had no desire to go out much, "especially since TV." He seldom dreamed of anything in the last half of his life. He had absolutely no telephone calls.

The clinical psychologist found no evidence of anxiety or depression. He judged the respondent to be "a modal family centered case," a judgment made independently of our concept of style of life. His daily round remained the same throughout the study. The significant others, mostly family and two friends, including a thirty-five-year-old neighbor, spoke of him with real affection, and expressed concern for his health, about which he himself never complained. His doctor said the respondent never had been troubled with health problems, and, in June 1961, he had not seen him in two or three months. However, a significant other mentioned heart attacks in July 1961, and the respondent died of a heart attack in December, just at the close of the field work for the study. He was in no way alienated, anomic, or isolated, and he coped extremely well. The exchange of energy between himself and his wife appeared in good balance, and certainly he gave as much or more into his social system than he took out of it. Although he was clearly Familistic in style, its saliency was not as great as for several others in the panel, and he was rated 2 in this respect. He is a very good example of successful aging through disengagement and has been placed in the top section of the autonomous-persistent group.

Pain and Giving

This sixty-seven-year-old school teacher remembered a pleasant childhood. Her mother was sweet and quiet and her father, who raised tobacco, was quick, energetic, and home-loving. She also had an aunt to whom she was deeply attached while growing up, and whom she described as a perfect lady, for whom she was the favorite niece. This aunt had been dead for only ten years at the time of the study.

She contracted malaria at the age of twelve. In her late teens, her fiancé died and she had a nervous breakdown. She was sent to a well-known clinic and the prognosis was that she might live a few years in a sheltered environment. However, she recovered from this illness, continued her education, and started teaching in her early thirties. On her very first day of teaching, she was in an accident and became crippled for life. However, she continued to teach. She was engaged to be married two other times in her life and each of these times the fiancé died. Her mother lived with her until the respondent was in her fifties.

When she was first interviewed, in October 1956, she was living with her sixty-year-old brother and a female friend of about sixty. She had a very bad hip and had to walk with a cane or crutch. Her eyesight was poor. However, she could hear well, and the interviewer described her as a cheerful person.

She had lived in Kansas City for forty years and liked it very much. She particularly enjoyed the relations she had developed at church. She disliked seeing real estate being sold around her to colored people and changing the racial makeup of the nearby school at which she was teaching. She expected that she would have to move soon, but she dreaded leaving her home, friends, and church. She guessed that eighty is "old."

She had a sister living in another state and a brother living in still another state; she felt quite close to both of them, as well as to the brother living in her home. She had gone to visit her sister recently with a view of retiring there, but decided that she would be a "third party," and so would remain in Kansas City as long as she could care for herself. Her brother was sick when he came to live with her, and she had to do a great many things for him.

She told the interviewer quite frankly that she suffered terribly from her hip but that she had long since gotten used to it. She was also anemic. She enjoyed staying home and liked to keep house. She did most of the household tasks. She rarely went out, other than for her teaching, except to church, and there she was chairman of the social committee for a Sunday school class. She also belonged to a canasta club and a teachers' club and mentioned seeing a close group of female friends very frequently.

When she was asked how she had been, in June of 1957, she said, "It is just as well not talked about." The children in school had been rather obnoxious. The white children were leaving, and the colored children were just getting used to white teachers. However, she did say that the principal of the school was very nice, as were some of the new teachers. They were all very cooperative and made a good "school family." She was enjoying her friends and talked about a particular canasta party with a good deal of enthusiasm. We then learned that a group of twelve women, including herself, had been meeting to play together for twenty-three years, thought of each other almost as sisters, and helped each other out in many ways. She said she looked forward to compulsory retirement in a year or two and would enjoy doing such things as sewing for the Red Cross and having more time for plays, musicals, and good shows. She would also enjoy her home, as she was quite a "homebody."

In April 1958, we learned that she had undergone an operation the preceding summer and was not able to go back to school until February. She had been in traction for ten weeks. She was now able to walk around the house without a cane. When she first came home from the hospital, her sister-in-law stayed with her for three weeks and her sister for two. All but two of the forty members of her Sunday school class came to visit her in the hospital. She now said she would continue to teach as long as she was able. She had twenty-nine Negro and nine white children in the class. On the other hand, she had only been to church three times since she was out of the hospital; she felt too tired to go. She claimed that her health was better than it had been at age forty-five. The interviewer rated her 90 per cent on her morale at this period.

In April 1959, we learned that she had been back in the hospital again the preceding summer. She said that she was better, but would always have one leg shorter than the other. Her brother had died in January. A woman had been living with her for three weeks. She preferred to stay alone, but the family would not hear of it. She commented at this point, "I used to be a baby, but it fell on my shoulders to be a protectorate [of her family]." Her brother's death had been a great shock to her; he had been a wonderful friend, and she had done much for him. Her comment was, "I have been without responsibility since January [the time of her brother's death], but I will find another responsibility." She looked back at the last twenty years as being very pleasant because of her friendships. If she had only six months to live she would spend the time with her family.

In October of 1959 she had retired. Another friend was living with her as a boarder, which she said really cost her money, but the family would not let her live alone. She was now watching television more. In response to the question about Jones, she said without hesitation that he would not take the job because his family would mean more to him. There was only one other white family left in the neighborhood, and she mentioned, with some pride, that she had learned to visit over the back fence with a Negro family next door.

In April 1960, she was spending a great deal of time settling her brother's estate. She was particularly concerned that her work would be disapproved by her other brother and sister. She indicated that it was a big job and that the lawyer was an old friend, but the brother did not like him and that made it very hard on her. She planned to sell the house that coming summer and take an apartment.

The clinical psychologist saw her in November of 1960. She was still living in the same house. He found her very well oriented, intelligent, and poised. She indicated that most of her friends were teachers, retired or nearing retirement. She had the serious hip condition, anemia, and some eye trouble, but no "overreaction" to health problems. He also noted that she had always felt very close to the children whom she taught. She now felt wise and capable about teaching, and entered into a very interesting and enlightened discussion about teaching methods.

In December 1961, at the age of about seventy-two, she was recuperating from a cataract operation and faced more to come. The house was for sale. She had established a fairly good relation with the Negro family next door, but her family was concerned about her continuing to live in that neighborhood. Her operations had removed the constant intense pain, and she was sleeping much better and had fewer responsibilities. She spoke warmly of her twelve close women friends. These "girls" did her shopping for her and came in whenever they could. She also enjoyed relating to people on television. She was particularly fond of one entertainer because he was "such a good family man." She was buying whatever she wanted because she did not know how much longer she would have to live. At the end of the study she said she had many friends, and that she had "always had the home but not the husband." She admitted that there had been a lot of sorrow in her life, especially with three fiancés dying.

This respondent's type of Familism involved persistent relations and decision-making with her family of orientation, no marriage (in this case by adversity), real familism through a small circle of close friends and through her relations with her children in school, and vicarious familism on television.

It is eminently clear that she is in the top level of the autonomous-persistent category. She gave to others during all of her life in spite of physical adversities and had overcome many obstacles. Also, she was having no trouble with disengagement. She showed no signs whatever of anomie, alienation, or isolation, she coped remarkably well, and she had a very strong familistic style in spite of never having had a family of her own. This respondent will be commented upon again briefly in Chapter Nine, in the section on health and well-being in relation to the theory of action.

THE LESS SUCCESSFUL AGERS

Not Quite With It

This fifty-six-year-old woman lived in a suburban home with her husband, who worked for a utility company. She had two married children and some grandchildren. At the beginning of the study, her parents were still alive, and her eighty-four-year-old father was still employed full time in newspaper work. In this instance, the analysis is best done in terms of the flow of impressions gained from the data over the five-year period. In 1956, we got the impression of a very languid person. Her husband worked the late afternoon and evening shift. She "fooled away the day" with him and did such housework as necessary after he left. They had no TV or radio. She claimed no set schedule and played the piano "to waste time." Her husband ate dinner out and "loved his work"—same job for thirty-five years. She did not go to church. They often had big family Sunday dinners, but she claimed they tired her. She had taught Sunday school when her son was still at home, but he, as a teen-ager, had been her assistant, and now she found it too hard to do it alone. She belonged to no clubs. The only friend mentioned was her sister, who did not live in Kansas City.

In March 1957, she was pleased that her son, a professional man, had returned from abroad with his wife and child. She thought of her mother, now eighty-five, as much more energetic than herself. Looking five years hence, she said retirement would be hard on her husband, and she hoped she would be "feeling better" (though no illness was mentioned).

In October 1957 she seemed a bit brighter and said she got most satisfaction out of "doing things you like to do by yourself at home." That same year, a senior member of the study, doing intensive interviews of a few cases, perceived her as a "deeply dependent" person who had led a somewhat sheltered and "sickly" life. As a girl, she had had vague thoughts of becoming a musician but had given them up.

In April 1958, she noted that she resented having to make choices and having to organize her thoughts. She loved to garden, had chicks and rabbits, and greatly preferred being outdoors. She had bought a television set, but had not yet looked at it.

In October 1958 she said her trouble "never happened"—that she just worried. She claimed her marriage was a happy one. In March 1959 she said she felt better than she had for many years. She organized a reception for her parents' sixtieth wedding anniversary. She had kept the grandchildren for two weeks the previous summer and found she enjoyed it.

In November 1959, her father had died, and she was working many hours with a lawyer straightening out her father's estate.

The clinical psychologist saw her in September 1960 and said she *appeared* helpless and naive and considered herself a failure. But she was not upset by her father's death. The psychologist did *not* see her, as had some others in the study, as a weak, schizoid, or infantile character; he thought this was all a facade which had been very successful for her.

The husband was interviewed in January 1961. He enjoyed most "going to the office—at least the wife says so." They were now going to church. Of her, he said the best thing in her life now was her grandchildren, and the worst was having himself around so much—"I'm much slower; she doesn't like to see people move slow." The best time recently was a vacation trip they took together to the west coast, "one of the most thrilling three weeks ever put in." In another interview with her, she mentioned the same trip with about the same enthusiasm.

A daughter was interviewed in July 1961 and revealed that having neighbors as friends, and having other friends, was quite a new experience for her. When the daughter had been growing up, the only "friends" had been family. She saw her mother twice a week.

A friend, who had been bridesmaid at the original respondent's wedding, was interviewed in March 1961. She had not seen the original respondent for over a year and described her as a "little withdrawn." In that same month, the clergyman was interviewed, and did not know the respondent at all well, even though the respondent's daughter was the first to be married in the new chapel. The lawyer who had been working with the respondent concerning her father's estate, interviewed that same month, described her as "a very energetic person."

In December 1961, at the age of sixty-one, the respondent looked fine. Christmas decorations were all in place. She said she still watched the sunrise every day, and would live outdoors all the time if she could. There were still no "typical days." She now watched television if there were any good programs. She claimed, "I don't really know very much about myself." She said that her son-in-law, of whom she was mildly disapproving at first, "seems nicer every day." She said she was going to church now and enjoyed it.

This case illustrates the importance of two dimensions of data in understanding the style of life and immediate or primary social system of many persons: time and the perspectives of others. She was a more complex person than would appear from the first interview. She had established a dependent mode of life which was successful for her, but could rise to the occasion in a crisis, such as her father's death and the settlement of his estate. Her primary social system was confined to family. She showed some tendency to be anomic, alienated, and isolated, although not in the extreme, and her familism was not outstandingly strong. She was rated 2 on all these variables. On the other hand, she was rated 1 on coping and illustrates the point that, although dependent in the sense of exchange of action energy, one may cope very well with life. She has been ranked at the top of the success scale within the dependent-persistent category.

Frustrated Familism

In October of 1956, this fifty-seven-year-old widow was living entirely alone. She was the daughter of a man who had been very wealthy but died penniless. Her husband had been on the managerial level. She had divorced him several years previously, and he had died shortly thereafter. She had one daughter who had nearly finished her Ph.D. in a distant university. She, herself, had graduated from high school. She was struggling to earn her living through real estate sales.

One of her brothers had been confined to a state hospital for nearly twenty years. He was ready to come out but had no place to go. Another brother lived in a nearby city and had periodic alcoholic episodes. She had one friend who came to stay with her when the friend's husband was out of town. Otherwise, she had very few friends. She did go out some in the evenings and said she did "almost everything including going to a Pullman porters' convention." Her days were taken up with business telephoning in the morning and sitting home in the afternoon. Saturdays and Sundays were her busiest days. She enjoyed making a sale but she disliked killing time on the job, because her eyes were such that she could not read. She was fairly active in one group in a liberal church and continuously emphasized freedom of thought. She occasionally attended meetings of business clubs.

In May of 1957, she had changed real estate firms. Business was very bad, and she expected her money to run out in July. Again she talked at length about the problem of her brother who was ready for release from a state hospital but had no place to go. The brother wanted to go back to his wife, from whom he had been divorced for twenty years. She also said that she had obtained tranquilizers for her other brother in a nearby city who went on alcoholic binges. She carried on some correspondence with some cousins and nieces. Her daughter did not write to her, and it was understood that, if anything important occurred, she would telephone. When asked what she would be doing five years from then, she replied, "I may be dead." She said that her daughter was the one bright spot in her life.

In December of 1957, her big worry was still her brother in the state hospital. Earlier she had spoken of the death of her husband, but now she told the interviewer that she had divorced him after nearly thirty years of marriage because he had not been faithful to her. She had been in the hospital for a time and commented that only one friend had stood by her while she was there. She said, "People do more depending on me than I on them." She did not plan to retire and said she would hate to go back to a small town. She had joined a "great books" club and was attending lectures on the New Testament in her church. She said that her mother had been overly pious and that she, the respondent, hoped that she had always managed to be truly liberal.

In December of 1958, business was somewhat better, and she had taken a trip to a western state and had flown to another city to see her daughter get her Ph.D. The brother had been moved from the state hospital to a county farm, where, she said, he had essentially the same life that he had had before in the hospital. She expressed strong skepticism about the morality of most men. Her older brother had been laid off because of alcoholism and had now come to live with her, and, as she put it, she had him "on her hands." She claimed nothing good had happened since the last interview and added that her life had been dull for the most part, although she had enjoyed a long trip with her daughter a few years previously. She sometimes ate out in order not to come home and see her brother drinking.

In July of 1959, she had thrown the alcoholic brother out. Her daily round looked about as it did at the beginning of the study. The younger brother was still at the county farm.

In March of 1960, she said she did not consider her life's work to have been anything. She still wanted very much to do something for her brother on the county farm, but had about given up hope. We learned that this "little brother" was the most important person in her life when she was young. She had treated him as her own child. She admired some things about her father, who was known for his philosophy and for being "fifty years ahead of his time." However, the father had never been a pal to either of his boys and had given more time to the community than to his family. Her mother had never displayed affection to anybody. Her own daughter also showed no affection to anyone, but had concern for the respondent. The daughter had been married, but she, too, was now divorced due to a "clash of intellects"—her husband was also a professional man.

In October 1961, the respondent seemed very anxious to talk, but it was difficult for her to stick to the questions. She showed pictures of her daughter, indicated books she was reading on mental illness, and appeared somewhat nervous. The daughter had moved and was now teaching in a university in another midwestern city. She considered her mentally ill brother's case now as hopeless, and that he would continue to live on a poor farm under medication. The alcoholic brother had come back to live with her. He had stopped drinking for three months and then had started again, and she was at a loss to know what to do with him.

The respondent was still working in real estate. She talked at some length about her daughter's divorce because of the "clash of brains" and said that her daughter and her daughter's husband had remained friends. She did not go out very much, and her daily round looked about as it had five years previously. She claimed there had been no great change in her health in the last ten years. She would very much like to have family gatherings. Her daughter was her main source of pleasure, but her daughter led her own life. She had few real friends. Things were more uncertain financially than they had been ten years ago. She said that church was a very good outlet for her.

For a time, we thought she might not fit any of the six styles, and we might have to invent a new one. In fact, this is the case which led us to consider the style Struggling Through Life With Maximum Frustration, a style which we decided against for reasons given in Chapter One. Then the Familism became quite clear, beginning with her relations to her younger brother, whom she had treated as her own child while growing up. Her life centered around her daughter and her two brothers. Both of the brothers had serious problems, and the daughter, who maintained a rather distant relation with her mother, had an unhappy married life herself. The respondent had a most unhappy married life, and at one point commented that she had never met anyone she could stand through her husband. This case illustrates that one does not have to be successful or happy in one's style to have the style. It is a clear case of frustrated Familism.

Her statement that "people do more depending on me than I on them" is quite good and accurate. She was clearly autonomous. In her case, the autonomy-dependency balance in her action system was a conscious problematical issue, whereas for most people it is not. She had tolerated an enormous amount of frustration and could probably tolerate more; however, there was the danger that when, for any reason, she could no longer help others in her network, mostly family, she might have serious difficulties, and hence the precariousness. She showed a high degree of anomie as well as considerable alienation and isolation. We have rated her 2 in relation to coping and, in spite of the rather unusual circumstances, we have rated her 1 in relation to style. The style was very clear, even though it did not have the amplitude or richness usually associated with Familism.

THE LEAST SUCCESSFUL AGERS

The Onset of the End

Dependency is not always a voluntary state—it can be forced upon an aging person most cruelly. This eighty-year-old widow is a good example of what can happen when an older person becomes physically incapable of doing for herself and is left emotionally to her own devices because everyone else is too busy or too bored to care.

At the beginning of the study, she was far from this position. She lived with her widowed daughter, mothered the daughter's seventeen-year-old son, and pulled her share of the load in keeping house. Because the daughter was diabetic and worked long hours as a clerk, the respondent did most of the housework, including cleaning and ironing. Next to the family, the most important thing in her life was her religion. From girlhood she had been an active Roman Catholic and never missed Mass unless something important prevented it. Daily she read her Bible and said many prayers as she went about her work.

Even as a child, her life had not been easy. She was born on a farm, one of six children. She got some education, perhaps up into high school (she did not remember any more), but soon after she got out of school, she went to work helping sick people and taking care of children. In fact, if she had had her life to live over, she would have taken some nurse's training, she believed. At any rate, in 1900, she married, and after three children (and one child who died), her husband died when she was only thirty-one, leaving her to bring up the children all alone. She worked helping in homes whenever she could and finally got her children successfully launched on their own. The period directly following was surely the most pleasant time of her life. No longer was there a responsibility for the children, and yet she had the good health to work and enjoy herself. But isolation was boring. Familism was her style of life. Right away she started caring for the grandchildren, and when one daughter was widowed, as she herself had been, she moved right in to help her.

At the time of the first interview she was bright, hard working, and looked rather young for her age. She found it hard to think of herself as eighty, and yet, except for one physically disabled sister on the west coast, she was the only one of her generation left.

The following year, the interviewer found a much lonelier person, and some of the spark was gone. Her beloved grandson had married suddenly, and the daughter had taken a job working much longer hours, so the respondent was alone a great deal more of the time. Her health and eyesight were none too good, so the old pleasures of reading or watching television were beginning to be limited for her. She talked almost incessantly of how lucky she had been in keeping her health so she could work. Work and prayer were the answers to all her troubles—loneliness, boredom, and fear. The psychologist who interviewed her about this time found her:

> well oriented as to time, place, events . . . [and] above average in intelligence. Whatever morale problems there are, they seem to be primarily due to her loneliness and boredom. . . . Her religion is quite meaningful to her, and she tells me that not only does she not fear death, but will welcome it when it comes. This is said with little affect, and she undoubtedly means it.

The significant others offered very little additional information on this woman. They were aware of her and mildly interested, but there the interrelationship ceased. Perhaps this accounted for the helpless, hopeless picture the final interview disclosed.

The last interview, four years after the initial one, showed that the respondent had failed drastically. She had sprained her back and was confined to a chair or bed. A niece and a granddaughter were also living in the apartment, as well as a great-granddaughter, making a total of five in the rather small quarters. Noise and confusion abounded, and the respondent was left sitting helplessly in the midst of this bedlam. Her own role was clearly a nonparticipant one. Occasionally she was able to hold the baby and feed it the bottle or wash a few dishes, but there her service ended, of necessity. Everyone else was too busy or too bored with her to give her more than nominal attention, and she was dying of loneliness in this mass of people.

She described her daily round as one of deadly monotony—nothing she could do, nothing to do, just sit from meal to meal and then to bed for a poor night's sleep. They were all too occupied to take her visiting or to church, and although she did not want to resent this, she did. She did not want to be a "crank" and tried to guard her tongue, but this was hard, as she still seemed mentally alert to what was going on. For this reason, she really welcomed the interviewers. They were people to talk to who were interested in her and at least temporarily relieved the boredom.

This woman was now essentially dependent on her children for everything. This was a tragic case of aging, because when age really caught up to her she was left with no defenses. She did not want to be dependent-precarious, but she was. Her physical condition forced her to stay in one place and not seek other outlets, and her family would not accept what little she could afford them from her action system. Nevertheless, her chief concern was still with the family, and she chose to be a part of the family rather than adopting a style of living alone. Therefore, her style of life continued to be Familism— although weaker now that she was no longer an active participant. Coupled with this aging had come almost complete disengagement— both voluntary and involuntary. She did wish she could work and go to church, but her comments hinted that some disengagement was not unacceptable—that maybe taking it easy was not really that bad. Death could not be too far away. Several of our cases convince us that when the action system runs down, the biological system runs down even faster than it would otherwise.

Faded Familism

In August of 1956, this fifty-eight-year-old skilled worker was living with his wife and two teen-age sons. He had been living in Kansas City for over ten years. He had come there for a visit and had just happened to find a job which permitted him to stay at home, whereas before he had been on the road a good deal. He got his own breakfast, although he commented that he felt his wife should do this. His spare time was spent with television and visiting with his family. He said that, if there were no difficulties, there was no part of the day that he did not like, but indicated that he did have difficulties at home, at work, or both, on some occasions. He did most of the shopping, but his wife did the rest of the household tasks. He had gone into business at one time, but failed.

He did not do much over the weekends and did not go to church. He belonged to a union but rarely went to its meetings. In terms of friends, he mentioned his wife's two sisters and two other people. He had a twin brother, a half-brother, a half-sister, and a sister who all lived elsewhere, and another sister who spent about half of her time in Kansas City. His relations with these relatives did not appear to be particularly close. His father had been a midwestern farmer.

In June of 1957 he had had an operation and complained about being quite insecure financially. One son had been graduated from high school and was about to go into the armed services. He saw his relatives very rarely but did keep in touch with them. He could not retire for financial reasons, although he would have liked to ease up on work. He was much concerned about his lack of education.

In November of 1957 his health was better. One of his sons had gotten into some kind of difficulty, but it was not clear just what. He commented, "We are alone now, I mean almost alone." He did not have many friends and did not consider them particularly important. Again he indicated that he would work as long as he was able and was not financially able to retire.

In January of 1959, one son had come back from the armed services and was working his way through junior college. It was claimed that the other son was visiting an uncle in a nearby state. The respondent was working only four days a week, his sister was dying of cancer, and in response to the question about the best things that had happened recently, he said there were none. He complained of loneliness and lack of pep. The best years of life were, he said, around thirty-five and the worst from fifty on. They were the worst because his health was not as good as it had been, and he had had to give up his business and go back to work for wages.

In July of 1959, one of his sons was still in college and in the armed forces reserve. We now learned that the other son had been in serious trouble and had been spending some time in an institution. The respondent was now working five days a week, but had almost lost his job and did not feel at all secure in it. He blamed this difficulty on a deformity caused by polio. He still did not do much over weekends, although he said he and his wife tried to take in a show occasionally. His wife was not particularly fond of television. A neighbor's child of eighteen months enjoyed coming over and visiting with the respondent, which pleased the respondent.

In relation to one of the story questions, Jones did not take the job because of his feeling for his family. Another such story question we found to be indicative of style in many instances:

> James Franklin was a hard-working, law-abiding man who had worked hard all his life to improve himself and to support his family. He was now about to retire and had saved a sum of money which would take care of him in his old age. One day he was visited by his son, an only child who was unreliable, unable to hold a job, and given to loose living. The boy was obviously terrified. He told his father that he had taken a large sum of money from his company and had lost it gambling. If he did not replace the money at once, he would be found out and would face possible prison. What does James Franklin do? Why?

In this instance, the story came fairly close to home for the respondent, and he replied, without hesitation, that Mr. Franklin would help his son. In relation to still another of these stories, Mrs. Birch did decide to marry, over her daughter's protests.

He indicated that his life had changed about every ten years and that each time he had had to lower his goals. He had recently had some financial difficulties in relation to an insurance policy.

In October of 1959, he again lamented that he had not achieved his goals. He had wanted to accumulate enough money to retire, and he was a long way from that. He was recovering from an operation. He mentioned thinking of perfecting and marketing some "gadgets in my head." He had been off work for some time and did not know when he would go back. The company he was working for was temporarily shut down.

He thought of his mother as a very good person and indicated that he got along very well with his brothers. His father was a hard-working honest farmer. He commented that he wished he had the ability that his wife had to be well liked and make friends. However, he was somewhat reluctant to talk about her. He said they had been married for thirty years and that it had worked out well. The interviewer noted that the wife was attractive and that the couple seemed to get along well together.

During the summer of 1961, there was a series of observations by a university student. He described the respondent's old two-story wooden house, with the upstairs portion rented. He described two sons, one who was working as a semiskilled worker and the other who had just finished junior college. But by far the most significant event was that the respondent's wife had left him after more than thirty years of marriage and was living in an eastern state with another man. She had gone there to visit, returned, left a note, taken all the money she could get, and left a number of debts. The wife had had rather expensive tastes. The respondent had managed to get another job and had become quite active with a group of divorced and widowed people. The observer, in fact, accompanied the respondent on a date to a club for older people, where a dance was held. The respondent had been down in the Ozarks over a weekend with another girlfriend. The observer felt that he seemed much happier than had been reported in the interviews. The observer went to a ball game with the respondent and still another girlfriend. In fact, the respondent had been visiting various women through some sort of lonely hearts club and expressed surprise that there were so many lonely people. He was still experiencing some trouble in finding work. He did not know where he stood about the ownership of the house because it had been in his wife's name as well as his own. He did not have much idea what his sons were doing. His wife corresponded with the sons, but not with him, and the sons were not particularly communicative. At one point, he was found watching television with his younger son, but there was no interaction between them. The same observer saw him briefly in December 1961 and found that the respondent was working and had not yet made a settlement with his wife.

In January of 1962, the respondent complained of the many adjustments he had had to make. He had great trouble sleeping. He had had a serious nervous condition caused by his wife's leaving. Saturdays he spent in housework. The most enjoyable thing for him now was to be with someone who helped him to get along. He was desperately in need of companionship and was very tired of work.

This man's orientation to life had been familistic, but it had become very much faded, particularly after his wife deserted him. Toward the end of the study he was still plodding along, somehow managing to preserve a house for his two sons. After his wife left him, his familism diffused out into a series of relations with lady friends.

He was just barely getting along, taking more out of others than giving. He badly needed a companion to lean on, but such a relationship was complicated for legal and financial reasons. He was wearing out at work and had already had one nervous breakdown. He was clearly in a dependent-precarious position. He showed a high degree of anomie and considerable alienation and isolation. He did manage to cope to some extent, and we have given him a rating of 2 on that variable. In terms of style, it had become so faded that we gave him a rating of 3.

A LESS VARIANT FORM OF FAMILISM

In the preceding sections of this chapter, the cases were selected and presented to bring out some of the many forms that Familism as a style may take and, hence, to sharpen an understanding of this style. As a result, the cases illustrate such matters as familism persisting through adversity, familism without a conjugal family, frustrated familism, and familism fading away. They do not, however, bring out the flavor of more typical American familism, of which there were numerous representatives in the Kansas City Study. In this section, we are presenting a case which falls squarely within this more typical range. It happens to be a highly successful case, but it is not presented so much from the point of view of the analysis of success as to round out the picture of American Familism as a style of life.

American Familism in Pure Culture

This respondent was fifty years old at the beginning of the study, in 1956. She had been a housewife all of her adult life. Her husband was a skilled worker with some supervisory responsibilities, and her father had had a similar occupation. She had had some college education. She was a graduate nurse, but had not worked since her marriage. She had two children, one son and one daughter, both of whom had recently left home. She impressed the interviewer as being a happy and animated person.

She had lived in Kansas City for more than thirty years, and in the same house for more than twenty. She said she loved it there. She had taken trips, but was always glad to get back to her home. She lived in a part of Kansas City which had some of the characteristics of a smaller community, which she liked very much. The neighborhood had always been a very good one, and she had raised two very fine children there, of whom she was very proud.

Her daily round had no set routines. There were many household tasks, gardening, and sewing for herself, for friends, and for the children; she said she was always busy with many projects. The children came to visit once or twice a week, or the respondent and her husband frequently went over to the children's homes. She enjoyed all parts of the day, but the very best part was in the evening when her husband was home. She commented that her husband had been with the same company for thirty-seven years. He came home at noon on Saturdays, and Saturday afternoon activities varied a good deal. On Sunday, once a month, she visited her mother in a nearby town. She did not go to church, but commented that she "raised two very religious children." She belonged to no groups and had just a few intimate friends.

In April of 1957, there was no change in her status. Her son was living in an eastern state, going to college, and she had been there three times since the preceding July to see him. She saw her daughter about once a week, and a brother of her husband about once a month. She also had some contact with other relatives. Her own brother came to visit once in a long while, and she remarked that her family of orientation had been small. She did a good deal of over-the-fence visiting in the neighborhood, and there was one neighbor whom she could call a close personal friend; in fact, they had been on a trip together. She expected her husband to retire at the age of sixty-five, in 1968, and said he would probably set up a hobby shop and do some repair work. She emphasized that she and her husband were very congenial, and she foresaw no problems in relation to retirement. When asked what life would be like five years from that time, she said she hoped to have some grandchildren, and added, "The family is the most important thing in life now."

She seemed very much the same in January of 1958. It was clear that she felt very close to her children, but was not possessive of them. Both of her children were married by that time, and she thought a great deal of her daughter-in-law and her son-in-law. She indicated that she had become closer to her husband's brother during the past year, since his parents had died. She saw her friends practically every day or talked with them on the telephone. She was friendly with the neighbors, but most of them had small children, and their interests differed.

In December 1958, she said she was fine; her son had had a boy, and the daughter was expecting a child soon. She commented, "All our life is wrapped around the children now." She said she was never lonely because there was always something to do. The best thing that had happened in the last five years was seeing her son get a college diploma, and the worst was when her husband had pneumonia and was on the critical list. When asked what she would do if she had only six months to live and could do anything she wished, she said she would visit her grandchildren, "back and forth, fast and furious." She still visited her mother, who was actually her stepmother but the only one she ever knew and to whom she felt very close.

In July of 1959, she and her husband were spending some of their evenings and weekends working on the daughter's house. The husband's brother came to dinner regularly on Sundays. She was very proud of the fact that the children had borrowed money from them when they were married and had paid it all back. In relation to the aging process, she said that she had not thought of herself as getting old until they brought out the family album one evening. Then she was shocked and begged the children to put it away. Things remained the same in October of 1959; she mentioned her life's work as raising a family and spoke of her husband as a "sweet old guy." She spent a good deal of time sewing for the grandchildren.

In October of 1961, the interviewer noted that they had a very good stereo console and many records. The respondent said she was fine and very happy. Her husband's brother had moved in with them, and she was very happy about this; she thought it was particularly nice to have three people for whom to cook. She said, "I perked up." She said the husband's brother "worships our children and grand-children." Her daily round was still varied, but housewifely. Her son and his family had moved to another midwestern state, and she saw them about three times a year. She said they seldom ate out and "don't go to be going." She now had four grandchildren and said that the daughter's two were "about the happiest you ever saw."

This respondent represents a pure case of strong familism, centered in a small conjugal family, but reaching out to some extent. This mode of the style tends to have Couplehood as a secondary style, giving the primary style a very strong underpinning.

This case also illustrates the important point that, even though the style is centered in the conjugal family, the children's leaving home is not necessarily a crisis. This respondent remained close to, but not possessive of, her children and was delighted to see them graduate from college, marry, and have children to whom she also felt very close.

Her action system was in good balance, and she has been rated autonomous-persistent at the top. All of her characteristic modes of action were rated 1.

ANALYSIS

The very large number of respondents with Familism as their style of life have social systems which are opposite to the World of Work in one crucial respect: functionally diffuse and affective rather than functionally specific and neutral relations predominate. Again, within the style, there are many variations along the same dimensions: degree of commitment to the style, its saliency, satisfaction obtained from the style, characteristic uses of action energy, and degree of successful aging.

"Successful Disengagement" illustrates a mild familism, which easily mellows and disengages with age. "Not Quite With It" also illustrates mild familism, which runs in the same general direction, but in a dependent-persistent, rather than an autonomous-persistent, category.

"Pain and Giving" emphasizes that living arrangements and immediate social relations, on the one hand, and style of life on the other, are essentially independent. This woman had never had a family of her own and had lived with members of her family of orientation only part of the time, for a while with her mother and for a while with her brother. Were she to move to an apartment and live entirely alone, she would still be strongly familistic. This relation between living arrangement and style is also illustrated in "Frustrated Familism," which also illustrates the fact that one does not have to be happy or successful in one's style to have it.

Another case illustrates this latter point, plus an important theoretical point in relation to successful coping with aging in the familistic style. "I Want to Retire" was a fifty-nine-year-old man, a specialized skilled worker in a small enterprise where he had worked continually for more than thirty years. He was divorced and had one married daughter who lived in a nearby state. He had an eighty-eight-year-old mother and one older sibling in Kansas City, and three older siblings not in Kansas City; he felt quite close to all of them.

The enterprise where he worked was rather familistic in atmosphere. He was well liked by the owner and had very friendly relations with the girls who worked directly with him. He had a large network of close friends and relatives, whom he visited often. He spent long summer vacations on a northern lake with his daughter and son-in-law, and sometimes with a sister, fishing and visiting with friends there; he looked forward to retiring and spending half of the year in that fashion. If he had his life to live over, he said he would marry young and have more children (which his divorced wife had not wanted). The most important thing in life was family— "We all care for each other." He regretted the divorce and said that he had not gotten over it until recently. In fact, by the end of the study, his strong familism had convinced him that his wife had been a wonderful woman who had died some years ago. One sister gave him a small fishing and hunting lodge where he expected to spend much time in retirement, and he enjoyed fishing with the sister and her husband, who had no children.

"Married life is the thing, and nobody should have to live alone." This divorced man, living alone in an apartment, was in no sense Living Alone stylewise. He was in excellent health, had saved adequately for retirement, and would persist in his mode of life. He was rated in the top group of the autonomous-persistent category. He would have sorrow as his immediate family, mostly older than he, died. But his familistic orientation would easily diffuse out into a large network of friends.

We have found that Familism as a style of life is most likely to be successful if the style is more open than closed. If the familism is dependent on the presence or absence of specific, usually primary, family members, the ordinary passage of time threatens the persistence of the style by the moving or dying of the crucial members. If it can diffuse generationally, to children or grandchildren, the chances of persistence are better. And if the person views his total life space in a familistic manner, the chances of being and remaining autonomous-persistent are best. "I Want to Retire" and "Faded Familism" make a sharp contrast in this respect.

It is possible to be trapped in familism and forced into a dependent-precarious position. "The Onset of the End" is a case where dependency was created by ill health. She was confined to a chair and bed and was waited upon to meet needs minimally. But, as we emphasized earlier, a person could be bedridden and dying and still be autonomous-persistent. In this instance, both the dependency and the precariousness lay in her action system, which was conditioned only in part by her health. She was unable to relate to others around her. But the source of this situation appeared to be in the others in her social system and not in herself. The family had closed ranks on her and forced her to be an island of loneliness in a churning sea of family activities. In short, we have an interesting case where her social system became a condition of action, rather than a system of action itself, from the point of view of herself as the actor. How much of this situation, in turn, had been brought on directly or indirectly by herself, we could not judge because of insufficient data.

Although our analysis is concerned primarily with the social dynamics of aging in small-scale social systems, our data occasionally suggested a few points of social structure. We were struck by the fact that, although sons-in-law and daughters-in-law were significant persons in the lives of many of the respondents, there were no relations between the parents of the son-in-law or daughter-in-law and the respondents. At least, such relations were not important enough to be mentioned over seven rounds of interviewing, in spite of many questions on relatives, friends, and the whole network of relations in the social life space of the respondent. In fact, American kinship terminology contains no words to designate this type of relation. This point would bear systematic checking in studies of the American kinship systems.

FOUR

❧

Living
Alone

Twenty-one of the respondents had achieved the style of Living Alone. This is the next to the least frequent style. Yet it does represent one-eighth of the panel. If our assumption of comparability on distribution of styles of life in Kansas City and other parts of the country is correct, it would mean that appreciable numbers of people in our culture, fifty and over, have this style.

It is a style that has some theoretical interest, because such things as living singly, loneliness, alienation, and isolation have been linked together, and all of them, in turn, have been linked with social and psychological pathologies in one way or another. But, as was emphasized in Chapter One, Living Alone, as a style of life, is not necessarily directly related to living arrangements and need not be associated with loneliness, anomie, alienation, or social isolation. It can relate to successful aging as defined here; its ratio of successful to unsuccessful aging is in the middle of the scale of distribution of styles.

THE MOST SUCCESSFUL AGERS

A Minimal Social System

This fifty-nine-year-old man lived entirely alone in a hotel room. He was an office worker and had been at the same job for thirty years. He claimed to read history and economics and had accumulated over two hundred books for his "old age." His company had no retirement provisions, but he had fixed that for himself, and he looked forward with pleasure to retirement at sixty-five.

He was an only child and still thought of himself as such. Until he was about fifty, his parental family was intact, and he went to see his father and mother in a nearby town every weekend. When his father died, his mother came to live with him in the hotel room. She became senile and was placed in a nursing home. At the beginning of the study he visited her there two or three times a week. In July 1957 she was worse, and in the summer of 1959 she died. We learned a little later, from the clinical psychologist, that the man had been severely nauseated at each visit and was much relieved by his mother's death.

This man had absolutely no friends and interacted minimally at the office. In addition to reading, he enjoyed shows and concerts; in fact, he saw *My Fair Lady* five times, in different cities, during the course of the study. He liked to go to Chicago occasionally to look around, but visited no one there. Most of the interviews took place in the office, but the clinical psychologist saw him in his hotel room. It was cluttered. Prominent in the clutter was a set of toy soldiers and other toys. He collected well-made toys, but also played with them. At one point he said, "There seems to be a wall between me and most people."

This respondent was one for whom there was a series of participant observations over the summer of 1961. They confirm the general picture, but are especially interesting in that they temporarily increased his social life space quite a lot, yet did not change his basic style of life at all.

It was virtually impossible to find any significant others to interview, except his barber who knew only that he was well read and went to shows, his lawyer, who thought he was a lonely man, and an aunt, who had not seen him in thirty years, who said he was a "mamma's boy."

He was a pure case of Living Alone, as a style of life. He was not the usual isolate; he was not alienated, defeated, or a blamer, and had not been forced into isolation late in life. However, he was very high on isolation itself and was ranked 3 in that respect. It took essentially nothing from others to keep him going, and he paid his own way. He was prepared to persist in this style of life indefinitely, although the clinical psychologist noted an element of deep dissatisfaction.

From Orphan to Aloneness

This respondent was orphaned at, or shortly after, birth. A relative placed her in various orphanages and convents while she was growing up. In this fashion she got some elementary education, but it is not entirely clear just how much. She was married in her middle or late twenties to a man twenty years older than herself. Her marriage and family life were not happy. Of her husband she said, "He wasn't much, he had other women, was mean to the children, and let the money run out." The children did not get along with each other or with their mother. The husband failed in business and then died, while the children were still growing up.

At the beginning of the study, in November of 1956, she had been widowed for about twenty-five years. She was living alone and doing manual labor, which required her to stand up all day, at the age of sixty-five. She impressed the interviewer as looking younger than her age but, at the same time, being lonely, isolated, and crushed by deprivations. She regarded forty-five years and on as being "old," a much younger age than mentioned by the vast majority of the panel. She said she rested a good deal, on doctor's orders, because of a heart condition.

She occasionally saw her children, one daughter and two sons, and talked to them by telephone. One son took her to church about every other Sunday. Otherwise she did practically no visiting. She had no other relatives. She mentioned two close friends, both of whom lived out of town, whom she rarely saw; in fact, she had not seen one for six years.

In May of 1957, she said she was feeling better physically and mentally, but had been quite sick the preceding January and had been hospitalized for three weeks. The children had rallied around her temporarily at that time. She was thinking of changing jobs for health reasons. She was watching a good deal of television, and as for reading, read only the newspaper. Of her children, she said she felt closest to the daughter, but did not see her very often and commented that the daughter was busy with her bowling league. One of her out-of-town friends had moved to Kansas City but had not called her yet. She did not know her neighbors. She also said that, if she had her life to live over, she would live it completely differently, and would have "a nice happy family, friends, and places to go." In August 1957, her situation had not changed, and she was still working at manual labor in the same job that she had held for sixteen years.

By November of 1958 she had had to stop working for health reasons. A few friends had called on her, and she wished that her children would visit her more often. She said that she "got the blues" often at the age of forty-five, but now she was used to it. She now felt the need to be alone more. She felt tired, needed rest, was less patient, and more nervous. In this same context, she commented again that she really regretted having married.

By December 1959 her daily round was all at home. There was some occasional visiting, and she went to church now and then. In relation to the story question concerning Jones, he would clearly take the job. She was not very happy.

In January 1961 she said her life's work had been keeping house, raising a family, and doing manual labor. She admitted that she did not, and had not, liked taking care of children; they got on her nerves. She had acquired a bird to keep her company. She commented that if she lived with her daughter they would not get along at all, and said, "My daughter acts older than I do; that's why she is divorced. I tend to my affairs, and she tends to hers. The children never got along at home before and do not get along with each other now. I just lived my own life and never thought of anyone else." To the interviewer she seemed despondent and nervous and to feel deserted by her family.

In December of 1961 she said she had been fairly well. She was doing a lot of sewing as she was alone during the week and on weekends, except she still went to church occasionally with one son. At times she visited the older son and his wife, who, she said, had "no time for me—just for their parakeet." She also commented that her older son had not wanted responsibility for children. She had not been in the younger son's home in more than a year, because the younger son's wife did not like her husband's family. She was putting aside money for her funeral, because she did not want anyone to help her. Often she thought she might like to go to a Catholic church because she had been raised in a Catholic school.

During the first interviews there was some impression of a frustrated familism and living alone of necessity. But certainly toward the end of the study it became clear that she had achieved Living Alone as a style of life. She had never really liked raising children, who did not get along with each other or with her. She felt some resentment of their desertion of her, but, for example, she was very critical of her daughter to whom she felt "closest." She had never had a family in childhood and could not achieve familism in adulthood.

She showed some anomie, with her low mobilization of action energy, and some alienation, and was rated 2 on both of these variables. Her isolation, due to the alienation, was rather extreme, and was rated 3. She was given the middle rating on coping and on style. In relation to success, she was placed in the autonomous-persistent category, in the middle. This degree of success was achieved in large measure by her very low level of involvement in interaction with others. She put virtually nothing into her social system but took nothing out of it.

"From Orphan to Aloneness" contrasts in an interesting way theoretically with another respondent, also sixty-five years of age, who was also orphaned in infancy, and whom we have called "Familism Persistent in Hardship."

The sharp contrast was clearly due to the fact that this respondent was brought up by her grandmother and her grandfather, a retired farmer, of whom she had very fond memories. She had many contacts with aunts, uncles, and cousins. In short, she was brought up in a distinctly familistic atmosphere, even though she did not have parents of her own. During part of the study, she and her husband lived with her daughter, son-in-law, and five grandchildren, and later on in the study they moved to an apartment next door, owned by the son-in-law. Her husband was a skilled worker. During the study he contracted two quite serious diseases and was unable to work for long periods. By the end of the study it seemed clear that he would not have long to live. In spite of considerable hardship, she was persistent in her familism and gave a lot to her loved ones. She was very close to her husband, to whom she had been married for fifty years; his death would be a great sorrow to her, although not a blow, as she expected it. We would expect her to persist in her mother and grandmother role and rated her autonomous-persistent at the top, with a clear style of Familism. Being an orphan can be a relative matter, and the type of individual social system the orphan has has a profound effect on style of life and successful aging.

THE LESS SUCCESSFUL AGERS

How Little I Do

This seventy-eight-year-old widow had grown up in another state. She married at about age twenty, but her first husband died on their honeymoon. She went into business and amassed what was, in those days, a considerable fortune. She then married a local businessman.

However, it turned out that he had married her for her money and, although they lived in the same house, they had no real married life together. She put up with this situation for about eighteen years and then left him, after he had managed to get all of her money.

She moved to Kansas City and, with the help of friends, bought a small apartment house, which she was running at the time of the beginning of the study, in September 1958. Her daily routine was rather humdrum. She did not care for television, did a small amount of letter-writing, listened to sermons on the radio on Sunday, and did a very small amount of visiting. She had no relatives in Kansas City. She spoke rather freely of her regrets and unhappiness to the interviewer, and at the end of the first interview stated, "You've made me realize how little I do."

In January of 1959, she had had a cold, and again talked about her allergy to dust. She had stayed to herself at Christmas and claimed that she had turned down invitations. She was bothered by the "shape the country is in." One of her tenants had become mentally ill.

In September 1959, we again saw a daily round of minimal managing of the small apartment house, resting, reading, and occasionally sitting on the porch with tenants. In relation to the story questions, Jones would not take the job because home was more important, Franklin did help his son, but Mrs. Birch did not remarry. She stated that her present job started about twenty years ago, at the age of sixty, and she did not consider herself to be retired. However, she had a strong desire to give the house to some church group and turn it into a home for children with some rather strict and unusual rules. She had found no takers, and this had become very upsetting to her.

The clinical psychologist saw her in July 1960 and indicated that the outward impression of a well-contained and adjusted individual changed quickly with the interview. By that time she was not accepting any new tenants. She talked of her shame about her second marriage. She had tremendous preoccupations with fire and fear of children being burned. In fact, the psychologist wondered how much longer she could remain in the community.

In November 1961, however, she was still in the community and the interviewer remarked that the small apartment house was a "wonderful old home." But it was no longer profitable. The respondent had not been as well that past summer and said that she had had considerable emotional upset for the past two years. She had the same preoccupations with children, accidents, fire, and smoking. Her lawyer had persuaded her that the house was not suitable for children because of its construction. She had recently lost one long-standing friendship through a quarrel and was upset about that.

She had developed a clear-cut style of Living Alone, but was not particularly happy about it. There was some underpinning of World of Work. She would have liked to have been familistic, but was completely frustrated in this respect, and had never experienced familism in her adult life.

She showed some signs of anomie, alienation, and isolation and was rated 2 in these respects. On coping she was rated 1, as she was on style. On success, she was placed in the autonomous-precarious middle category. We again have an example of a respondent with a minimal interaction system, but in balance. The precariousness comes from her emotional upset of two years' standing. Nevertheless, she was still "in the community" a year and one-half after the clinical psychologist had seen her, and on the basis of the three and one-half years she was seen in the study as a whole, we did not place her in the most precarious rating in this category.

The Almighty Dollar

Here is an unusual case of a seventy-eight-year-old married man with many social contacts, whose basic style of life is one of Living Alone. Perhaps his own words speak best for how this might be.

> There was no one I admired as a child. My guardian, who took me when I was made an orphan at seven, was a lousy, no-good, dirty, mean devil. I still get mad when I think of him. I get sick when I think of him. I had the worst life a young boy could have. . . . I ask nothing from nobody and I don't want to give nothing. I'm a sick old man, in pain all the time, and I'm ready to go anytime. Neighbors? I can live without 'em. I never had too many friends. I can get along just fine alone. People expect too much of me. My wife expects me to do all the shopping in the cold, and all the cooking. The only friend I've got is the almighty dollar.

This old man was orphaned at an early age and had lived a life trusting no one and believing in himself alone. He had married once and his wife had died; he married again at seventy-four, and for a while it looked as if he would find some real companionship with this woman, but in a short time the glow wore off, and he went back to snarling and spitting at any human who tried to get close to him. This was a very special case of Living Alone, because he continued to go to the Golden Age Club dances, named several friends (but made it very clear that they were not close), and did not really want to retire when he did. His work had been mostly semiskilled, and his latter days were being spent in a low-rent housing project, so he had little of his "almighty dollar" to comfort him in his waning days. There were strong undertones of minimum involvement in this case, because once retired due to ill health, he found retirement very satisfactory. He expressed this in his description of an ideal day. "I would like to feel good, to go somewhere where it's warm and hear music for dancing."

This man was panicky at the thought of becoming dependent because he trusted no one, and dependence requires a high degree of trust. As his health became worse and he became more lonely in greater isolation, he found his old self-reliance insufficient. This is the reason for the autonomous-precarious classification. He was classed as Living Alone, despite the numbers of people he contacted, because there was not a strong specific affective relationship with anyone. He showed a high degree of anomie and alienation, yet not social isolation. He was rated 2 on coping, as he was on degree of style.

THE LEAST SUCCESSFUL AGERS

Cats and Filth

As indicated in Chapter One, the sampling for this study was such that the very top and very bottom of the socioeconomic scale were excluded from the panel. But a very few of the respondents came rather close to these extremes, and in this instance, the respondent presented a picture of slum squalor.

In September 1958 she was seventy-two years old and was living in a small apartment which she owned, in a building in poor condition, in a run-down section of the city. Her brother lived on the second floor and her sister on the third, but they interacted very little, except for occasional squabbles, and she said of them, "They are old and sick too, and don't go anywhere." The interviewer said she looked her age and appeared rather tired. There were two cats tied up in the apartment.

She had lived in Kansas City for fifty-one years and had come from a small town, where her father was a farmer. She said she preferred a large city because there was more help for the needy.

She was divorced. She had one son who was in a mental institution, and one daughter who had married a professional person and lived on the west coast, and whom she had not seen in several years. At this time, she said of her husband, "He was a good husband, a tobacco chewer, a good provider who told stories that made me laugh." But she added, "We weren't too much together. We worked different shifts and sometimes argued." She had been a hotel waitress, but had not worked for years.

Her daily round consisted of resting, taking care of the cats, shopping, housework, and listening, occasionally, to the radio. She had very few friends, and they were people who did things for her. She said she felt a hundred and six and rather unhappy. In response to a question about the nicest things that had happened recently, she said, "Nothing, I just live plain and common." The most important things in her life were doing things by herself at home, and just sitting and thinking about things.

In February of 1959 she had not been feeling very well and had had the flu. She said the church people had been nice to her during Christmas, and had brought her things. The nicest thing about being old, she said, was that "people want to help me." She would not admit that she was lonely, but said she did feel weary and blue. She felt that way especially when her brother and sister argued with her. She said, "That gets on my nerves. I am tired of being bawled out." The best time of her life had been in her thirties, when she was in excellent health. The worst time was when she was divorced.

In October 1959, the situation was essentially unchanged. She had stopped going to church because of some difficulty she was having with her leg. She still did a little shopping, but said that would have to stop when winter came; she would depend on others to shop for her. She thought any age up to seventy was all right, because she had been happy and healthy and had gone to church a great deal up until that time. During this interview, we learned that she had been married and divorced twice. Her daughter had finished school on the west coast, where she lived with her father, and the respondent was not sure how many grandchildren she had, if any.

In February 1960, the situation was about the same, although perhaps a bit more deteriorated. When asked about her life's work, she said she had worked as a waitress, housekeeping for others, and in stores. She also commented at this time that she had been married and divorced "several times." She said her second husband and his wife always looked her up when they were in Kansas City. She was feeling particularly blue during this interview because of a sick cat. The interviewer reported that the stench in the apartment was almost unbearable. By this time she had five or six cats. Her life revolved around the cats, and an elderly man, a neighbor, brought her the cat food.

By January of 1962, there had been a fire which had destroyed her original home, but the respondent was living in a similar type of apartment in the same neighborhood. The sister was living behind her in another apartment, and the brother somewhere nearby. All three lived alone and hardly interacted at all. Seven cats were now noted. The one friend who had gotten the cat food for her had now died, and this caused her considerable inconvenience. She now indicated that she had had four husbands, one of whom she had married twice. She had no company and said she did not want any. Her final comment in the study was that she did not want to go to funerals any more and that she had "got outta watching husbands die."

This woman had a very marked style of Living Alone. By piecing the bits of information together, it seems quite clear that she had managed to live alone through four marriages and two children. She was rated 1 on style. Her characteristic uses of action energy were rather disorganized and demoralized; she was rated 3 on anomie, 2 on alienation, 3 on isolation, and 2 on coping. Her interaction system was minimal, but she gave little, if anything, to others, and it was somewhat of a burden on others to keep her going. She had managed to be rather persistent over a considerable period of time, but toward the end of the study had moved into a more precarious position as the very few people she depended on died or drifted away; she was thus rated dependent-precarious, at the top of that category. As with most people with this style, disengagement was no problem due to the low level of engagement.

Don't Want No Friends

In contrast to the case of "The Almighty Dollar," this seventy-four-year-old man was an isolate who had had a warm, happy childhood but had deteriorated in his old age to a stage barely distinguishable from paranoid schizophrenia.

Semiskilled labor in heavy construction had been his life's work. He had never made more than a subsistence income and was living on social security in a tenement hotel with his third (common-law) wife. Somewhere in the city he had a son and a daughter. "I used to live with 'em. Hell no, I don't see 'em now no more—they've got to make a living."

He missed work very much. His forced retirement left him with no idea of how to spend his time. Had he had the style World of Work he might have turned his energies to some use, but as it was, he spent his days just sitting and listening to the radio or walking around the block. "It's all the same to me," he said, when asked to list the best and worst aspects of his day. The best thing he could find about his present age was that people were more respectful, and he had fewer responsibilities.

He recalled his childhood as a good one. He was the older of two brothers in a farm family and had had a large group of friends as he was growing up. He started work at thirteen and regretted that he had not gotten a better education, because for the rest of his life he was bound to semiskilled jobs. His mother was the most important person in his childhood. "She was good to us children, kind to me. I tried to listen to her and do what she asked. I think of her every now and then. Dad was my hero. He seemed to know all the answers. I respected him and obeyed him and tried to listen to him."

His description of such a good life as a child was hard to fit with the contentious old man of the interviews. Perhaps there was a clue in his description of his father as his hero and the interviewing psychologist's comment that the respondent seemed to prefer the world of fantasy. He might have lived on dreams for most of his life. But there was little left of heroes or dream world in the respondent's old age, and perhaps this explained his withdrawal and discontent as much as anything.

The psychologist further described him as very reluctant to give out any of his feelings. He appeared depressed, withdrawn, and unreasonable when pressed to do things or when faced with reality.

He became increasingly suspicious of the interviewers. He felt they were trying to investigate him to change his social security check. The final interview was achieved only after a real "Keystone Cops" kind of chase through a rooming house. Both his common-law wife and his landlady hid him from the pursuers. When finally caught, the respondent showed he had become far more bitter. He was belligerent throughout the interview and refused to answer many of the more personal questions. When asked whether he would like his son to be different from himself, he replied, "He is just what he's supposed to be. I don't want him to be like what I used to be because I don't want him to kill people." This statement remained unexplained. He had become aggressive toward his wife and friends and proclaimed with conviction, "I don't want no friends." He had no affective relationships left and sought none, so he had achieved a style of Living Alone. He was in, but not strongly of, the World of Work most of his life, and had depended on his succession of wives to keep him going. He was becoming increasingly demanding and unwilling to meet even the most reasonable demands from others. This made him dependent-precarious, with an outlook of institutional care in the near future.

ANALYSIS

In most of these cases, success is achieved by maintaining a minimal social system but remaining in balance in exchange of action energy within this system. In this sense, the style is related to social isolation, and most of the respondents in this category are rated fairly high on this variable: eight rated 3 and eleven rated 2. However, this relation is not absolutely necessary, and two of the respondents were rated 1, as is illustrated by "The Almighty Dollar." Alienation bears a functional relation to isolation, and the *distribution* of ratings is almost identical (although the individual ratings on a given respondent were not always identical on these two variables) : two were rated 1, twelve were rated 2, and seven were rated 3.

Anomie, including personal disorganization, does not bear any consistent relation to this style, with six ratings of 1, eight of 2, and seven of 3. And, in relation to coping, persons with this style do rather well, with nine rated 1, eleven rated 2, and only one, "Don't Want No Friends," rated 3. It is a somewhat deviant style, suitable for persons with a tendency toward alienation and isolation, but not a style strongly related to general demoralization. Occasionally it is, and "Cats and Filth" is a prime example, but clearly she represents the exception rather than the rule.

In a few cases, notably "The Almighty Dollar," Living Alone as a style was clearly related to failure to reach the stage of trust, in Erikson's sense, in personality development. In this instance, there was no florid development of paranoid schizophrenia, and he managed to live in the community without being a serious threat to himself or others. His style acted as a protective coating against the outbreak of paranoid tendencies.

When it is the style that is adopted in waning years, Living Alone is rather closely related to total disengagement. Often these people belong in the class of those who have loved and lost rather than of those who have never loved at all (such as "The Almighty Dollar"). There are some people who never make warm affective relationships in their lives and live in a world alone from childhood on. For them the style of Living Alone dominates past, present, and future, as was true of "From Orphan to Aloneness" and "A Minimal Social System." But, in the case of an aging person who has had a style such as World of Work for much of his active life, the disengagement process may continue to a point where he accepts the style of Living Alone in a minimal social system. Such was the case with "Don't Want No Friends," and there it was clearly associated with unsuccessful aging in the sense of dependent precariousness.

FIVE

❦❦❦

Couplehood

Couplehood was the second most frequently encountered style in this series, with thirty-three respondents who had developed this mode of living. For it, as for Familism, the core area of life is characterized by functionally diffuse and affective bonds, this time focused in a two-person group. Many of the respondents whose style was Familism had Couplehood as the secondary style, reinforcing it. When we add these two categories there are eighty-eight respondents, or more than half of the panel, whose lives were absorbed in close personal relations and for whom the distinctly dominant core of their social systems was a primary group.

This style is associated with a relatively high degree of success, with twenty-three respondents classified as autonomous-persistent, two as autonomous-precarious, five as dependent-persistent, and three as dependent-precarious.

THE MOST SUCCESSFUL AGERS

Goodbye Miss Chips

At age fifty-five, this woman was medium in height, on the heavy side, and had straight iron-gray hair. Her face was characteristically pleasant and kind. She lived in a room rented from another teacher who lived with her retired brother.

The respondent was born in Kansas City, the oldest of three sisters. Their father owned his own small business, but it was not enough to support the respondent and her sisters when both of her parents died. This necessitated her leaving school at seventeen and getting the first teaching job to help support her sisters. She had remained in teaching until the beginning of the study and had gradually increased her education until she had completed her master's degree. Over the years, she had worked so hard at teaching that she became a beloved figure not only in the school, to everyone from the custodian to the principal, but in the community as well.

During the first interview, she described the importance of her close friendship with the teacher from whom she rented. They traveled together during their summer vacations—usually back to the roommate's old New England home. She loved to travel, but spoke disparagingly of the New Englanders they met on these trips because, she said, "They don't get things done like people in Kansas do." Her regular days were taken up with her little pupils, and weekends and evenings she often prepared special material to interest or amuse the children. Even the few groups to which she belonged were all teacher-connected. As a faithful Roman Catholic, her religion was very necessary to her, not only as security and solace in time of trouble but also as a preparation for life hereafter.

Seven months later, things had not changed much. She watched more TV because her health had not been good, and she needed to take it easy. She had not changed a great deal since she was forty-five, except that her health was much worse. Her contact with her two sisters was still warm and close, even though one lived far away. She dreaded retirement—no plans had been made for it other than routine financial ones.

Over a year elapsed before the next interview, and in that time her life had been severely jolted. The roommate's brother had died of cancer, and the respondent herself had been operated on for cancer. This threw her even closer to the roommate, who had retired, and they spent far more time together. In addition to this one special friend, she reported having four or five other close personal friends (who were not as close as relatives) and countless other people she considered friends. Friends were very important to her and always had been, but neighbors were not important at all.

Her attitude toward retirement had changed significantly. Now she looked forward to it since her roommate was retired—"There are so many things we'd like to do." She still liked to do a good job at her work, as teaching had always given her great satisfaction.

Four months later, very little had changed. She described herself as loved and esteemed, which was just the way she wanted it. She made clear in all her answers that she reached out with love and affection to others. She clearly expected and received love in exchange.

A year later, a new school year had started, and the respondent was working again. She said she was a little happier than at earlier periods in life and was now looking forward with special pleasure to spending the summer months in the New England home that her roommate had just bought. She was still busy with her teaching, but she found the work getting harder and talked frankly of retiring. She wished she could see her relatives more, but still found herself very happy.

In May of that school year, she suddenly retired. The combined pressures of ill health and age had forced a sudden decision. It was in this period, following her retirement, that the significant others in her life were interviewed. They gave a picture of a fine, kind, dedicated teacher, beloved by everyone. They all substantiated the picture of a woman with strong values who had been supremely happy in her life's work, but was finding retirement difficult.

In the final interview, some months later, she reported that now she was a great deal more content with retirement. Her days were quiet—no routine, no pressure. Mostly she shopped a little and took care of an ancient dog. Weekends she and her roommate went visiting and did chores. Sunday she regularly went to church, even getting her Protestant roommate to drive her some miles to church when they were in New England, where they were soon to live permanently. She accepted all these changes with characteristic good spirits, but did mention how she missed the children from time to time; mostly she missed being needed by them.

She had clearly begun to disengage but was not disintegrating. She made fewer new friends, had fewer responsibilities, was less concerned with making a good impression, and bought fewer new clothes. She was clearly, determinedly autonomous-persistent. She took a lot, but she gave back even more. Her style of life had appeared to be oriented to the World of Work, but in reality she worked for economic necessity and not for style. Her style was basically a familistic one in the way she related to pupils and co-workers. There was also Couplehood underlying it as a style. Thus, at her retirement she was able to be strongly couple-oriented in style, letting her familism become secondary and so aging successfully.

Couplehood Though Alone

This seventy-two-year-old man came from a rural background, as did so many of the respondents in the panel, especially those in their seventies and eighties. His father was a farmer and a school teacher. He had admired his parents while he was growing up, and he remembered them as agreeable people. He had gone through the fifth or sixth grade; he could not remember which.

He went to work for his uncle at a rather early age and became a skilled worker with a trade. He recalled the period from 1912 to 1918 as the best time in his life. Business was good, and he was married and enjoying life. He referred to his first wife frequently throughout the study. He remembered her as a very pleasant person who "liked parties, was good looking, and a good cook." She died in the flu epidemic of 1918. He was subsequently married and divorced twice, married a fourth time, and widowed in 1951. The worst period of his life was when he lost an eye and was out of work. He did not begin getting work again until about 1935, and did not have much work until World War II, so he had suffered considerably from the Depression.

At the time of the first interview, in October 1958, he was living in a three-room apartment, part of a two-story house which he owned. He rented the upstairs portion. He had lived in Kansas City for thirty-nine years and liked it. He liked his neighbors, whom he described as good working-class people like himself. His last full-time job was in 1949, following which he worked part time for a considerable period, but by the time of the study he was fully retired and living on social security and rental income. His daily round consisted of watching television, playing the fiddle, puttering, going to card parties, and sometimes going to a dance. He visited his daughter every day as she lived just two doors away. He spent a good deal of time with his daughter and son-in-law on Sundays, and occasionally went to church with the daughter. He described his last wife as a very fine woman and frequently talked about his daughter as a very lovely girl. He had one grandchild whom he also saw every day. He mentioned four friends (three ladies and one man), and said that he knew ten neighbors by name, and visited them now and then. He occasionally visited the people with whom he had worked. However, he told the interviewer that, if he had his life to live over, he would not have gone into this type of work. He would have gotten a better education and become a professional man so that he would not have had to "work so hard."

In March of 1959 he said things were fair. He had been playing cards quite a bit and enjoyed that very much. He had taken a trip to a western state to visit his sister. Things looked about the same in November of that year. When asked what he would do if he were suddenly given $25,000, he replied, "I would give it to my son—oh, that's right, I don't have a son—I would give it to my daughter." In response to the story question about Mrs. Birch, he said without hesitation that she would marry.

The situation remained unchanged in January 1960 and again in November 1961. At the time of this last interview, the interviewer recorded that the respondent had a long telephone conversation with a lady friend and commented that, at the age of seventy-seven, the respondent still thought of himself as a ladies' man. He was still playing cards and going dancing.

This respondent represents an interesting variant of Couplehood as a style. He had clearly achieved it with his first wife, with his last wife, and possibly with one of the others. His four marriages suggest a strong need to be "coupled." During the period of the study he had transferred the focus of couplehood to his daughter and to his lady friends.

He was clearly autonomous-persistent and has been ranked in that category at the top. He contributed a good deal to his significant others, and took little from them. His charactertistic modes of use of action energy were all well organized and in balance and have been rated 1. His style, although clear, was not quite as salient as for others in this group, and he has been rated 2 on that variable.

THE LESS SUCCESSFUL AGERS

Trapped in Couplehood

At the beginning of the study, in the summer of 1956, this respondent was a fifty-eight-year-old woman, Protestant, and a college graduate. She lived with her sixty-eight-year-old retired husband, who was a professional man. She had two sons and one daughter, all of whom were now away from home. The interviewer described her as a tall, thin, youthful woman, who spoke freely and had an appearance of relaxed vitality.

At the very beginning of the interview, she impressed upon the interviewer that her husband had gotten on her nerves since he had retired and that she wished he were not around; she returned to this theme many times during the study. She said the house was too big for them. She did a lot of sitting and pacing the floor and was a very heavy smoker. She claimed she was not relaxed enough to read. She belonged to no clubs and went to no meetings. She claimed that her outside interests had dwindled during the ten years that her mother had lived with them.

She then told the interviewer quite freely and frankly that she was under psychiatric care for what she said the doctors called a "depressed psychosis." She had been hospitalized for two weeks three years previously. Her illness had developed after her children left home. Recently she thought she had been much better; she had been lacking in incentive and drive, but had begun to feel she might recover. She said her husband was the calmest, most contented person imaginable, who had not complained during the three and one-half hard years of her illness. It was apparent, however, that his very calmness disturbed her. Her weekends were no different from the rest of the week. She did not go to church, although years ago, before her marriage, she had been active in church and had taught Sunday school. She had one very close friend, an older woman, whom she saw about once a week and talked to frequently on the telephone. She frequently confided in this friend and found that it cheered her up. She mentioned two other friends, one of them fairly close, whom she rarely saw but talked to on the telephone. All three of these friends had stood by during her illness. One son was married and lived in Kansas City, the other lived in a nearby city, and her daughter lived in a southwestern state. In April 1957 she looked better. She had spent a month in the southwestern state with her son and new daughter-in-law. She had started to go to church and went to a monthly meeting of a church group. She also did telephoning for another group. Every other week she took one of her neighbors to a home for the mentally ill to visit the neighbor's sister. She was watching television a little bit more and enjoyed at least one program per evening.

The husband was present during the first part of the interview. He then left and the respondent commented, "Whew! Thank goodness!" She said her husband flourished in retirement, that he read a great deal, and that his retirement had been voluntary.

In the spring of 1958, she kept putting the interviewer off but was finally seen in May. She had been depressed and nervous and had spent five weeks in a hospital for shock treatment during the preceding summer. She now saw one friend every day and another one once a week, and she wrote lots of letters. She said she felt about ninety and would like to be forty-five, a period when all the children were home. She again commented that her husband really did not need her and that his retirement had been extremely hard on her. Her husband liked to listen to ball games, which she could not stand.

In November of 1958, when asked about the nicest thing that had happened, she said that her husband, a nonbeliever, had gone to a church supper with her. Also, she had spent a lovely week with her daughter. The worst thing was a rather disappointing trip to the southwestern state to see her son again. She said there was nothing good about being the age she was. She was never lonely, and when she felt depressed, she wanted to be alone. She still had spells when she hated everything about the house for a day or two. The most irritating thing was when her husband tried to pressure her to do something. Up until about six years before, they had gone out a lot with friends, but the friends had died or moved away.

The best years in her life, she said, were in her middle and late thirties, when she had her family, was active in club work, and had many friends. Shortly after that, the older boy married against her wishes, and things started going badly. She stated that the worst time in her life was when she lost her mother, but then added that this was her psychiatrist's idea. She said things had never changed for the better, but then added, "Oh, it's not all bad, we sometimes have good times on trips." She again claimed that she liked being alone and did not know what to talk about with her husband: "He has such a darn practical outlook on life." She again told the interviewer flatly that she was tired having her husband around, adding, "It's a good thing he's deaf and can't hear me." She had "blown up" recently at her husband because he could not adapt socially. He sat reading a book on a visit and had not entered into the conversation. Then she added, "My doctor told me to blow my top."

She said smoking was her greatest temptation in life, and she did a lot of it. She was also tempted to buy a high fidelity set. Among her regrets were having been a "bridge fiend" at one time in her life, to some neglect of her family. She admitted that she thought of death and occasionally had death wishes.

In November 1959, her daily round looked about the same, except that she had bought the high fidelity set and was listening to records a great deal of the time. As a result, she no longer watched television. Her husband occasionally annoyed her considerably by trying to read aloud to her. In response to the story question about

Jones, she said that he did take the job and added, "If he read aloud to me, I'd be glad he took it."

Another story question which we found quite revealing of style and other characteristics of the action system was: "Mrs. Smith was outraged when a cousin of hers insulted her one day. She spent the whole day fuming about her cousin and daydreamed of ways to get back at her. The next day she heard that her cousin had been killed in an auto accident. How did Mrs. Smith feel?" This respondent replied, "I don't want to know this namby-pamby Mrs. Smith. I hate her." If she suddenly acquired $25,000, she would save it for the children. She was doing considerably more reading than previously, and she had taken a programship of her church circle. In response to the story question about Mrs. Birch, this respondent replied that Mrs. Birch would marry, then hastily added, "But I wouldn't."

In January of 1960, she said she was not sure what people, even her children, thought of her. Her husband stifled her initiative. It had cost lots of money to get her back where she was then, and she said that her spells were farther apart and not as severe.

She spoke of her father as the grandest person who had ever lived. He was an entertainer and at one time had had an outside love affair. It was her mother who had held the family together. She was proud that she had always behaved perfectly toward her father, although she resented that he had interfered in her choice for marriage. She admitted dreaming rather frequently and described a dream of being in an elevator from which she could not get out. As to daydreams, she said she sometimes speculated about whom she would call first if her husband died.

The clinical psychologist saw her in September of 1960 and noticed a flatness of affect and tight control. Consequently, he decided not to probe deeply. He commented, "She is much more emotional than her husband, who has ceased to be anything for a long, long time." He felt she had a real goal of getting back to good health. The son who had lived in the southwest had now returned to Kansas City, and the psychologist reported good relations with a granddaughter during the interview. He noted that she was losing some of her friends, but felt that perhaps she would begin to adjust to having her husband around the house.

An interviewer called at the house in March 1961 to interview the husband, who was not at home. She did see the respondent and was shocked by her appearance. The respondent was neatly dressed, but very pale, with her hair disheveled and a strong odor of liquor on her breath. The respondent told the interviewer in that brief encounter that she wanted to get away and did not want to go to the doctor or to the hospital. She had only slept two hours the night before, and she felt that she and her husband were about to separate.

In April 1961 the husband was interviewed. He was quite abrupt and did not smile throughout the interview. The original respondent was away attending a church meeting. He said that the best time of life for him had been when he was in the Army, but also added that the period when they lived in a nearby city and the family was growing up was also a good time. He said that the present period was the worst for him because of his wife's mental condition. She had a depression about every week or ten days; at these times, he could not sleep and was afraid that she might commit suicide. He said that he could not afford to let himself get upset. The interviewer noted, too, that he was obviously very fond of the dog. He said the "kids" visited fairly frequently, adding, "probably too frequently." They ate quite a few of their meals in restaurants. Sunday was the worst day of the week because his wife was always depressed on that day. He commented that his wife could not reconcile herself to getting old, and also that she loved to drink beer. He said, "Music thrills her, but not me." He claimed that retirement had not changed their relationship!

A friend and neighbor was interviewed at about this time. She had been in the business world. She had been married twice and the first marriage was very unhappy. She was struggling to try to keep the second marriage "halfway livable, serene, and bearable." She and her husband occasionally went out to dinner with the original respondent and her husband. Her own life space was rather limited, and it was apparent that the original respondent filled a gap in it. She said that the original respondent hated getting old. She had known her for six years. She and the original respondent drank beer together, and she commented that "she *loves* beer." The friend claimed that she herself did not drink much. They had no mutual friends. She then told about an episode when a house plant was broken after they had had a couple of highballs. She thought the original respondent had no life goals and commented that she had depressions "for no good reason" and would be "way high and then way low." She thought the respondent was about forty, although she seemed about sixty; her actual age at this time was sixty-three.

The minister of her church was interviewed during this same period. However, he knew very little about her life—"Just a handshake on Sunday." The visitation minister from the same church was interviewed. He had known the respondent for about two years and saw her twice a month. He said he thought the respondent was about sixty years old. "She shows pain in her face, and it is not all physical." He said she was in a state of confusion "between outgoing and retiring." He thought she did lots of reading, and he had encouraged her to enter a study group. He had seen her that same day, and she had seemed reasonably oriented. He said, "She doesn't strike me as being mentally disturbed." She had always been very warm and cordial to him.

There was also a rather remarkable interview with a beauty shop operator, who had a tiny shop where the original respondent had been coming regularly for the past three years. The operator said she very much liked the respondent and that it always gave her a lift when she came in. She thought the respondent was about sixty, but looked younger. She said the respondent was interested in everything, pleasant, had a sense of humor, a great deal of common sense, and never complained. She knew that the respondent had been in a hospital and not well, but the respondent had never complained about this. She also said that she had done a great deal for a sick friend. She thought she led a normal life, knew that she read a lot, and enjoyed visits from her family. She said the respondent had "almost" had a nervous breakdown at one time.

The daughter was interviewed in November. She said she had been giving a lot of thought to her mother lately, as to why her mother had so many foibles, fears, and desires and what her mother's real relations were with her father. She said her mother was very emotional and her father was taciturn. Her mother needed to be needed, whereas her father was self-sufficient. She thought that her mother visited quite frequently with her neighbor friend, and added that sometimes the men stayed at one house to watch television and the women went to the other house. She knew that her mother was depressed on Sundays and thought that this had been a habit of long standing. She said that her mother belonged to the mothers' group of her own sorority and that she attended meetings once a month.

The respondent was interviewed again in December of 1961. She announced that she had had a beer and was an inveterate smoker. She talked at some length about Christmas shopping being a terrible chore. She had made a trip East the summer before with her husband to attend his fiftieth college reunion. She had also made a trip to Dallas with her husband and seemed to have enjoyed both trips. She said that some nights she did not sleep very much. If she felt well, she would "go like a house afire, if not, I do nothing." She had become treasurer of a group at the church and secretary for the sorority mothers' club. However, she also said that she almost never went out and spent most of the time reading and listening to the hi-fi. The big house got her down, and she still wished that they could get an apartment. She again made a big point that her husband's retirement had been "a pain in the neck." She said her daughter was like herself, "very nervous." Describing herself, she said, "I have no strong points —oh, perhaps a determination to do things for myself. I've never slept well because my brain is too active. I have never pampered myself. I have not grown old gracefully. I am not like my husband who can sit by the hour." She said she had all she needed, but they meant less to her than they did to her husband. She and her husband spent a good deal of time in different parts of the house. Family gatherings were all right once they were over, but it was getting harder and harder to get ready for them. She had fewer friends and did not make new friends. Her main extravagance was on books and records. An ideal day for her would be to "be alone just one day," by which she meant not having her husband around the house.

A year and one-half later, in the spring of 1963, one of the authors requested the field office in Kansas City, which had not yet been closed, to interview this respondent briefly by telephone, largely to see how she was getting along. The report that came back was indeed interesting. The interviewer said:

I called and talked with R via telephone. Her voice sounded strong and vigorous, and she seemed in excellent spirits. Comments were made in the background from time to time by a son. These comments were apparently humorous, and R laughed gaily at them. In response to a question about how she and her family had been since the last interview, she said, "We have been most fortunate—we have had no serious illness." When asked how she was feeling personally, she said, "Fairly well for a person of my age. Some days I have no pep at all, but that's to be expected at this time of life. On the other hand, I know and see a woman ninety-three years of age, and she never seems to run down or have a bad day." When asked what she had been doing lately, she said, "For one thing, I bought a combination FM radio I can move about with me. I had a time finding it." The neighbor friend with whom she used to visit quite regularly and with whom she drank beer had died about a year and one-half previously.

When asked about any changes in her social life she said, "There really is no change in our social life. We just don't get out socially, and I really feel we should. Some of our friends join these age clubs. I don't want to join the Golden Age club. I hear in St. Louis they have a Silver Age club, which is a younger group, and if they get it started here I would like to join that."

When asked about the nicest and worst things that had happened in the last two years, she first said, "Nothing I can think of really," but when asked about trips, she replied strongly, "Yes! we had a *nice* trip to Florida in March. My husband took in the A's spring training, and I had a visit with an old friend. Last year we had a nice trip too. . . . As for bad things—you know we lost our old dog. She was blind and deaf and had lost all control of toilet habits."

When asked about what she was doing in her spare time, she said, "Well, I have been knitting. When I last saw you, was I making the squares for General Hospital? Well, I don't know how many squares I have made to make covers for the indigent patients. My daughter got me started knitting sweaters, so I have made eight or nine and give them to friends. . . . I'm still reading like mad!" When asked about new clubs, she said, "None, I still attend just church circle, and I am secretary of the sorority mothers' club. I don't do any bridge playing yet—I haven't gone back to that *yet!*"

We have classified this respondent as dependent-persistent, toward the bottom of the category. She liked to think of herself as autonomous and as doing everything for herself, but she took more out of her social system than she put into it. She had been treated for manic-depressive psychosis, and showed both manic and depressive traits at various points during the interviews. But she managed to live in the community, except for one very brief hospitalization, and even increased her activities to some extent. She was fairly successful as a mother and began having her mental difficulties after the children left home. She complained bitterly about living with a retired husband, and found the adjustment rather difficult. Actually, she protested too much. She leaned heavily on Couplehood as a style of life, and, although she was trapped in it, it acted as a strong protective coating which made it possible for her to persist and to keep her psychosis relatively well controlled. And there were periods, especially on trips, when she obtained a good deal of satisfaction from the style.

She did show considerable anomie and was rated 3 on that. There was a moderate amount of alienation and isolation, both rated 2, and she coped moderately well and was rated 2 on that. She could probably persist for several more years with this general mode of life. Her speculations about her husband's death reflected some of the ambivalence and, at the same time, expressed some fears of what would happen to her when he did die. She might move into a precarious position, but, on the other hand, there would be a possibility that she could re-establish Couplehood with one of her children.

The Duke and the Duchess

This sixty-four-year-old railroad engineer and his wife lived in a comfortable old six-room house in a good middle-class neighborhood. The respondent, a tall silent type, was complemented by his giggling, overanxious, overtalkative wife, who answered for him at any chance. Their two grown sons, one divorced and one married and with children, also lived in Kansas City.

He was born in a small town in Kansas and his father was a car repairer for a packing house, but he had been in Kansas City for forty-nine years and had been with the railroad all that time.

At the time of the first interview, he had reached the envied position of senior engineer and was working only every other day. This gave a special flavor to their life together, for on his days off he and his wife had a taste of what retirement would be like. They found each other's company wholly satisfactory, and their social life was limited to couples' activities. He stated he had no "buddy," but liked all kinds of people. He had two railroad group affiliations, but mostly he and his wife just sat around the house and watched TV. They went to see the children once in a while, and the children came to see them, but he was glad to see them go. His attitude toward them was best described as detached. Most important in their values was their weekly attendance at church. He was brought up a strict Roman Catholic by his father, and he still attended church regularly although he belonged to no church groups as he had some years previously. To him religion meant making sense of this world, and he felt special need of a guardian angel as he risked his life at the throttle of his engine. The important thing, he said, was not the church, but what went on inside a man—his faith was all important. "You have to live by the golden rule and the Ten Commandments."

Seven months later, the interviewer returned and found the couple coldly opposed to continuing the study. They had wildly misinterpreted the Christmas card the lady interviewer sent to the respondent as an attempt to seduce him. The wife said she had been subjected to all kinds of ridicule by her children. She was so angry she told how she sent the interviewer's husband a card from her alone to get even. This was typical of how the respondent and his wife were inextricably bound up, and how, in emotional situations, she called the moves. The interviewer explained the study again, and finally, somewhat mollified, they agreed to go on with questions.

The respondent said he did not want to retire, but might be glad to in five years, when he thought he would "just tinker around." He did not seem to think there would be much left to do when he retired. Most important to him was that he and his wife stay in good health.

A year later, a new interviewer (male) began seeing the respondent, and the respondent answered more fully since the wife seemed satisfied all was well. They still led about the same life, he said, and the most exciting thing had been a trip to Hawaii. It was from these trips, recounted at Lodge get-togethers, that they had acquired the nicknames "Duke" and "Duchess." They were the ringleaders in square dancing, fun, and general merriment. Friends were more important to them than relatives, and casual contacts were not particularly important. He still enjoyed work very much (even though there had been a fatal accident with his train recently), and still disliked the idea of retirement. He planned to continue as long as he was able. He took the accident in stride as an occupational hazard.

In January 1959, when the respondent was sixty-seven, life took a very different turn. The younger son died of multiple sclerosis, and the wife had two serious operations. With one boy's death and the divorce of the other, this man and his wife had no family to divert them. They had nothing left as important to them as cultivating life with each other. The death of his son had brought death to the husband's mind more often, but he accepted the idea without much fear. "I'm older and nearer," he said. "I've lived my life, now I kind of expect it."

His value system was clearly one of the acceptance of work and doing a good job at it. His values came directly from Christian ethics which had surrounded him since boyhood.

By the final interview, when he was seventy, he had resigned himself to his retirement, and he and his wife had bought a home in a western town of retired people. This was significant, because this town was the kind of community that stressed the couple-centered life and group recreation that had meant so much to the "Duke and Duchess" in the past. They could avoid casual associations that made demands on them (including grandchildren's visits) and would have maximum opportunity to disengage from work and community responsibilities into those phases of life that pleased them most.

Because of this close emotional tie between the two, the respondent's style was classed as Couplehood, and because of the wife's two serious operations, one for cancer, which made her long survival questionable, he was classed as precarious. The balance in exchange of action energy was on the side of the wife. This situation, together with the precariousness, could eventually make him a problem in his retirement community.

THE LEAST SUCCESSFUL AGERS

The Frustrated Inventor

This fifty-six-year-old man lived with his wife. He was a machinist and jack-of-all-trades with steady employment. They had no children, but in the recent past, and especially during the Second World War, there were many children in the house as they ran a day-care arrangement for children of working parents at no profit and probably at a loss. They lived in a working-class neighborhood; they had a "ranch" in the basement, consisting of some three hundred chinchillas, on which both of them, and especially the wife, spent a great deal of time. His wife thought he would never retire, and he doubted whether he would, except for physical disability, but his wife would have liked for him to retire and be around the house.

His father left the family when the respondent was about ten, and from twelve on, he was working and helping to support the family. He tried hard to get a higher education, but found he could not manage working and studying at the same time. He went into business for a while with his brother, but this did not work out well because, as the brother told us later, the original respondent's wife wanted him at home too much. But he had always had considerable mechanical ability, taught machine work for a while, and had been in his present job for several years.

In each of the interviews he talked about his various inventions, which ranged from those in automatic transmissions and programmed learning to a new method of swimming, whereby he could swim for hours. These inventions all appeared to have been too little or too late, and he had constantly lost money on them. During his middle years he thought he could "turn the world upside down." By the start of the study his expectations had become much lower, and they became even lower during it.

In December 1958 he seemed changed, did not think as clearly, and said he did not think his mind was as good as it had been. In later interviews, however, things were much as they had been, and the episode was probably reactive to serious conflict with his supervisor, who was subsequently fired. The respondent then became supervisor.

In March 1960 he admitted he had fallen way short of his goals in life. He had wanted to establish a big home for orphans and had just "taken it for granted that he could make all the money he wanted." He had made two rather complicated inventions since the previous interview but was about to give up inventing because he was trying to save money for his wife.

In October 1960 the clinical psychologist wondered if he could believe much of what the respondent told him. (A reading of the entire series, however, indicates that most of it, if not all, was true and checks out.) The psychologist noted two physical breakdowns, the one during school and one at the time of the respondent's marriage. He also noted signs of depression and some danger of suicide.

The wife, who was not only interviewed but also present during most of the interviews with the original respondent, had devoted her life to finding ways of being useful to other people. They had lost a child at birth. Of the chinchillas, on which she worked very hard, she said, without complaint, that they would never make any money on them because her husband was too soft-hearted to kill any of them. She spoke warmly of him and said they had no close friends because of the way he lived. They never spoke of aging, but she said her husband realized he was getting old. They "went out" three times the preceding year.

The chiropractor, who thought of him as a nice fellow who seemed younger than he was, said he visited his mother in a nearby state every three months and was a person who made friends. The butcher, who had known the respondent for fourteen years, thought he was gregarious and liked to talk to people. He had been aware of a change, however, which he accounted for by saying that friends had moved away and that the respondent's wife no longer took in children.

In November 1961 the respondent said he was fine. He had begun to watch television, which he did not do at the beginning of the study. He said his "deft" for inventions had decreased. He had given up his swimming method because of a back injury and this, too, represented the failure of an invention.

This couple were highly dependent on each other, and his style is clearly Couplehood, although she put much more out for him, and he was just around, highly disengaged except at work. Work, for him, however, had never been the World of Work, as a style of life. Except for a brief and unsuccessful period in business, it had been a way to express his inventiveness. His attitudes toward retirement, expressed early in the study, were an expression of this relationship. The inventiveness was beginning to disappear. When it was gone, it might not be possible to sustain him as a going concern, wife or no wife. He has been rated 2 on anomie, alienation, and isolation, and 2 on coping. The clinical psychologist's judgment of some danger of suicide is probably correct.

Rejected and Hurt

Sometimes a person spends a lifetime trying to find himself, and by his search achieves a noble and satisfying style that wins for him a deep, enduring place in the affections of those in his life space (for example, "Pain and Giving"). But sometimes, the harder a person seeks to find himself, the more elusive becomes the quest, and the frustrated searcher becomes hopelessly enmeshed in trying first one scheme and then another; often, in this case, he pathetically succeeds in alienating the ones in his life space he most desires to hold close. That is the story of this respondent, a sixty-four-year-old woman, who, but for the love of her husband and the consequent style of Couplehood, would have been totally alienated and isolated by the end of the study.

She had grown up in the midst of a large family, among whom she felt she could have been the best had she not been unloved and inept in interpersonal relations. She was marked by this outlook from at least the age of thirteen, and it grew worse rather than better as the years went by.

Her father died when she was in her teens, and she went to work at once to help support the family. Outwardly, she was willing, but inwardly she was greatly annoyed at the lack of aid given by her other siblings. She had her happiest time of life in her adolescence. She felt her peer group enjoyed her and accepted her fully. The psychologist reported that this left her with a feeling that she could do no wrong, that she had a sort of total strength, a feeling she never lost completely. It took the form, in her adult married life, of extending herself for others, but so annoying was her attitude of omniscience, that she received nothing in exchange, which was highly frustrating to her.

Her husband understood and worked hard to help her try to understand herself, but with little success. At the time of the study, she was fighting a heavy burden of physical ailments which were aggravated by her personality problems. She and her husband had never had children, but had given a great deal of time to caring for near relatives. She had also tried to keep a tight bond between herself and her nearest sister, but at the beginning of the study all these relationships had broken down. The respondent was also alienated from her church family by repeated personal conflicts. Similarly, despite the considerable advanced education she had acquired, her civic efforts soon were found unacceptable by those with whom she worked.

She used the study and the interviewers as a sort of self-analysis on the installment plan and actually came to sufficient insight to heal some of the intrafamily breaches, but she was unable to make more than superficial changes. At the end of the study she was growing worse physically, mentally, and socially. Her only close permanent relationship was to her husband, and she was terribly dependent on him. This gave her a rating of dependent-precarious, at the top of the category.

ANALYSIS

Couplehood illustrates the same principle of successful aging that Familism does. Particularism, in Parsons' sense, tends to be closely associated with functional diffuseness and affective relationships. If the particularism in Couplehood results in narrowing the field to one particular person in what might be called a closed system, there is an element of precariousness simply due to the probability that something could happen to remove that person from the field (death, desertion, divorce). This situation is well illustrated by "The Duke and the Duchess." On the other hand, in "Beyond Couplehood," a case briefly reported in Appendix Two, a woman is also totally unable to transfer her couplehood to anyone else after her husband dies, because of the closed system of her life style. Nevertheless, she maintained her couplehood and autonomy by a rare device of living chiefly in her memories without losing her hold on reality. The fact that her style rating was 2 certainly made it easier for her to maintain her primary style than if it had been more strongly held. This form of Couplehood is also more likely to be associated with dependency, as is well illustrated in the case of "The Frustrated Inventor." If the person is able to develop one or two alternative focuses for this style, that is, other partners, a possibility which is enhanced when Familism is a secondary style, both precariousness and the probability of dependency are lessened. "Couplehood Though Alone" is a good illustration of this situation. Finally, if a person is able to diffuse this style beyond its immediate focal point, the chances of autonomy and persistence are best, as illustrated by "Goodbye Miss Chips."

This style is predominantly, but not exclusively, associated with marriage; twenty-four of the thirty-three were married at the time of the study. It is clearly a style open to the widowed, both men and women; there were seven respondents in this category, five women and two men. Two single people developed this style, both women. It is possible that fears of homosexuality or being charged with homosexuality prevent this style from developing among men to any great extent. One of the single women developed the style with her single brother ("The Retired Working Girl"—see Appendix Two). It is interesting to note that none of the people with this style was divorced at the time of the study, although a few had been divorced earlier and remarried.

Success and misery can be linked in this style, as it can in the others. This situation is vividly illustrated by "Isolated Couplehood." This seventy-six-year-old semiskilled worker lived in a small apartment in a rundown hotel with his semi-invalid, seventy-four-year-old wife. At the beginning of the study he still did a little work on occasion, but was soon prevented from doing so by his wife's incapacity, and later on by his own poorer health. They eked out a living from social security. The wife never left the apartment, and he rarely did. They belonged to no group, did not attend church, had no relatives, no relations with the neighbors, and no longer saw any friends. They had had two children, but both died in infancy. He spoke of his wife as a very good woman and said they were always together. At one point during the study he had a severe cold which nearly went into pneumonia, but he could not afford to see a doctor. Throughout this entire period he took excellent care of his wife, whom one of the interviewers thought to be senile and perhaps feeble-minded as well as physically handicapped due to a hip condition. He was a drain on no one. He was classed as autonomous-persistent in the top category. He did show a considerable amount of anomie, some alienation, and extreme isolation. He coped reasonably well, given all the adversities, and he was rated 2 on that. The style was very distinct and was rated 1.

"Trapped in Couplehood" is a good illustration of how a clearly developed style can be a protective coating against mental illness, as is "The Almighty Dollar" in the preceding chapter. In this instance, the two personalities were complementary: the husband was a calm, taciturn person, who was able to tolerate a considerable amount of disturbance on the part of his wife.

"Rejected and Hurt" represented a variant of Couplehood in that the respondent really wanted to achieve a style of Living Fully. Occasionally, a style is clearly not a first choice, but is the style the person is able to achieve under the circumstances of his action system. Thus, Couplehood for this respondent was infinitely preferable to Living Alone, and she was grateful for it, but she was far from satisfied with it because what she really wanted was a wide circle of diffuse affective relationships. Her growing personal disorganization in the face of the discrepancy between her achieved style and her preferred style was a major factor in her precarious rating.

In two instances the sample happened to pick up two members of the same family who turned out to have joint Couplehood as a style of life. There are certain aspects of joint Couplehood that are of theoretical significance in studying styles of life.

The first pair, "Baby Sister" and "Successful Widowhood," were two widowed sisters who lived together. The older, "Successful Widowhood," stayed home, ministered to "Baby Sister" and her needs in every way, and sacrificed herself, her time, and her money. She cooked and sewed for the younger, and did all she could to make life pleasant for her sister, despite her own numerous physical hardships. "Baby Sister," on the other hand, went to work and took all her older sister's efforts on her behalf quite for granted. She rarely helped with even routine chores, and in reporting on events in the household she never thought to mention her sister's illnesses unless she was inconvenienced by them. This was a clear example of an autonomous-persistent person coupled with a dependent-persistent one, both of whom had a style of Couplehood with a strong base of Familism. This arrangement was relatively satisfactory to both parties, for each filled the other's need. Because one party has a style of Couplehood, the partner does not necessarily have to embrace the same style. But when both have achieved Couplehood, the relationship tends to be a satisfying one.

A second example of this type was "Husband" and "Wife," who had achieved joint Couplehood in their seventies. In this case, the husband was the dependent one and the wife autonomous. Their Couplehood was so complete that each listed couples only when asked to list best friends. The delicate balance between the autonomous and dependent partners, both of them persistent, was shown in many small ways. She had active church interests outside the home, he had none. She reported that she made up her own mind when faced with serious problems; he reported he asked his wife. But both agreed they were very happy, and one said, "We're just about equal."

The husband adhered to this style more strongly than did his wife, and he had made Couplehood evident in all aspects of his life. In his work as a clerk, before he retired, he made clear that he had enjoyed working with others, but usually worked with just one man. In fact, the only hero he could recollect from his childhood was Robinson Crusoe, a man for whom Couplehood as a style surely meant a great deal. He even turned to his wife throughout the interview to help him answer his questions, whereas she answered hers alone. In summary, he said, "The best of this age is that I'm still alive and thankful we can be together."

The romanticized idea of an old couple walking hand in hand into life's sunset does have some basis in couples such as "Husband" and "Wife," but it is not typical of most of the cases in this study. Joint Couplehood is far from a universal style of life, even among the married.

SIX

❦

Easing Through Life with Minimal Involvement

The smallest number of respondents, twelve, developed the style of Easing Through Life With Minimal Involvement. All but one had married, but their commitments to marriage and the family were minimal. All of them worked, or had worked, but their involvement in the World of Work, with one exception, was minimal. It is a style found in all three socioeconomic categories, and one which can be seen in all the age groups in this panel. However, there were eleven men, and only one woman, and we are convinced it is a style which is much more likely to develop around male rather than female roles in this culture. The style is found in all the success categories, and about equally divided among them, with four autonomous-persistent, one autonomous-precarious, four dependent-persistent, and three dependent-precarious. There is, again, variation on the other variables within the style, although in this instance the two dependent categories are rather strikingly associated with anomie, alienation, and isolation.

THE MOST SUCCESSFUL AGERS

The Crony

It was difficult to get a good image of this man during six full rounds of interviewing because of the kind of life he led. Fortunately, some later material of a different kind gave us a vivid picture.

He was sixty-five years old at the beginning of the study and lived with a female cousin in her mid-fifties. He was an only child and had

93

grown up in the East. His father had died when he was about nine years old. He spent a few years in business college and tried a number of jobs before coming to Kansas City. A relative urged him and his mother to come there. He came on first, happened to find a job operating a streetcar, and worked at that for more than thirty years. His mother joined him shortly, and he lived with her for many years. He was married briefly when he was in his early forties, but divorced two years later. At the beginning of the study, in 1956, he was retired from his job. He was medium height, thin, wrinkled, and gray. He wore glasses and had false teeth that did not fit well.

The small home where he lived was owned by his cousin, and he paid room and board to her. He did all the grocery shopping, which he did not especially like, and also washed the dishes. He said he enjoyed "TV and shooting pool, and that's about it." In the evenings he usually watched television with his cousin.

In April 1957 he talked more about pool and the pool hall. He felt it was important for him to go to the pool hall because they might want him to work. He kept his own record of all the pool scores. He said he never did make friends with the neighbors. If he inherited money, he would like to travel.

In August 1957 the picture was essentially the same. His eyesight was beginning to give him trouble and he missed being able to read all that he wanted to. He was thinking of taking a part-time job so that he could get enough money to take a trip to the East to visit some old buddies of his that he had not seen in more than thirty years. He stated, "I never get too friendly, lest people get inquisitive and want to know your business."

The picture remained unchanged in January of 1959. His eyesight was his only problem. He said he was lonesome only when he could find no one with whom to play pool. He did not like to be told how to do things, at the pool hall or by his cousin. Another cousin, the married sister of the cousin with whom he was living, was thinking of moving to a southwestern state with her husband, and he thought he might possibly go with them. He thought the best period of his life was "probably the last twenty or twenty-five years. Nothing exactly happened. It seems to me I enjoyed it more than the early part." If his cousin were retired, he might stay home a little more than he did. He was somewhat diabetic and had not had a beer in two years, although he was tempted. He added, "I do smoke." If he had six months to live, he would travel and spend all his money (partly to keep his cousin from getting any of it). The interviewer rated him as satisfied with his way of life at that time, and noted that he helped just enough around the pool hall and at home so that he did not feel useless.

In August of 1959 he was working at the pool hall. As a result, he was hard to find for an interview. He said he was taking care of the pool hall, but business was going to the dogs. The fellow who ran it had taken a paper route, and the respondent took care of the place during the periods the proprietor was away. He was permitted to play pool as long as there were empty tables, and there always were. Now, instead of watching television with his cousin, he went out every evening and was rather mysterious about where he went. The cousin did not know. He was always home for dinner. He proudly stated that he went to bed between 11 P.M. and 1:30 A.M. His pool hall was closed on Sundays, so on that day he went to another one.

In relation to the story about Jones, the respondent said that he would take the job and it would suit him very well. He added, "I like to roam." As to the story about Mrs. Birch, he thought that she ought to stay single.

In November of 1959 he had come back from a visit to the East where he saw old haunts and visited with childhood friends. In regard to life goals, he said, "I am passé for goals." He also commented, "I am happy because I've got nobody to bawl me out." He recounted a dream of having to climb walls and jump fences to get where he was going, but said he had waked up before he got there.

Participant observations, which began in the summer of 1961, gave a vivid picture of this respondent's style of life. It took the observer some time to win the respondent's confidence. He finally was able to go to the bar with him. There he immediately observed that the respondent and the bartender were very good friends. When the respondent had used to run the streetcar he would toot every time he passed the bar. The observer found that the respondent was not working regularly, but ocasionally did work the night shift in a parking lot. He usually went to bed after breakfast. He still did all the shopping. He also kept all the scores on the Kansas City Athletics and told the observer that he did not know why he did it, saying, "I don't know why I do anything."

On the second trip to the bar with the respondent, the observer pretended to be the respondent's son. "Everyone got a bang out of it, and the respondent went along with the gag." From then on the observer became a true crony of the respondent. He played barroom shuffleboard and bowled with him. The respondent used profanity and told dirty jokes with relish. He took particular delight in quarreling over a point with one of his buddies just for the fun of it.

During July, the respondent worked full time in a parking lot. The observer found him on one occasion complaining bitterly that "some s.o.b." had just stolen his transistor radio. His cousin had warned him not to take it to the parking lot, and he did not know what his cousin was going to say about the theft. He indicated that he was still playing some pool, with a seventy-five-year-old Jew with a glass eye. He emphasized, in particular, that he never played favorites with his friends. The observer noted that he always dressed like a retired doctor or lawyer, generally much better than others in his circle. A couple of days later, the observer again found him at the parking lot, and he had bought another radio. He said that his cousin did not say anything about this although he had expected she would, and the observer surmised that probably "she thought he was way beyond the stage where reprimands would do any good." He talked somewhat humorously of people, including himself, as "curling up and dying."

In August of that year he was still working in the parking lot, and the observer saw him there several times. The respondent said that he had used to go to the movies with his cousin every Saturday night, but four years ago they had bought a television and had not been out since. The cousin was now rather lonely at lunch, he said, because he could not be there. The observer noted that the cousin's married sister visited occasionally but the respondent was always either napping or out somewhere when she came. By this time he rarely went out in the evening; he watched some television with his cousin, although he could not see very well, and was going to bed a lot earlier than he had a few years previously. The observer also took the respondent to a ball game.

The observer saw him briefly in October of 1961 and learned that the respondent was going to have an operation on his eyes, as he had become almost blind. The respondent had not gone East to see his old friends because the operation would cost too much. The observer saw him in November and December. He was still always well dressed. His eyesight was failing. The observer also noted that the respondent was very fond of the cat. In January of 1962, the respondent was confined at home. He had had the operation but could not yet see. His cousin had visited him once in the hospital, and the parking lot attendant, whose place he had taken when the attendant was in the hospital, visited him every day and brought him cigars. During the observer's visit, the respondent's friends from the bar stopped by to see him and brought him cigars. He regretted that he was unable to play pool, but seemed to be taking his lot rather well.

He was interviewed again in January of 1962. He seemed to be in fairly good spirits, but said that time hung heavy on his hands. He could not see much on television, although he did listen to it. He was happy about his leisure because when he was working he had had the night shift, had slept during the day, and had not had much leisure time. The respondent commented, "I haven't any home, only a room in my cousin's home; even the furnishings are hers." He said he had fewer friends than he had had at the age of forty-five, because many of them had been connected with work. He saved some money every month for emergencies. He had not had many sorrows in life, although his mother had been sick for several years. He talked with fondness of the gang at the pool hall and said he had known them for years.

Fortunately—to complete the picture—the observer, who had become very fond of the respondent, saw him again in April of 1962. The respondent said he could get about quite well then. In fact, the observer went to the bar and played games with the respondent and said it was obvious that he could get about. The respondent commented that he would rather have Negroes next door than some white people. He was beginning to play a little pool again, and did some of the shopping.

This man represents one of the clearest cases of Easing Through Life as a style. This case also brings out the sharp contrast with Living Alone. This respondent was highly adept at the crony relationship, a joking play-oriented relationship that never gets very close. It is a diffuse-neutral and yet somewhat particularistic relationship.

This style made it relatively easy for the respondent to be autonomous-persistent, and we have rated him at the top of that category. He contributed to his system expressively, through humor and playing games, and, to the minimal extent necessary, instrumentally, by doing the shopping and the dishes in the small household he shared with his cousin. He could even take over an instrumental role, such as filling in as a parking lot attendant for a friend with whom he was not deeply involved. He took his eye problem very well indeed, and his cronies came to visit, joke, and give him cigars. We predict that he would persist in good balance as long as he lived, even if his eyesight failed him again. He was rated 1 on all his characteristic uses of action energy and 1 on saliency of style. One can age successfully by moving through

the interstices of the social system in a jocular manner, provided there
has been rather long practice in the style of Easing Through Life With
Minimal Involvement.

Keep on Living

This eighty-four-year-old man was first a farmer, then a small
businessman, and had then retired. He did not particularly enjoy being
retired, yet said he had no problems and could not think of any problems older people might have. He got up at 5 A.M. (as did many of
the people interviewed), puttered around the garden, watched a lot
of television, took several naps a day, and went to bed at 11 or
11:30 P.M. He said the day was "gone before you know it." He saw
little of his children, two of whom were on the west coast. The most
important thing in life, he said, was eating when hungry—a classic
expression of disengagement.

In October 1958 he said he was fair, but felt he was getting old,
which was odd to him because he had never felt that way before. He
was never lonely. His main goal in life was to conserve his energies
and emotions to keep on living and not be a burden to anyone. If he
had had his life to live over, he said, he would have stayed at home
instead of getting married and eventually would have traveled. His
seventy-two-year-old wife did most of the household tasks, although
he shared in some. He visited a local store daily, where he was known
affectionately as "Dad" and was considered to have a good sense of
humor. He kept up with the news and was an avid baseball fan. His
wife said of him, "If he ever had a goal, I never knew it."

In the summer of 1961, a participant observer said that the respondent's daily round was the same, except that he had given up
hedge trimming; his mind was clear and his memory good. The picture
was the same in an interview with him in December 1961. His wife
answered the questions for him whenever she was in the room; she
did not smile, and he did. The clinical psychologist had observed
earlier that the respondent's main concern was for his wife, who, although twelve years younger in chronological age, seemed in many ways
older.

Although a simple count of daily tasks would suggest that the wife
did more for him than he did for her, in terms of action energy the
situation was reversed. As the clinical psychologist observed, this was
"a remarkable old man." Disengagement came easily to him, as he
had never been highly involved. He showed no signs of anomie or
alienation, and he coped very well. He was mildly isolated, but it did

not bother him. Again, aging was an easy matter for him, because he had learned long ago to ease along.

THE LESS SUCCESSFUL AGERS

Then She Married

This respondent gave us the most complete data of all the panel members, particularly in relation to her life history. At the same time, she presented us with the opportunity to refine the basic concepts of style, success, and both style and success in relation to the process of aging. The case history will be given in more detail than for other respondents because we have the rare opportunity of seeing the full life trajectory in all of its important ramifications. It is almost as if she had been the object of an intensive longitudinal study from early childhood, rather than just for the five and one-half years of the study. The retrospective material on her life history, obtained largely in two long interviews by a member of the senior staff of the study, comes through with a strong impression of accuracy with no important distortions.

Childhood and family of orientation. The respondent was born and grew up in a medium-sized New England city. She was the eldest of three daughters.

Her father was of New England Methodist background. He started as a cashier in a bank and rose to be its president. She described him as being:

> quiet, controlled—not exactly reserved. He liked people very much. He was sure of himself and achieved his goals. He was very strict, but of a kindly strictness. He had a great deal of common sense. In the early part of our lives he was perhaps a little unbending in his ideas but as he grew older he softened a bit. He was outstanding in town and had the respect of the people. No smoking or drinking—Sunday was a special day.

He was also a gifted amateur musician and served as organist and choir director in the Methodist church. He had somewhat dominated the respondent's mother, who was a Quaker. He came from a long line of New England storekeepers and musicians.

The mother came from a long line of school teachers. The respondent described her as a:

> *wonderful* person. She was a born actress, and I have always thought she could have made a great success in the theater, if

she had gone into it professionally. As it was, she organized the Little Theatre group and was very active in it. She was the sort of person who dramatized everything. She could make an exciting story out of anything that happened. She was quiet in manner, but she had a perfectly marvelous sense of humor. She *fascinated* father, the staid New Englander—they were so *different*.

She was a very energetic woman who participated heavily in community affairs, including the board of education. The respondent said:

> My sisters and I, when we get together, remember our childhood as the happiest time in our lives, and a lot of that is due to Mother. She read us things; and later, when we read things she hadn't read, she'd sit right down and read them herself. She'd say, "I must at least keep abreast of thee, even if I cannot be ahead of thee." Mother kept us going mentally—she entertained and instructed us.

Both parents were thus well-educated people, and it was assumed without question that all three girls would go to college and be trained for some profession and career. The respondent went to the local public grammar school and from there to a Quaker boarding school in Pennsylvania. She was quite talented musically, both at singing and playing the piano, and her father wanted her to attend a relatively new college, noted for its progressive approach, to prepare for a career in music education. But at this point there was considerable conflict with her father on the problem of career choice.

> There was some conflict with Father—maybe I felt frightened of going into something he was so good at himself. I danced, too, of course, and I suppose I could have been a music and dance teacher, but I just didn't want to teach, and I wasn't really good enough to be a professional dancer or musician. I sang in choirs, I've done that all my life, and I played the piano at parties—jazz, too, so of course I was delighted to party—but I decided to keep music an avocation. [Father was] pushing me, and he did something that always made me want to do the opposite. I wanted to go into musical comedy—but I didn't have enough money and not a *strong* enough desire to starve to do it.

Thus, she decided against a career in music, but still, on completion of boarding school, had not decided for anything in particular. So she went to a local college for women, on a scholarship. Because she had to select a major and a minor, she decided vaguely that she might like to be a writer, and majored in English and minored in modern languages.

After two years of college, a family friend wrote from France and offered the respondent a summer job in a school she conducted for children of parents who traveled. She accepted this, first spent a month in Paris leading a rather Bohemian life on the Left Bank, and then went to the province where the school was located. She spent six months in France and thought she might like to continue her education there. She was offered a job in a Paris dress shop, and spent some time trying to decide whether to take it. Her parents finally decided— and she did not fight the decision—that she was too young to live alone in Paris, although she was twenty-one at the time. So she returned to the United States, but decided not to return to college, and instead enrolled in a business college in another state, where she took a nine-month stenographic and bookkeeping course.

During her childhood she participated in the activities of three religious denominations. She attended the Methodist church, her father's regular church, went to the Episcopal Sunday school in a church where her father was choir director and organist for a time, and joined in Quaker meetings held in the family home. Ultimately, her father was converted to Quakerism, and, at eighteen, the respondent chose that denomination. At the time of the study she was a member of the Episcopal church, for reasons which will become apparent later, but she had never rejected her Quaker background.

At the age of fifteen, when she was in boarding school, she developed what she described as "a very deep and very close relationship" with one of the girls in her class. This relationship continued over the years, including the years of the study, and they had kept in close touch by writing "very intimately." She described this woman as "a fine, strong individual. She had a fine family and was a good mother and has done a great deal with her life. She has a sister who is schizophrenic and has taken care of her. Very strong person. I always pictured her turning out as a social butterfly—but she has done so much for her family."

The primary adult pattern. The respondent's first job after business school was in her home state, but in a different city, where for six months she taught in an insurance agency's employee school. This job, like the one in France, and most of her subsequent jobs, was gained through a family friend or relative. The school went out of business and the respondent then went to a large city in another eastern state to become secretary to the head of a consulting firm. There she established one aspect of her pattern of life which persisted over the years. Her jobs were mostly secretarial, but she seemed always to have professionalized them by being close to the top man, having subordinates of her own, and taking special interest in the work of the agency or firm for which she worked. She worked with the firm for three years in the eastern city, and then followed her employer to a large midwestern city when he was transferred.

She remained with this firm in the midwestern city for two more years, 1929 to 1931. She described her life during this period as "burning the candle at both ends," working hard all day, then going out to parties at night, frequently until dawn. During this period she met a woman whom she disliked intensely.

> She was a writer—a southerner. She used all her wiles, southern wiles—got men to work ideas up and then suddenly take them for herself. She was out to get somewhere and she did—stab people in the back. I'd never want to be successful if I had to do it that way—cute, attractive, feminine, but using people as she went along for her own ends. Her first husband committed suicide—she drove him to it.

The two women were in the same organization, and the other woman did not like the respondent's independence and self-assurance.

> She wasn't jealous, but didn't like the way I ignored her and protected my boss. We got along very well [on the surface]. She invited me to her home and to stay overnight and out to lunch. She played up to me as to others, but I was determined not to let her work on me against my boss. She never talked to me about business because she knew I wouldn't tell her anything. I admired her brains. She prostituted her brains. She could have gotten there without doing it that way.

It was also during this period that she had her first frustrated love affair. The man had a Quaker background like her own, but had become a Christian Scientist, and she claimed that this religious difference broke up the affair. But she also added that the affair was largely "physical" and that she had emerged from it "disgusted with men" and on the edge of a "nervous breakdown."

At this point, she established another pattern which became a recurring theme over the years. She gave up her job and went back to her New England home "for a rest." She withdrew almost completely from the outside world for six months, spending most of her time in her room and hardly stirring from the house. Then, partly at her parents' urging, she took a part-time job in a local store, and when this grew tiresome, she took a series of temporary office jobs in New York, filling in for regular employees on vacation. During the summer of 1932, she worked as social secretary and office manager for a Quaker resort in the Catskills.

She was then asked by her former firm to return to the midwestern city in a special capacity, and she went. Once again she had a stormy love affair. This time the man was an architect and artist—"a perfectly fascinating person"—but he wound up marrying one of his models. The respondent was again ill and depressed, and returned to her New England home. For about another year she took temporary fill-in jobs in New York, to which she commuted from her home.

In 1936, she went back to the other eastern city, where she had worked earlier, as secretary to the vice-president for another counseling firm. Her boss was, she said, an erratic man—jumpy, brilliant, demanding—who had already precipitated a nervous breakdown in one secretary. The respondent liked and respected him, but she had to leave her job after nine months, she said, "for the sake of my health. I was a high-keyed person myself, and working for him was giving me chronic indigestion and making me terribly nervous."

This time she did not go home but followed a variant of this pattern by going back to her alma mater, the boarding school, where for a year she was secretary to the principal and ex-officio member of the faculty. She loved attending faculty meetings, counseling students (which she did in an informal capacity), and being among Quakers. Most of the Quakers there, she said, were very broad-minded, in contrast to the "old-fashioned kind" who, like her father, frowned on smoking, drinking, and staying up late. One of the respondent's few acts of rebellion against her father concerned smoking in the family home. She said, "The Methodists are even worse than the Quakers on things like that, you know. For years, father wouldn't permit smoking in his house. But I faced up to him on that, and I did get him to break down—not on drinking, but on smoking at least. As a matter of fact, he got more liberal on matters of personal conduct as he got older."

She decided to leave the boarding school after a year because, she claimed, she was dissatisfied with the pay. However, she also added, "of course, all this may indicate that I wasn't sure where I was going or what I wanted to do." She always liked city living and felt isolated in a small country boarding school.

Her next move was to a university in a relatively small community in New York state, where from 1938 to 1941 she was secretary to a librarian and a music teacher. Her middle sister had been to this university in the late 1920's, and had raved about it for years. During this period she sang in the a capella choir and associated with musicians, artists, and architects. She had particular respect for one of the men for whom she worked.

In 1940 her father became very ill. He had an operation which was followed by unexpected postoperative complications. He nearly died and was hospitalized for five months, during which time the respondent dashed back and forth between her job in New York and her home in New England. She said, "I had to postpone resigning my job, because we needed the money for Father's medical care. And after he got out of the hospital, Father had to go to the southwest to recuperate." The respondent stayed on at the university until her parents returned home. In the meantime, she had had another love affair and broken down again. She said, "I got very thin, and, as you know, the climate in that town is very bad. So I finally resigned and went home for a while."

In 1942, she went to the west coast, because a friend of her father's offered her a job as secretary in another counseling firm. She hated it there and said it was particularly hectic because the Second World War had just started. In addition, salaries were frozen, and she felt underpaid. So she resigned and went to an employment agency. Because of her knowledge of Spanish she was sent to a secretarial job in a Latin American country. She stayed there for a year and lived in a rented house with three other "girls." She described this experience at some length during one of the interviews, in response to a question about best times in her life.

> It was an unusual job and a congenial bunch of people, and the kind of life you wouldn't lead anywhere else. We had servants and all that—a big house. It was interesting to learn about other kinds of people. We entertained a lot. I played an awful lot. It was a growth period for me. We were helping the war effort too. They picked older girls to go down. The young ones would go haywire. Four of us had a big house, and we had a ball. It was a lucky break that I got that job.

After that year she again went back to her parental home, and then held some temporary jobs in New York. After that, she went to work for a small concern in a southern city. On this job she traveled with her boss and a consulting engineer to various industrial plants in the region, working hard and playing hard, and learning a lot about engineering and engineers. She ultimately quit her job because she did not like her boss. "He wanted me to play night and day, and I'm just not that kind of person." However, she stayed on in this city for several more months, on another job, because, as the interviewer readily guessed, she had fallen in love with the consulting engineer. This romance was also ill-starred, and was complicated because the man already had a wife, whom he felt he could not divorce. The affair did become sufficiently serious that the respondent took this man home to meet her parents. They seemed to like him very much, although it is doubtful whether they fully understood the situation. She then went to an eastern city where she helped set up an office for the company with which she originally worked in the south. This company eventually went out of business, and she went back to her parental home.

She worked in her father's bank for a while and then drove her parents to the southwest where they had been spending every winter. This particular winter she stayed there with them and worked as a free-lance hotel stenographer. Her mother had a heart attack that winter and was hospitalized for a time. As soon as the mother was released, they all drove back to the parental home in the east, and the respondent stayed at home for another six months, keeping house for her parents. She then went to work in New York as secretary to the publisher of a women's magazine in "a very fancy suite of offices on Park Avenue." This magazine went out of business after a year and one-half and in 1948 she took a job as secretary and research assistant to an official of a professional association. Her employer, a woman, was making a survey, and the respondent worked on analysis and write-up.

"In the meantime," she said, "I'd become engaged. My fiancé was a fascinating man, charming, very musical, and brilliant—teacher at a progressive school in the New York area." But he had been married twice before, and this affair did not work out, she said, "because I found out he was unstable." She was "very attracted to him," and the romance lasted for two years. Also, her parents were quite fond of him. "Father had always wanted a son, and that's the way he treated Bill. He liked Bill very much, and I think Bill took advantage of it." In the midst of all this, her father began to show signs of mental illness and did, in fact, develop cerebral arteriosclerosis. The parents were in the southwest at the time, and the youngest sister sent them back to the east. The father had developed some grandiose ideas. The respondent said, "Bill and I were still engaged at this time, and Bill really was just wonderful with Father. Father trusted Bill and thought of him as a son."

Her father was committed to a state mental hospital in 1950, and the respondent, fatigued and strained by her love affair and her parents' troubles, went off to another city for a brief "rest cure period." Her fiancé had become rather possessive and resented the fact that she was living at home and commuting because that would break up their evenings. When the respondent returned to New York she found a letter from her fiancé announcing that he had gone off on his honeymoon. Her reaction to being thus summarily jilted was severe shock, but, she added, basically she was relieved. At first she told no one about it except her employer and her middle sister, a professional woman. The sister "got absolutely hysterical over it" and this lifted the respondent's spirits. She wrote to her former fiancé and said it was all for the best.

In ruminating about this love affair the respondent said, "It isn't that I didn't want to get married. I always wanted to get married, but I was interested in other things, too, and I never met the kind of man I wanted to marry." She added quite quickly, "I don't think my father had anything to do with this." And, after a pause, she said, "And then, I never was conscious of any particular drive to have children."

For several months following this episode, things went from bad to worse for the respondent. Her work was not going well, with her own and her parents' personal problems. Her employer was "very understanding, but she could see that I was getting more and more irritable and distracted. She suggested I take a leave of absence, but I wanted to stay on a while longer. I needed the money, and I needed to keep busy." Her father's stay in the mental hospital "was hell for Mother," who suffered a stroke a month after his commitment. The respondent again took over management of the family home, but this time she hired a housekeeper and kept working in New York.

The siblings in the later years. The respondent's middle sister had obtained a Ph.D. degree and had worked for a number of years in a southern state, dealing with mentally retarded children. But she had had a "nervous breakdown" and had had to give up her position. The senior staff member, who obtained most of the life history material, met and talked with the sister. She got the impression that the sister was quite a competent person in her field, but a very unhappy woman who had had more than one emotional breakdown.

The staff member found the sister to be quite "winning" and warmer than the respondent, who was also charming but rather cold. The sister was rather homely, but she had an extremely pleasant smile and a social style that indicated humor and enthusiasm beneath the subdued, somewhat self-effacing surface. As the sister was leaving the room, the respondent said, "She's the one with the degrees, and I'm the one that traveled." The sister added: "Yes, and I'm the one who never got married."

The respondent commented, "My sisters are far and away more fascinating than I." Then she launched immediately into a description of her youngest sister whom she greatly admired and probably envied somewhat. Her remarks indicated that she could always control the middle sister, in spite of her superior education and knowledge, but the youngest sister was the only one genuinely independent of the family. This sister had always been artistic, and the respondent said, "She's by far the most brilliant of the three of us." The sister had been married for twenty years to a man of aristocratic European origin, who was also an artist. They owned and operated an art shop in a middle-western city where they painted and did picture framing. Her sister and sister's husband were always very close. "They do everything together. I couldn't be that way myself, but it's really wonderful." They were childless because the husband "never wanted children, and he feels very strongly about it. My sister knew this man when she married him and knew exactly what she was getting into. But they are perfectly happy, and they are just fascinating people, both of them." It had been planned that this sister would go to an eastern college of considerable prestige, and she had taken the entrance exam on which she made the highest marks until then recorded. But, with characteristic independence, this sister decided she wanted to be an artist and packed herself off to art school. This sister never really returned to the ancestral home, unlike the other two, both of whom spent long periods at home during their adult lives. In this connection, the respondent commented, "I'm not really *dependent* on my family —it's just that I have always *loved* them so much. When we were growing up, we were a very close-knit family—so much so that people thought we were snobbish. It wasn't that; we just liked each other better than anybody else. Now my middle sister really depended. She always needed the family more than the rest of us. But my younger sister! I think she could get along without any family at all. Always could." The younger sister, in addition to her talent as an artist, also was able to sew beautifully, was talented musically, and was a gifted mathematician.

Of the middle sister, the respondent commented further that she "was quite unhappy as a child. She was the middle child, you know, and she thinks a lot of her trouble has been due to that. She knows a lot of the theory about that sort of thing, though I must admit I don't quite see the connection." As children, she and her middle sister were never close—both sisters were closer to the youngest sister. In later years, however, the respondent and her middle sister had grown considerably closer, and they had spent many hours discussing their early years. The respondent said, "My middle sister told me just the other day that she always felt that I favored the younger sister over her, and that all I ever tried to do for her was to boss her—of course, we were all inclined to be a bit bossy. We got that from Father." She described her middle sister further by saying that she was always the most studious and scholarly of the three, and was the best educated by far, but she was not brilliant, like her younger sister, nor socially outgoing like herself, and, therefore, felt painfully inferior to both.

The late marriage. In the fall of 1950 the respondent was still working for the professional association in New York when she agreed, at the request of a friend who was an engineer, to attend some social functions connected with a convention of engineers. She met one of the delegates, and they saw a good deal of each other for the next few days. The respondent liked him, "although he was a much older man; he was sixty-five when we met, you know, and I was forty-seven." He apparently made up his mind immediately that he wanted to marry her, and as soon as he got back to Kansas City he began a campaign of daily letters. The respondent commented, "That's very unusual for him; he never writes letters." This courtship by correspondence continued for several weeks, and finally, in December, the respondent consulted her minister and her doctor. "You see, I was thinking about my mother and father. I didn't feel that I could leave them. I felt they needed me." However, the doctor informed her that her father would not live longer than another year, and her mother would not last much longer than that—predictions which came true— and she decided to accept the proposal. They were married early in 1951.

Her husband's first wife had been dead for three years. He had three children, all grown and with families of their own, and no one to keep house for him. She said, "He's a family man. He needs a

woman, and when he met me, he was just ripe for marriage." The respondent was concerned about the reaction of the children, but they
accepted her immediately.

> In fact, I think they may have been relieved to have me on the
> scene—my husband was a strict father, though he has mellowed
> a great deal as he has gotten older. He is very much like my own
> father. I was brought up the same way my husband brought up
> his children, so perhaps that's why his children and I got along
> so well, right from the start.

The first year of the marriage was depressing and anxious. It was
the year of a big flood and her husband was quite involved with that.
She did not like Kansas City and knew no one, so she spent months
sitting at home with a Negro maid as her sole companion. The respondent put a bright aspect on the situation by saying:

> Well, of course, I was wholly occupied just learning to run a
> household and generally adjusting to marriage. I'd never spent
> much time in the kitchen, in my life, because I had never been
> married. You don't do much cooking when you are by yourself.
> That maid was really wonderful, she taught me a great deal about
> cooking and household management. I don't know what I would
> have done without her, that first year.

There was a stern and tough quality in her husband, and he was a
highly instrumental type whose almost exclusive preoccupation was
with his work.

She had to change her ways in several respects after marriage.
For example, she said her husband was:

> very, very intelligent, but he's slow and deliberate. I'm quick, and
> I'm always interrupting when others are talking. It's not that I'm
> trying to get the center of the stage, but just that I'm interested
> and always have something to say. But it drives my husband wild
> to have me interrupting him, and he's let me know it.

She had a great deal of difficulty with the menopause and attributed the loss of her singing voice to it. She joined the Episcopal
church because she believed her husband was an active Episcopalian;
she found out otherwise. "Oh, he talked about being a, you know,
'pillar of the church' but it turned out that he didn't mean in Kansas
City; he was talking about a small town where he used to live." She
joined another musical club mainly because she would have felt guilty

about wasting her musical ability if she had not. And she made a desperate effort to find social activities that she could enjoy with her husband. When the Episcopal church failed to provide this link, she joined the Shriners' Auxiliary. Then she rather apologized and said, "Organizations aren't as important to me as life with my husband."

She did not make friends, only acquaintances who were friends of her husband. She said, "Oh, I don't make *real* friends any more. I've already made them, and I don't really expect to make any more."

The senior staff member summarized some impressions of the situation by saying, "She thought she was marrying her father, but she has, I think, been cruelly disappointed. What she got was the authoritarianism without the indulgence."

The five years of the study. In October 1956, she was living with her husband in the lower part of a home which they owned; they rented out an apartment upstairs. She spoke of Kansas City, Kansas, with little enthusiasm, although she said that Kansas City, Missouri, was a fairly interesting growing town. She herself was living in Kansas City, Kansas, and did not like it. She preferred a large city with art galleries, lectures, music, and opportunities for many activities. She was not particularly happy about living in a neighborhood in which most of the people were Catholic.

She was somewhat uncertain about the future. She expected that she would stay in Kansas City until her husband retired and then they would probably buy a trailer and travel, keeping Kansas City as home base.

Her daily round was quite housewifely, interspersed with a great deal of letter writing. Her husband came home around 6 P.M., they had a couple of drinks, then dinner, and the husband went to bed immediately thereafter. She spent the evening largely in reading. When asked what part of the day she enjoyed most, she replied, "Night— I'm a night girl. Morning, it takes me two hours to get started."

She played golf twice a week. The division of labor on household tasks was normal for this culture. Saturday was no different from other days because her husband worked. Saturday evening they did usually go out to dinner, sometimes dancing, or to a baseball game. They occasionally went to church on Sunday, and watched a good deal of TV. When asked about things she enjoyed most on weekends, she mentioned watching TV with her husband, but when asked about the less interesting and enjoyable things on the weekend she also mentioned "programs on TV I don't like that my husband does."

In May of 1957, her husband was not working. He had not retired, but was between jobs. This situation made it somewhat difficult to arrange the interview, because the husband somewhat objected to the study. She had started working, but intended to give up the job because it was a teaching job in a business school, which meant that she had to be gone at night. She commented that not working was quite hard on her husband, and there was a great deal of adjustment to be made at home. "He does the work here at home while I've been working. He's very good at it." She had to give up playing golf, which she missed. As to social life, she said:

> We entertained at Christmas; about every two years we have a big open house. It was partly for business reasons. But outside of that, we don't do too much entertaining. This is a queer town. There are only a few people of our level—educationally speaking. I don't do things like we would in the east. I had lots of friends and saw them often.

She mentioned having many cousins, but not being close to any of them. Some of them were rather famous people. She did do some correspondence, and kept in touch with them at Christmas time. As to friends, she said, "I told you before that most of my good friends live away from here." She did have two fairly close friends in Kansas City. As to neighbors, she said, "The less said the better! We are Episcopalian, and they are Catholic, and they always band together. A lot of them aren't our type. They aren't as well educated and have different likes and dislikes." However, she did know six or eight families, "I suppose through my husband. They were marvelous when his wife died. And his wife was a very friendly person—I suppose she was friendly and they liked her." As to her husband's eventual retirement, she said, "He'll work as long as he can, and he's very capable of working good. He couldn't stand it. He'd die." But as to what she would be doing five years hence, she imagined that her husband would be retired by then and they might sell the house and go to California. When asked if she had her life to live over again, what would she do, she said, "Well, I don't know. I think perhaps I'd like to have married earlier and had children. I'm sorry none of us girls have had children. But that's the only thing I would change."

By September 1957 her husband had gotten another big job. She planned to work as his secretary and had been serving in that capacity at home until he got his office. She was excited and happy over the situation. The job would take eighteen months to two years for completion. The husband, who was then seventy-two years old, came in just as the interview was terminating. The interviewer commented that he was a very healthy and vigorous-looking man and looked at least ten years younger than his actual age. As to other people who were important in her life, she mentioned the bank teller and storekeepers, the hairdresser who was a very good friend of hers, and the doctor. When asked about things that gave her the most satisfaction, comfort, or pleasure in life, she listed doing a good job at work, visiting with family or relatives you do not see often, and just being with your family at home, in that order.

Unfortunately, she was not seen again until October 1960, so that the fourth and fifth interviews were out of order. That was the period when she was working with her husband and another engineer, and it was probably impossible to interview her because of the husband's objection. Apparently it was a fairly satisfactory period of her life. In a later interview, she spoke with pride of her performance at work during this period. By the time she was seen, her husband was no longer working, and was essentially retired. She had gone back to work, as a secretary in a small department of a local university.

When asked about satisfaction in achieving her goals in life, she replied:

> Well, I don't know if I had any definite goal except to earn my living. I didn't have any burning desire to do anything special. Yes, I've done what I set out to do, not necessarily monetary, but I'm satisfied that I've done a good job. I feel I've gotten along very well, because I've had very interesting jobs. In periods of depression I never had to go on relief. I always took temporary jobs and pulled through. I always felt anyone who really wanted to find work could—I did.

When asked about type of work or occupation that she had always wanted to avoid, she said, "Nursing—I don't think I could take care of people that way. It's too intimate, too much drudgery. I don't have the knack. I like to help people but not that way. I get too sympathetic and too wound up in it. It's too personal. Too physical maybe." When asked about her present goals or aims in life, she said:

> Just to earn a living—right now it's very necessary that I work. I might like to get into more of an executive position, but because of my age I don't think I can. I feel if I had to do a real high-powered job, I couldn't take care of my retired husband. It can't be too good a job because then I couldn't take care of my home —a retired husband is a problem.

When asked about things she found herself thinking about, she gave a rather vivid answer.

My family—the three of us left—my husband and our problems and my middle sister who isn't well, needing psychiatric help now. I wonder how to write to her. Think about my future days. What I'll do if my husband dies. He talks about it all the time. Our plans to sell this house and move—and my job. Can I ever work out having a piano? I miss it. The problem that my husband watches TV all the time, and I don't like it. Wish I could have more time with my friends and family. My grandchildren—their real grandmother [mother of stepchild's spouse] is here and she is jealous. Think of my friends in the east and wish I could see them more. I think of the world situation, the United States news. I'd like to have money enough to travel—travel and do jobs in different parts of the country. Sometimes I think of controversies I've had with my husband and wish I'd done different—a disagreement. If my husband died, what would I do? There is no one home—east—the three of us are out here. Would I stay here or go back east?

At the end of the interview she made several informal remarks which led the interviewer to observe:

Although she continued to talk glowingly in the interview about her happiness and her husband, she made several remarks of things that aren't going so well because he's so old. She said he's like all engineers and she'd known three of them—they don't like people. He didn't do much but sit and watch TV, and she was bored with it. She missed her piano very much and somehow, someday, she would find a way to get another one.

In November of that same year she said that things had been going quite well. Her husband had been ill over a year ago, but was now fine. She herself was feeling very cheerful. She had heard that her middle sister had been much better. The respondent had had a raise in her job, and her husband's son and daughter-in-law had visited them from the west coast. On the unpleasant side, there had been some trouble with the husband's daughter. She was moving into a new house. She and her husband overextended themselves, and the respondent and her husband became involved financially. "I'm not the parent, so I just had to sit and listen. I can't say a word. There was lots of—shall we say—conversation.' "

She mentioned that she still had the problem that "I interrupt my husband all the time—he gets very upset by it, but I do it all the time. I get enthusiastic and forget. He's deliberate and slow thinking. That's all my fault, and I try to quit it. I'm working on it." She was seldom in a bad mood, but occasionally she was: "When I think the men in my life are impatient and unreasonable, I get perturbed. I mean my husband and my boss. I can't stand, in general, unintelligent, dumb people." She also mentioned that her husband had a constant nervous cough which bothered her. In earlier interviews she had said that she did not enjoy cooking or any kind of housework. Now she claimed that she liked to cook but hated to wash dishes.

When asked about the best time in her entire adult life, she replied, "The past ten years—since I've been married. Because marriage was a fulfillment for me and I married a very unusual, fine, stimulating man, and since we are mature it worked out very well. When you marry later in life, there are not so many problems as when you marry younger." However, the interviewer had the distinct impression that she did not really mean what she had said and felt she must or should say that. Consequently, the interviewer asked about the next best time, and she enthusiastically talked about her life in the Latin American country. When asked about the worst time in her entire adult life, she described the period when her father became mentally ill, the years just prior to her marriage.

When asked whether she was the kind of person who circulated among a lot of people in a lot of situations, or was more inclined to spend a good deal of time alone, or with just a few people, she replied,

> I'm not living my natural way. There are few people here that I like to know, and my husband's health and age. I am a social person. I am with people all day at work but otherwise not much. We spend a great deal of time alone. Mostly with a very few good friends. We're not antisocial, but selective. I did prefer circulating a lot. I don't know if I do now. Yes, I'd like to go out and be with people more. I like to entertain, and I do very little of that now. I used to do a lot of that.

She saw the stepchildren who lived on the west coast about once every two years. The ones that lived in Kansas City, stepchildren and stepgrandchildren, she saw about every two weeks and talked to them on the phone two or three times a week. She said she felt much better than she had in years, since she had gotten over the menopause, and said, "Perhaps I don't worry about things as much as I used to." When asked about things that tempted her she said, "Drinking—I enjoy it— can't say I'm an alcoholic, but I can't hold as much as I used to. I shouldn't smoke so much either." As to regrets, she said, "I'm sorry I didn't do more with music. I had a gift and I didn't use it as I should have. I did something socially that upset my family. I went with the wrong kind of men." She thought of death from time to time, but said, "I'm not afraid of dying. I wouldn't want to be crushed by an automobile. I'm not afraid of death—but the way I might die."

Her daily round in this period was rather different from what it had been four years previously; now she was working and her husband had retired. The evenings were rather similar. Her husband, even in retirement, went to bed considerably earlier than she did. Saturday she went to the beauty parlor in the morning and did cleaning or yard work in the afternoon. Saturday evening they often went to a friend's home for dinner or called on the children. They frequently went out for the day on Sunday, sometimes to her husband's sister's farm for a cookout. They went to church once in a while. Sunday evenings were taken up with television.

When asked what age she would most like to be, she replied thirty-five to forty, and referred to her trip to the Latin American country and to a love affair. "It's a good peak at that age—I was very keen. Felt confident." When asked about the less interesting or enjoyable things on weekends, she said, "I suppose having the routine of meals. Having to do it—especially with an older man." She wished she could see friends more and still did not like the neighbors.

In October 1961, she said they were both in very good health. Her husband, now seventy-five, was building a curb. "So you know he's well. He's a marvelous person—but engineers never give up." She now had a little car of her own and was very proud of that. Her daily round looked about as it had a year and one-half previously. When asked about her strong points, she said:

> I enjoy people and get along with them well. I have a good sense of humor. I think I have good judgment about my work, and I am very adaptable. I have worked for many temperamental men and have learned to get along with them. I have a temperamental husband, and I've made a success of my marriage. When you are a second wife, you have to work at it. I'm not decrepit and still get a kick out of life. In my work I get along with women.

There were no family gatherings on her side of the family, but there were on her husband's. "On his side, I'm the leader. His sister, the children, and grandchildren get together four or five times a year. That's important to me because it's important to him. That's one of my duties and pleasures. It's both." She still said that her real friends are mostly in the east. "I think as you get older you don't make real friends. You have more acquaintances than real friends." She said her responsibilities had increased over the past ten years. "Yes—of necessity, my marriage. I've taken on a ready-made family of three grown children, nine grandchildren, and a husband." Her attitude toward money had changed too. "I think I should be careful—because my husband keeps talking about dying, and the estate. I think I am more conscious too because I'm spending from a joint account. We have two lives to consider. You want things when you are married. Some things are more important. I am much more conscious of saving than I was when I was single."

When asked about the most important thing that had happened to her in the last five years, she said it was starting to work again. When asked about the best and the worst things, she said, "I think that we have grown very close as a married couple, and have accomplished some of the things in our married life that we wanted to. The worst thing is that my single sister became ill, had a nervous breakdown. She's getting better."

Analysis. On the surface one might be tempted to say that this woman has had all six styles of life at one time or another. But, we believe, careful analysis reveals otherwise, and it is important to understand her true style in relation to the problems she faced with aging. She had almost always been in the world of work, but not really of it. Work was just a way of earning a living, helping her family, and later her husband. She thought of her early family life as a happy time, found some identification with and some ambivalence toward her father, kept in fairly close touch with her sisters, reached out with moderate success toward her husband's children and their families, and kept in occasional touch with a large network of cousins. But she never achieved a Familistic style of life, nor did she ever seriously try to do so. She had, at least on a conscious level, made a valiant effort to develop the style of Couplehood, but the difference in age from her husband, his personality, and perhaps some deeper feelings of her own made it impossible for her really to develop Couplehood as a true style of life. She had lived alone at various times, but generally not for long, and only as a living arrangement, not as a style. Her preferred style of life was something approximating Living Fully, and perhaps at times she thought she was, as during the experience in the Latin American country. But again, she was never able quite to consolidate this mode of living as a style. Certainly her mode of life during the five years of the study was inimical to the style of Living Fully. Thus, in essence, she achieved a style of not achieving any other style, and had eased through life with minimal involvement.

The senior staff member who obtained the life history judged that she was a very "dependent" person. This judgment may possibly be correct in some psychological sense, although we have doubts about that. It was made mainly on the basis of her frequent returns to her parental home. We believe that her own account of these episodes, and her own statement about her relations to her parental family, were more accurate. She did not "depend" on her family. She returned because she "loved them so much," although "liked" might have been a more accurate expression. Her trips home were essentially a rational way of resting up after an intense period of work and play, and of getting ready for another such intense period. As we are using the concepts autonomy and dependency, she was and remained essentially autonomous. She contributed a great deal to her parents, especially during the time of their illnesses, to her middle sister during her nervous breakdown, and probably also to the youngest, highly independent, sister, simply by remaining good friends with her and her husband. After she married, she put a great deal of energy into her new social system, especially her husband and her husband's children, and got very little from them in return. Thus, she had always made her way into the world and helped others when they needed it. However, she has been classified as autonomous-precarious, in the top third of this category. The precariousness, which was not great, lay in the fact that her accustomed ways of getting along in life, especially friendships, entertaining, and participation in some group life, were withering away due to circumstances largely beyond her control. If her husband were to live for several more years, and when he died or when she was forced to retire, or both, these accustomed modes of living might have atrophied to a point where she would have few resources of action; she might move into the dependent-precarious position or, possibly, right out of the system and into institutionalization.

As yet, she showed no signs of anomie or alienation. Her social life space was certainly constricted in comparison with her earlier life, but she had not yet approached even a rating of 2 on isolation. She was clearly coping remarkably well. She was rated 2 on saliency of style, for she clearly had not developed this style as fully and distinctly as, for example, "The Crony."

Thus, we have the case of a woman who had worked out a way of life for many years which permitted her to ease through life with minimal involvement. Late in life she moved herself into a situation where this mode of living was no longer possible, and where she was forced into somewhat more involvement than she had ever had before. She was then living in a comparatively constricted system, which she did not quite accept but with which she coped very well. In terms of her personal characteristics, she might conceivably develop a "crony" role, although the social base for this was certainly not apparent by the end of the study. We agree with the judgment of the senior staff member, although for a somewhat different set of reasons, that she may have some difficulties with aging. On the other hand, having done so well in the interstices of the social system for so long, she might ease on to the end with comparative success.

Nearly Styleless

This man had retired from a semiskilled job just a few months prior to the beginning of the study. His age was given as sixty-five, but at the end of the study, just five years later, he referred to himself as being seventy-two. The interviewer described him as short, small, bent, and feeble, with white hair, glasses, and false teeth, and added, "He looks old." He was not a man of words, seemed rather indifferent to the study, and impressed the interviewer as being characterized by passivity and mousy timidity. He lived with his wife, who was about ten years younger, who still worked as a skilled industrial worker. His daughter and her five-year-old son lived in an apartment just below them.

He commented that now that he was at home, he was "the maid" and did most of the cooking and cleaning. He also took care of the daughter's child after school. The day was spent in puttering around the house and looking at a little television. He was in bed by 9 P.M. and up at 5:30 A.M. His ninety-seven-year-old father, eighty-seven-year-old mother, a brother, and three sisters lived in small Missouri towns. Relatives visited occasionally on weekends, and he went to church about once or twice a month.

In April 1957 he went back to work for a brief period, but just a few hours a day, at the place where he had worked prior to his retirement. He said he did not feel very close to his relatives but he got along with them. He had done "a little of everything" during his working life. He was a little bit bored and missed his work some, particularly because he liked to have people tell him what to do. He commented that, if his wife were at home, she would figure out things for him to do. A little later in the study, on this same theme, he said the only thing he didn't like about retirement was that "I get 'notness.'" At another time he said, "a fellow gets like a dried up weed if he don't do something." We also learned that he enjoyed going to a cabin on a nearby lake with his wife for a weekend.

He had lived in his parental home until he was thirty-five years old, doing full-time farming. He left home at that age and married at thirty-six. He said age thirty was the best time of his life because he was running around and having a good time. He could think of no part of his life that was the worst. If he had his life to live over, he thought he might marry a little younger and was not sure whether he would marry the same woman, although he added, "I still want her." He thought of his life work as farming, although he had stopped farming at the age of thirty-five.

By September of 1959, the family had bought a little cabin on the lake and spent weekends there fishing. When asked about the most important people at various times in his life, he gave very flat answers. When he was growing up, they were his "parents, I guess." His mother was quiet, and his father was easygoing. Both parents died during the course of the study, but this was discovered in response to a very direct question, and not in the context of best and worst things that had happened. The most important person now was his "wife, I suppose." He commented that she was nervous but acted "O.K." toward him.

In December 1961, the main change was that the daughter, who had been divorced, had remarried and moved out of the downstairs apartment, which was then rented to nonrelatives. The respondent said that he suffered some pain in his leg, but he thought he was in "fair shape" for a man of seventy-two. He said his wife was "poorly" with rheumatism, and she had had her teeth pulled and the new ones did not fit. A granddaughter was living with them temporarily, but was about to be married. His daily round looked exactly the same as it had five years previously.

The interviewer noticed that the kitchen was in a mess and that the respondent seemed to enjoy this situation. He was vaguely unhappy over the extra work caused by having company. At one point he opened up rather suddenly on the subject of the amount of beer which his new son-in-law drank, but then quickly became withdrawn again.

He was rather vague on things that he liked to do and mentioned reading (which was somewhat doubtful) and going to the lake. His main comment in this context was that his wife had always made the plans. He said again that he did not have any close feelings for his relatives, except perhaps his daughter.

The interviewer appended a note on a "streak of rebelliousness buried under a deluge of henpecking. He would really like to give his son-in-law a good thrashing. And his only way of striking back was by not doing things, such as keeping the kitchen in order, and showing a certain amount of pure cussedness."

This man came about as close to stylelessness as it is possible to get. Yet he did ease along all his life without becoming involved in much of anything. We have thus given this style, with a rating of 3 on its saliency.

He showed a moderate amount of anomie, and was given a rating of 2 on that, and also on isolation. However, he did not show alienation, largely due to his low level of involvement, so he has been rated 1 on that variable. He was more or less coping with his situation and was rated 2 in that context. Although he did most of the household chores, was henpecked, and might appear to be autonomous on the surface, he was essentially dependent. Basically he wanted to be henpecked, as long as he could have his little rebelliousness on the side, and he admittedly wanted to be directed. Thus, at this low level of involvement, he was taking a little more out of his system than he was putting into it. Also, the fact that he lived at home until he was thirty-five years old suggests that dependency was a lifelong pattern for him. There was a strong probability that the few significant others in his social system would outlast him and that he would persist in his mode of life until death. We have thus rated him on success as dependent-persistent, at the top.

THE LEAST SUCCESSFUL AGERS

A Life That Was Not Lived

This man was born in Boston. He spoke with a somewhat affected accent, and his one interest in life, at which he worked sporadically, was genealogy; he used this largely to establish that he came from a long line of Boston Brahmins, which, from other evidence, seemed rather unlikely. He had been considered brilliant in his early high school days, but suffered a major defeat in a contest and seemed completely to have lost his motivation. He did not go on to college, a matter which he deeply regretted. It would be rather pointless to give his life history in detail because, in a sense, there was no life history. Until about two years prior to the study, he thought of himself as practicing for life. Then he had a heart attack and realized it was later than he had thought. The best image of this rather remarkable man is obtained by giving impressions from the succeeding interviews.

At the time of the beginning of the study, in October 1956, he was fifty-five years old and living with his wife. A married daughter lived not far away, and a married son lived in the east. He was a middle- to lower-level executive in a large company. The interviewer described him as thin, short, and lacking in muscular tone.

His daily round consisted of reading the paper, which he considered a waste of time, going to work, coming home and wasting time reading the paper again, and in the evening reading or sporadically trying to learn to play the organ. He was not certain that he enjoyed any of it except possibly lying in bed and listening to music. He insisted that he was not suited for his work and got no support from his boss. In fact, he claimed that he did not really do anything at work. He had nominal supervision over four employees, but did not supervise them; all he did was sign orders. He had no friends at work, or anywhere else, except a few people he considered more or less friends, with whom he corresponded about genealogical matters. On Saturdays, he generally went to a junk shop but usually did not buy anything. Otherwise, there was "not much doing" over the weekend and he did not particularly enjoy anything. He thought he would like chess, but he did not play it any more. He had no religion and claimed that all life is rather futile. He belonged to a few organizations but never attended meetings.

In March of 1957, when he was probed about any pleasant things that had happened to him since the last interview, he finally mentioned a trip to California, but said it was rather tiresome. His wife, in the background, commented that she had enjoyed it. Nothing unpleasant had happened, but everything was boring. He said he did not do much but go to work and rest. When asked about relatives, he said, "All my folks were peculiar and didn't like each other." The only people with whom he seemed to interact were some children from next door who would come over; he would play records for them. When asked what he would be doing five years hence, he said, "Unfortunately probably the same thing," but added, "There are too many variables and I can't predict."

When he was interviewed in August of that same year, a new high fidelity set was on and four children were sitting around listening to it. Commenting on his own children when they were small, he said, "I never liked children." His son and family had moved out from the east. This meant that he occasionally saw grandchildren, but considered them to be a bother and preferred the neighbor children, commenting, "The children next door are easier to get rid of." When asked about friendships, he said, "Everyone should have a friend—I had one back east once." His work associates were definitely not friends, and he attributed that in part to his lack of a college education. He occasionally sent cards to sick people, but never went to see them. He said he had been rebuffed on that once.

In February of 1959, he had gone back to genealogical work and was pleased to have proved, at least to his own satisfaction, that a town in Missouri was named after a close relative of one of his ancestors. He was less worried about his heart and, in fact, he and his wife and daughter had been bowling. He was on tranquilizers and had been to a psychiatrist. He said that by nature he was a reformer, but if he had enough pills he did not get irritated. He used to be more irritated at age forty-five, he said, because they did not have tranquilizers then. When asked about boredom, he said that that happened frequently. And, when asked about the best time in his life, he indicated that it was the four or five months after he had his heart attack because he did not have to go to work. One of the questions used to probe the respondent's orientation to interaction read:

> Now a different kind of question. Here are four general types of people we see around us in our daily lives. Look these descriptions over carefully, then tell me which *two* of these descriptions resemble you most, as you actually are. First tell me the one you think resembles you *most,* then the one that resembles you *second* most. (a) A person who is *esteemed* by others, and takes a continuous interest in human welfare in general. (b) A person who is *enjoyed* by others, and takes his joys and sorrows as they come, from day to day. (c) A person who is *loved* by others, and takes a continuous interest in the personal welfare of all those who are dear to him. (d) A person who is *approved* of by others, and attends to his affairs conscientiously, from day to day.

This respondent could not think of himself in relation to any one of these four, and so invented another category, "a person who is *endured* by others."

Respondent was seen by a senior staff member the following September. Her usual approach was to probe rather deeply into the life history. It is interesting that in this case the reports of two rather lengthy interviews give very little life history material, other than the bad break he had in high school, that he had been called a little shrimp when in school, and that during a brief period in his life he had related to a group of Boston Jewish intellectuals. Her impressions of him included alienation, withdrawal, and vicarious interaction. He had never been of the business world and regretted its values. There was some anomie in his egotistic adjustment to life. He had episodic bursts of anger. She thought he was really not unhappy and that his inner life was satisfying. Lack of college was a real sore spot for him. He was ashamed of his son and sorry that the son had moved to Kansas City. He had wanted him to go to college and be a Harvard type. He, himself, had the fantasy of retiring and living on Beacon Hill in Boston. His father had been a good honest man, but the respondent had not liked him. The interviewer emphasized in particular that the respondent was not a phony and that he really did like music and mathematics.

In the second interview she had a "revised view of his morale. His defenses were down and I saw a sad, sad man." She imagined that he was quite dependent on his wife and thought that he was a passive dependent personality. He was afraid about his mental health, and talked about seeing a psychiatrist. He was afraid of death because he would then lose his whole unlived life.

Similar impressions were given in an interview in April of 1958. At that time he made the remark, "Never live with any relative if you can possibly avoid it, except possibly a husband or wife." He did not like his grandchildren because they asked to play the organ themselves, whereas the neighbor children asked him to play for them. He commented, "It doesn't take much to bother me."

He was seen by the clinical psychologist in September 1960, who thought that the other staff member had underestimated the disturbance in this man. He saw tension, anxiety, and "probably pure panic." The respondent had had another cardiac episode. He admitted to some hallucinatory experiences and displayed some paranoid reactions. The psychologist thought that they might be a toxic reaction to the medication for the cardiac condition.

By September of 1960, he was again bowling, which he said he thought was "rather silly," but his wife liked it. And then, most uncharacteristically, he talked about a pleasant Saturday he had had. He had gone bowling twice, had lunch with his daughter, and visited friends he had not seen in a long time. He commented, "It was nice to find someone who was really glad to see us." He also commented, "There are two ways of doing a job, my way and the wrong way."

In November of 1961, he appeared very nervous. He had given up learning to play the organ. He claimed he had always wanted friends to share his interests but that he was too peculiar. He had been demoted at work and felt they were trying to give him another heart attack. He said, "People don't like me." There was no use saving for a rainy day which may never come, he said. The best things in life were bowling, stereo, and having an air conditioner and FM radio in his car.

It is abundantly clear that this man failed to develop any of the other styles. It was in the study of this case that we were forced seriously to reflect as to whether Easing Through Life With Minimal Involvement is a residual category or a true style. We concluded it is a true style. His diffuse neutral and specific affective orientations to interaction, plus complete cynicism, permitted him to keep life at arm's length and ease through it with minimal involvement. In this instance, his wraithlike wife complemented the wraithlike marriage. This respondent also furnishes us with another instance in which the development of a very clear-cut style became a protective coating against the outbreak of obvious symptoms of mental illness. He also furnishes us with an important methodological observation. On round six, where he spoke about his pleasant weekend, he gave a very different impression from the total impression over the period of the study. Had we had only this one interview, rather than the longitudinal perspective, we would have had a very false image, at least in relation to the dimensions in which we are interested. Also, it is more than likely that different interviewers produced different degrees of style in the responses. In this case, as with all the respondents in this panel, we are fortunate not only in having interviews over time but also in having interviews by three, or frequently more, interviewers.

Staff members who saw this respondent commented on his passive dependent personality, on his dependence on his wife, and on his being babied at the office when he had heart trouble. We have placed him in a dependent category, but not primarily for these reasons. There is probably considerable overlap between passive dependent personalities and dependency as conceived here, in terms of balance of action energy with the individual social system. But the two concepts are not identical. In the present case, the respondent gave little, if anything, to anybody except to a very limited extent to the neighbor children for a brief period. He took a lot from his wife and probably took a good deal out of his co-workers. We have classified him as dependent-precarious, but toward the top. The precariousness stems from evidence of considerable disturbance in his action system which, to some extent, included his mental health. He might ultimately have had to be hospitalized, especially if his wife had died first. However, there was the bare possibility that he might realize his dream of retiring and leading a simple life in Boston where he could pursue his hobby of genealogy and pretend he was a Boston Brahmin. In this case he could become in balance with his action system at an extremely low level of involvement, and we would have the highly improbable, but not impossible, instance of a person moving all the way up from the dependent-precarious to the autonomous-persistent category. We rated him high on anomie, alienation, and isolation, and 2 on coping. His style was rated 1. As he had never really lived, it was most improbable that he could age successfully.

Living With the Children

The interviewer described this seventy-eight-year-old man as follows:

> The respondent was short and slim—salt-and-pepper hair. His face had rather deep lines, but [was] not "covered with wrinkles." He wore glasses and hearing was quite good. . . . He was alert and responsive—tended to ramble some, but mostly because he liked to talk, not from any semblance of senility.

> He was not a happy man. He felt very deeply the loss of his wife [six months before, after fifty-two years of marriage]. I suspect he has never been the jolly type, and that, considering the loss, his morale was pretty high. . . . He made remarks about the "condition of the world," but frankly, I thought he found it a good place in which to live. He had had quite an active life, and was keeping busy with rabbits and guinea pigs, completely redecorating the house, and so on.

This old man lived in his own home, with one room rented to a roomer. It was not too far from his only son, who was still in disgrace with the father because he had changed religions; the respondent felt it had broken the mother's heart and contributed to her death nine years later. The respondent was not religious himself, and even acknowledged he was of the faith his son had joined, but he could not abide the thought of anyone hurting his wife. He was seeing the son and his family only a few times a month, but that was better than it had been; for a while, the father had disowned the son completely over the issue.

He stated his intention never to move from his house, because it was on ground that had been in the family for many years. Only a year later, however, he had agreed to sell, for a price over four times the original cost. He stayed on the property for a while, meanwhile making plans to purchase some other property in town to fix up for rental or for his son and family to live on.

The worst thing about his age, he reported, was his inability to work. He remarked further that the best years of his life were in his thirties, when he was working hard and making a great deal of money.

He revealed a great deal about his early life. He was one of nine children in a rather strange family. He had the phenomenal record of having seen two brothers, a sister, and his father go into insanity and then death from the effects of drinking. Because of his adoration of his mother, who made him promise never to drink a drop, he did not follow the others and was able to avoid whiskey all his adult life. He apparently transferred his deep affection for his mother to his wife and continued to live as a sober, hard-working man right up to the time of the interviews. His philosophy of riding out the many tough times of life, especially his wife's death, was summed up in an unconsciously humorous remark made in all seriousness: "I just has to learn to live with it. Isn't any use committing suicide. Would just hurt yourself."

By the summer of 1959, he was living in a recently purchased old house with his son and family. He completed the interview at that time only after a bit of persuasion, as he felt the interviewer was going to sell his life story to a magazine. He reported a hernia operation and other assorted ailments, but also reported constant work on rebuilding and remodeling the house.

Almost two years elapsed between the time of that interview and the final one. The interim interviews did not give much hint of what was to come. But the old man's reporting of his daily routine in the last interview told a great deal about his change of style.

He was getting up around ten in the morning. He would go to bed around midnight, but stayed awake until nearly daybreak, and then slept until ten, eleven, or even one o'clock the next day. When he awoke, he just lay in bed, read the paper, and thought. His breakfast came while the rest of the family had lunch, and then he worked jigsaw puzzles all day long and into the evening. Sometimes he broke the pattern by watching the grandchildren a little, but he seldom saw TV. He just worked his jigsaw puzzles, which he had completed by the hundreds by this time.

Saturdays and Sundays were the same as weekdays. He did not like to visit with people, particularly as he had become quite deaf. He enjoyed only his puzzles and listening to baseball games on the radio. There was no more mention of house repairs or property interests. His daughter-in-law told the interviewer the respondent had always been a rather argumentative, friendless person, and now had become entirely so. He was ill-kempt, uninterested in anything, solely preoccupied with his ills, and antagonistic to friends or any overtures of friendship. In short, he had disengaged completely into a life of minimal involvement. He was in an almost desperate state of anomie, alienation, and, except for his family, isolation.

This case reflects retreat into a style to prevent total deterioration of the personality. By adopting this style, he could continue rather indefinitely in a marginal existence, so long as his family was willing to put up with his unpleasant company.

ANALYSIS

The reason we have relatively few cases in this style is that, basically, it is a difficult style to achieve at all, and even more difficult to achieve successfully in relation to the aging process. There is little in our religious and social ethics that lauds nirvana. In this time of social pressure to become involved, it is difficult not to do so. "The Crony" and "Keep on Living" achieved noninvolvement rather well in two different modalities. "Then She Married" did not achieve the style as clearly and would probably have more difficulty with aging. "Nearly Styleless" barely achieved any style and eased along in a dependent fashion.

If the style was held for a lifetime, as it was with "A Life That Was Not Lived," the person had never really become engaged with his action system. On the other hand, if it was a style achieved in the later years, as in the case of "Living With the Children," it represented a type of total disengagement and a complete denial of pressures. "Living With the Children" was an unusual case, in that he had had such an active style of World of Work for such a long time, even after his retirement, and had talked as if he were active in the final interview. However, his style at the close of the study was unmistakably one of least possible reaction to any people or events that impinged on his action system. The only activist thread left running through his life was his absorption with jigsaw puzzles, and this in itself was a kind of minimum involvement with reality.

The cases in this series illustrate points about compatibility of styles with types of relations and modes of interaction. Minimal Involvement can be achieved with either diffuse neutral relations, as with "The Crony," or specific affective ones, as with "Then She Married." In this latter case, even her strong dislikes were handled on a specific affective basis with minimum involvement and kept well contained, and insulation was maintained between socializing and the work situation. Her strong tendency toward specific affective relations undoubtedly played a very significant part in the ending of her stormy love affairs. When she finally did marry, and placed herself in a situation calling for a diffuse affective relation as its core, she found it rather difficult. Furthermore, she married a man whose style of life was World of Work. His orientation was highly instrumental and specific neutral. Neither their styles nor their accompanying orientations to interaction were complementary, which increased the difficulties for her.

This style should not be confused with Living Alone. In the latter case, the social system of the individual is reduced in scale, but there may be a high degree of involvement with what is left. In the former case, the scale is not especially important, and may be rather broad, as with "Then She Married," but involvement with all aspects of life is minimal. The two styles are somewhat deviant in our culture, and they have in common that they may serve as a protective cover that prevents the development or emergence of serious disturbances in the action system, including psychotic symptomatology. However, these styles do not guarantee successful aging, and, in fact, they do so less than any of the other styles, as indicated in Table 5: 25 per cent of the least successful agers fall in the Minimal Involvement category, and 14 per cent in Living Alone, as compared with 8 or 9 per cent in Couplehood, Familism, and World of Work, and only about 4 per cent (one case) in Living Fully.

SEVEN

❧❦❧

Living
Fully

Twenty-two of the panel members achieved the style of Living Fully. Their energies were not heavily invested in any one segment of life, but were spread rather broadly. Yet their involvement in most aspects of living was more than minimal. Twelve members achieved this style very clearly, and seven fairly clearly; only three achieved it somewhat vaguely. It is the style which is most highly related to success, with 78 per cent in the autonomous-persistent category, 18 per cent in the combined autonomous-precarious and dependent-persistent group, and 4 per cent in the least successful, or dependent-precarious group. Like the other styles, however, it was by no means an absolute guarantee of successful aging; there were cases in which it was associated with pre- cariousness in relation to the aging process, and even one case in which it was associated with dependency.

THE MOST SUCCESSFUL AGERS

No Aging

To every rule there is an exception, and this grand old woman broke every rule on aging that could be laid down. Aging had not yet caught up to her, even though she finished the final interview at a splendid eighty-six. Her disengagement was minimal and her physical condition was superb. She had been forced into technical retirement because of her age, but she was so fully engaged in so many activities it was hard to tell that she had "retired."

Perhaps her son described her best. "I'm proud of her—I think she's the grandest person alive! She has her own teeth, mind's clear— she can argue anybody out of everything. She's a very remarkable per- son—one in a million. I believe she doesn't act her age at all."

She was remarkably attractive in appearance. Her hearing was poor, and she needed a hearing aid, but she was not disabled. Her husband was dead, and all her children had moved away, but she had not let herself become lonely. How had she managed?

She got up at 7:30 A.M. for a big breakfast, then read the paper thoroughly. Following this she cleaned the house (she had a cleaning woman only once a month), then did errands and made phone calls. Every afternoon was crammed with clubs—literary, business and pro- fessional, garden, political, and church. She added, "When I don't attend club meetings, I spend my time studying for the literary clubs. I'm an awfully busy person." Evenings she read and actually took time to watch a little TV before going to bed around eleven.

Weekends were no quieter. Saturdays she *really* cleaned house and then went to town. She walked, of course! Sundays were almost quiet, comparatively. First she read *all* the Sunday paper, then went to church. The afternoon she spent writing to each of her children; then she went to her sister's, or her sister came over, for a regularly sched- uled game of cards and light refreshments. Any other spare time she had she spent with one of her many close friends.

The interviews do provide some information about her past that suggests reasons for her resilience. She was brought up and remained a regular member of the Methodist church. She was one of six children. Her father was a farmer, and the family was a warm, close one. The respondent's son remembered how he had enjoyed visiting his grand- parents, and the respondent, herself, said that her parents were like companions in the interest they took in their children.

She took her first teaching job at twenty, but kept on with her education until she received her master's degree. Her husband had been a teacher also, and they taught many of Kansas City's most out- standing citizens, a fact of which she was very proud. Their family life had been a good one, the happiest time of her life, she recalled. The four children had been at home, and she had not occupied herself with clubs and civic work then, although she did teach. The rest of the time she spent enjoying being a homemaker—baking cookies, fix- ing picnics, and the like. When her mother died, they had taken her father into their home, but he had died shortly thereafter. That was the worst time of her adult life, even worse than ten years later when her husband had died.

His death coincided with the children's moving into adulthood, and she compensated by becoming actively involved in civic and political fields. Several prominent political leaders became close allies and friends as she organized the women for political action. Over the years her work was honored by citations and awards of all kinds. She still appeared regularly at public affairs and on television to speak in behalf of various causes.

Her greatest trial was that one child had not been as successful, professionally or personally, as she would have liked for his own happiness, but she still offered this one her love and support in measure equal to that offered to the highly successful brothers and sisters. One son who was interviewed as a significant other commented how, since the children's youth, their mother had made very evident her love and pride, but had rarely offered criticism or advice on the lives they led. This conformed with her spoken philosophy that it had never been important to her to do what other people expected her to—nor had she made it a practice to speak her mind, if doing so would "make her unpopular." In other words, she had felt and acted on the idea that there was room for great latitude in people's behavior. Because she was neither a conformist nor a person who insisted that others conform to her, she liked other people and wanted them to like her even if she disagreed with them. Consequently, if she could not say something nice, she made it a point to say nothing at all—an adage she would be likely to quote—for quoting adages and poetry was a very characteristic manner of speaking for her.

The final interview with this respondent found her living alone in the big old house where she had lived for sixty years. She rented the upstairs to some teachers to provide both income and companionship. Reluctantly stopping to think about herself on the interviewer's insistence, she mentioned that she slept a little badly and had had some bowel trouble, but her over-all health was better than it had been in her forties. She was still enjoying her retirement because of the greater freedom to do as she pleased at her own pace.

There is much to be learned from this woman and how she filled her later years. She was not a social isolate and certainly was not alienated. She could never, by any stretch of the imagination, be called anomie-bound. Yet, she was no longer in the working world, and some age factors were beginning to impinge upon her. What would the future hold? Almost surely she would age as gracefully as she had lived. Her activities were not a protest, but a fulfillment. She had had problems, but had chosen to rise above them; she, herself, said that this was one of her strong points. As serious problems of old age did come upon her, if she lived to see them, she would undoubtedly disengage successfully and handle her problems with competence as long as she was physically able. The classifications here are clear. She was autonomous-persistent and living life fully. She was different from some of the older women who kept busy to pretend old age was not coming. For her, it had actually been delayed by living successfully.

The Competent One

At the beginning of the study, this sixty-six-year-old woman lived with her sister. She was a "customer's man," selling stocks and bonds. She considered herself in semiretirement because she could come home at 3 P.M., after the close of the stock exchange. Also, she had a "drawing account" and received commissions from her regular customers even when she was not at work, which gave her a great deal of freedom and flexibility. The sister, two years older, did all of the housekeeping. She, herself, disliked ironing and cleaning house, and said, "I have always had a man's attitude." She thought of herself as "older," not "old."

She had grown up on a small farm. At the end of her sophomore year of high school, at the age of sixteen, she had left school to teach school. She found she did not care for school teaching, and took some business courses. She then obtained a job in a bank which failed. She took another job in a larger bank, and from there, by dint of hard work and perseverance, particularly in the 1920's when several men had tried to block her promotion, she had risen to be a vice president. When she reached compulsory retirement age, she entered the brokerage business, at the suggestion of the president of the bank.

She had many friends and belonged to several clubs. She went to church, but was getting a little tired of Sunday school, which she had attended all her life. She went out frequently, played bridge with her friends, and played canasta with another sister and a brother, who also lived in Kansas City. She had gone to a university a few years previously and taken courses in applied psychology and English literature.

In April 1957 she had bought a new car and was also planning a trip to Hawaii. The sister, who had aged appreciably since the first interview, planned to visit in California. They had no television, because the sister was opposed to it. The sister knew more about relatives and did the correspondence.

That fall the respondent was back from Hawaii and had enjoyed the trip immensely. She claimed she had had a nervous breakdown four years previously. She also said that "things get better as you get older." By November 1958 the sister was no longer in Kansas City and had gone to help a friend on the west coast. A friend of the respondent's lived with her for a short time, and she bought a television for the friend's sake. Although at the first interview the style of life appeared to be Couplehood, over time it became apparent that this was by no means the case; when the sister was not there, she simply hired someone else to do the housework. The sister returned in 1959, but later left to live with another sister in the west. The respondent's style of life was scarcely affected by the sister's comings and goings. She had no thought of retirement and believed she could work until she was eighty-five. Her father had lived to be almost one hundred.

Her brother was a tall and vigorous man of seventy who had remarried in 1958. He maintained fairly close relations with his sister, of whom he said, "She has grown old as gracefully as anyone I know." A fifty-year-old friend told us that the respondent did not like to be kept waiting when she picked her up in the car. A beauty shop operator thought the respondent had led a "sheltered life" and stressed that she was a very fine person who had grown old gracefully.

In December 1961, at the age of seventy-one, her daily round looked about as it had in 1956. She still did setting-up exercises every morning. She worked somewhat later in the afternoon. She did not play quite as much bridge, and now had to write the family letters, as the sister was no longer there. She belonged to a service corps *for* senior citizens. She had been on an official goodwill mission to Latin America and was planning to go on another to the Far East. She had cut down on some activities, and did not mind it.

It was discussion of this case which first led the authors to the concept of the style Living Fully. She was certainly not oriented to Couplehood, nor to Living Alone. Whether she lived with her sister, a friend, or alone was quite secondary to her. She liked her family, and enjoyed the few relations she had with its members, but she was certainly not familistic. She had worked all her adult life and continued to work. But for her work was simply a means to have enough money to buy new cars, good clothes, travel, belong to clubs and have lots of friends. Unlike the case of the woman sixteen years older, "No Aging," she was aware of aging, and was aging slowly. The bare beginnings of successful disengagement were clear in comparing her at sixty-six and at seventy-one. She was clearly autonomous and persistent, and has been placed in the first rank on successful aging. She was rated 1 on all her uses of action energy, and on style.

Ministering to the Town

This sixty-seven-year-old man held a dual position in the government of an incorporated town in Greater Kansas City. He lived with his second wife, who was also his bookkeeper. Her parents were living with them, and her mother, eighty-six, and ten years older than her father, was somewhat senile.

The respondent was an ordained minister with three years of graduate training in theology. He was born in an Amish home and had had a work-oriented and stern father. He became the eldest son, through the accidental death of his brother, at age nine. He played football in high school, against his father's wishes. After the father reached sixty-five, he began reading novels and philosophy, and got new ideas. The respondent, himself, thought of retirement as a timetable for slowing down, with partial disengagement, gardening (which he loved), reading, and going to ball games. Like his father, he wanted to be active mentally and physically. (His father lived to ninety-six.)

He had gone into the ministry and was active in it for several years. Then he had had a serious throat condition which required an operation, and forced him to leave that profession. He had come to this suburban town, which he loved, and had lived there ever since. His first wife had died seven years prior to the study. He had been deeply in love with and devoted to her, and it was a terrible blow to him. His son had contracted polio while in college. Even his wife had given up hope for the son, but he had not. The son was crippled, but had gone on and was doing well. The respondent had come through all three crises remarkably well.

He knew a great many people in the town. He had many acquaintances, but few, if any, close friends, a pattern he learned in the ministry. He and his wife frequently visited sick or elderly people and took them baskets of vegetables or flowers from their garden. She was known as "Lady Bountiful." He did a great many things for people in the town, and for the town as a whole, and had actively had much to do with important decisions, although he was very modest about it. At the beginning of the study, he reported that he did not watch television regularly, because he did not want to get to a point where he had to watch.

In March 1957 he reported that the in-laws were going to move to the home of another daughter. Later in the study it became clear, from other sources, that the in-laws had been quite a strain on him. The second wife was a woman of tough-minded competence. One sensed there was a little tension there, too, although the relationship was essentially in balance, and he was glad that "Lady Bountiful" had made a home for him. The in-laws had left in August 1957. He reported at that time that he was not going to retire and would always do something.

In April 1958 there was not much change. He was not up to par because of a tooth extraction. In July 1958 he felt better, but complained that he did not like his wife going home to lunch to watch television. On the worst thing that happened in his life, he reported the loss of his first wife; "It nearly killed me." In March 1959 he had been in a hospital for an operation. He reported being made an honorary member of the Junior Chamber of Commerce as one of the best things that had happened recently. The worst, he said, not mentioning his operation, was that his son and the son's wife had had trouble. She had walked out, then later came back. There were financial problems, and he helped out. A grandson had had a severe accident, which had helped reunite the parents. The respondent said sixty through seventy was the best time of life; he was of service to the people of the town, and this was better than being a minister. The "change of life" had not affected his relations with his wife, he said; rather there was a deeper meaning of love.

An interesting thing, from a methodological point of view, happened in May 1959. Two professional staff members, interested in a special study of kinship, interviewed the respondent and his wife separately, but at the same time. They found the wife to be an appealing, forthright, and competent person, having a difficult role in competing with the dead first wife. The respondent had introduced them to his wife before the separate interviews. During the interview, tears came to his eyes when the original respondent spoke of his first wife. After the interview, he again introduced the interviewers to his second wife (although he should have realized one of the staff members had been interviewing his wife in the next room, all the while). He called one interviewer by the name of another professional staff member who had interviewed him earlier. These staff members concluded that the respondent was senile. Again, we see the dangers of making certain judgments in cross-sectional studies. The material we have subsequent to this indicates that the respondent was by no means senile, and was probably in a temporary emotional upset from the interview on kinship, caused by his deep attachment to his first wife.

In October 1959 the daily round had not changed. He enjoyed being seventy-two, and said his wife understood and loved him. By January 1960 he was thinking about retirement, but would wait until his wife became sixty-two, three or four years from then, so they could retire together. In September 1960 the clinical psychologist found him in fine shape, service-oriented, with no evidence of depression or anxiety. In July 1961, he had had no vacation that year, and regretted not seeing the grandchildren in two years, but planned to when he retired.

When the wife was interviewed in March 1961, she enjoyed it thoroughly. She mentioned at least one television program that they liked together. They loved to go to the zoo, but her husband tired more than she did. They had owned a larger lot, and had had thoughts of building on it, but sold it because it now appeared too big. Several other people were interviewed, all of whom thought very highly of the original respondent.

By December 1961 he had given up half of his town job, but retained the other half. He was fine, and his son was fine now, although he had taken to alcohol. He and others got the son over this problem. He explained with considerable insight that the son's wife was a Cinderella who had never matured. He planned to retire in a few years. He said he had "been a lot happier at home." He did not go to the Philharmonic any more and said with a twinkle, "I'm afraid I am slipping." He was still counseling Boy Scouts. He said he had always wanted to be seventy-five and would be soon. He had started a college fund for his three grandchildren. An ideal day would be to garden, live in a new house (they lived in a part of town in which businesses had grown up around them), watch a football game, and do something to help others. The formula for keeping young was moderate exercise and reading.

Some Familism and the World of Work are encompassed in his Living Fully and ministering to the town. He showed none of the deviances in his action system, such as alienation, anomie, or social isolation. He had coped with a whole series of crises very well. He was able to disengage gradually as a mode of coping with the inevitable and accepted slowing down with age. He was thoroughly autonomous, and was not likely ever to be a burden on anybody. He has been given the top rank on the success scale.

Slow and Easy

With one major exception, to be described below, this man's mode of life and social system remained unchanged during the course of the study. In his case, the major points can best be developed by a more analytical approach than for most of the cases, with less emphasis on the flow of time.

Life history. The respondent was born on a large farm. He was probably closer to his mother than to his father while growing up. Her people were all "hale, hearty, and well met." His father was a "hard-boiled Swede," and his people were very quiet. He had only an eighth-grade education, but started teaching school at the age of seventeen, and became the highest paid elementary teacher due to his meticulous discipline. He went into the army during the First World War. When he returned, he saw no money in teaching school, and so he went into a bank run by a man whom he admired very much. He married in his late twenties and continued in banking. The Depression hit him very hard, and he lost all, but managed to eke out an existence working for collection agencies for a time. During the Second World War, he obtained a middle-level job in a Federal Reserve bank, which made it possible for him to achieve security. By the time of the study, all his plans were laid, and the future looked secure. He had continued his education throughout his life and was very proud that in one of his courses he made a 99+. He was seen in his preretirement years, at ages fifty-eight to sixty-three, and he looked forward to retirement at sixty-five with much pleasure.

Characteristic uses of action energy. This respondent talked a great deal and was pleased to be interviewed. He revealed many characteristics of his life quite freely and fully.

He had always shunned high-level responsibility in the World of Work. Had he remained in the small town near his family home, he most certainly would have become vice-president or president of the bank. But he preferred living in a large city, where he could get more out of life. In his early years of banking, he was "scared to death they would make me manager." Similarly, he was active in the American Legion and took on the job of straightening out all of the personnel records of the Kansas City members (which also related to his meticulousness), but he did not want a high office in the Legion. In response to the story question about Jones, he said Jones would not take the job, but the reason given was that he would not want "top responsibility," rather than the usual more Familistic answers.

He was an extraordinarily meticulous man. After one of the interviews he proudly showed his garden to the interviewer. There were no weeds, and each plant was carefully placed in an absolutely straight row. He commented, "See what a meticulous man I am." In a later interview, when asked about his daily round, he said, "Exactly at 7:00 A.M. I open the bathroom door and walk out to the breakfast table." He made a ritual of saving and budgeting. During the last interview, in response to a question about his relations with people at work, he said, "I am referred to as old fuddy-duddy, the fussbottom." He liked to live slowly and described himself as "easygoing." In the fourth year of the study he commented that eighteen months from then, when he retired, he wanted it understood, particularly by his wife, that the word "hurry" had been taken out of the English language.

In spite of the slowness, he had some trouble with nervousness, and suffered with ulcers. He looked particularly nervous on the second interview, in May 1957. In November 1958, he had been in the hospital and had been afraid he had cancer. But no cancer was found, just ulcers. He said there was nothing wrong but tension, and he was given "slow-down" pills. He was often disturbed by food and things associated with food. In May 1960 he said, "I can't control tensions, and I know it."

He thus showed some signs of anomie, associated with his tensions, ulcers, and his relationship with his wife, to be described below. There was no alienation or isolation, and he coped reasonably well.

Relations with his wife. His wife was about the same age as he was, but there any resemblance stopped. At the time of the first interview, she questioned the study and looked at the interviewer with an intense stare. She worked as the secretary for an important civic organization. From the beginning of the study, the respondent made it clear: "My wife and I disagree. I am easygoing, she heads up organizations. I don't want to be the leader, she does. She never says 'I'm sorry.' Tangles don't bother her. When she gets fussy, I get up and go over to the club; she's probably cooled off by dinner time." She paid for the inside of the house, and he paid for the outside. They never had any children, and, at one point, he commented he was glad they had not.

In May 1957, the wife impressed the interviewer, also a woman, as a "pleasant, charming woman." She undoubtedly could be, and was in her work and in her many organizational activities, but was not with her husband.

In September 1957, he commented, "My wife was darned stingy with sex during the first twenty-five years of married life, and for the next twenty-five years, I will be the stingy one." In November 1958, just after he had been in the hospital, he said, "I can't slow my wife down. She has never been sick, and has no patience with slowness and sickness." His only qualm about retirement was that he would be in the way, and there would be "just that much more chance of being fussed at."

Two and one-half years before the end of the study, his wife had an operation. Cancer was found, and he knew that his wife was dying. This appeared not to change her characteristic behavior patterns appreciably, and he still complained of his wife's nagging and wanting to be "on the go." But he showed great concern for her and her health. At about that time, he showed his wife's picture to the interviewer and said he had always tried to please her but had not succeeded. The interviewer commented that the wife looked younger and very well educated. The clinical psychologist who saw the respondent during this same period, said, "The whole subject of women was a deep and perplexing problem to this man. She [his wife] can reduce him to tears, but on the major issues they are in substantial agreement." At one point, the respondent had commented that, when they went to a show and it was a little sad, he shed a few tears, but his wife thought that that was silly.

His wife again had surgery six months before the end of the study. The respondent said he was "blue" much more, because his wife was very ill. Her illness had canceled all plans for extensive traveling after retirement, which was to be soon.

Scope of the system—activities and interests. For all the meticulousness and slowness, his social system had considerable amplitude. He had some interest in his family of orientation and relatives, although he was not very involved in that facet of life. He said, "I like to visit the family on the farm occasionally, but just hello and goodbye are enough for me." He liked the outdoor theater, ball games, and good shows, and went frequently. That was one facet of life in which he and his wife could share. He belonged to one club, went there frequently, and played cards—he was not a "drinking man." He was quite active in the American Legion. He enjoyed taking different people to and from work, to get new ideas. (It is interesting that he was the one who had the car. His wife rode with him occasionally, but usually took the bus.) He was fond of gardening, another aspect of life in which his wife shared somewhat. He had some, but not extensive, relations with neighbors. He was one of the relatively few respondents in this panel who said life was made for pleasure and enjoyment, without any qualifications about their having to be earned or the like. During one period, he got into a "regular round of TV programs." At the beginning of the study he still went to church, but then began to listen to services on the radio to get more variety. He also enjoyed visiting sick people in hospitals.

Disengagement. In the first interview, October 1956, he talked at some length about retirement, and expressed the view that people should prepare for retirement and "give young folks a chance." One way to prepare would be to be given time off before sixty-five, to get used to it gradually. He usually went to Legion conventions, but during that same interview he said, "This year it is nice to be different," and he did not go. In May 1957, he said he was not attending organizations as much as he used to. He again emphasized that he looked forward to retirement, and commented, "I have had a pretty complete life." In November 1958, speaking again of retirement, he said he would "fool around and go over to the club more."

He had enjoyed teaching school, being in the Army, and working in the bank—"I enjoyed it all." He had always enjoyed the age he happened to be. But he was glad his life was not mainly ahead of him: "These are troubled times." At the end of the study, in response to a question concerning the best things about his age then, he said, "not having to do things unless I really like them. I wear a hat out of fashion just because I like to. I can play a lot of cards and not feel guilty"—a very good expression of the spirit of disengagement.

Style. This is another case in which it is quite clear that none of the other styles fit. However, he quite clearly had a style. He was Living Fully in relation to his own aspirations, which had never been very high. He would rather live fully in his own slow, meticulous way than take responsibility, be a huge success at work, fight with his wife, or reduce his life space and live essentially alone.

Success type and rank. He was quite clearly autonomous-persistent, in that he contributed a great deal to others in his system, and took little from them. We have placed him in the middle of this category. His wife's death would certainly cause him a lot of sorrow, but it is doubtful that it would affect the general functioning of his action system. He had looked forward to retirement for a long time and would continue to live fully at his own level and pace. We would not be surprised if he remarried and achieved some elements of underlying couplehood, which he had always missed. He could offer an older and slower woman a lot of security and contentment.

Forced Disengagement

At the beginning of the study, this sixty-two-year-old woman was living with her husband, who held a semiskilled civil service job. Her one child was married and living in another part of the country.

During the first interview in June 1956, and in many ways throughout the study, she was the most effervescent of all the respondents. Her husband, who was sitting in the background, said of her, "She just likes to be busy." She was very active in her church, in Grey Ladies, Red Cross, and in other groups, had many friends, and did a lot of visiting. One group put on banquets to raise money for the church.

In March 1957 we found that her husband had unexpectedly been retired for disability. She cried during the interview, then smiled through her tears and said, "It isn't so bad, but it's hard to take; this is our first great trouble." Later, in an intensive interview by a member of the professional staff of the study, we learned what had happened. Her husband woke up one morning complaining of severe pains in his legs, and was unable to go to work. No organic condition could be determined. The husband completely withdrew into a chronic depression. His co-workers lured him back to work on the pretext that they were shorthanded, but that did not last long. In her perception he had changed radically overnight.

At the beginning of this period she reported watching television more, which she said was "terrible," and having less company. Her daughter was having a third child. In August 1957 she said she was just fine, but continued to be worried about her husband. She could not get him to go out as he used to. The daughter's baby was born a spastic. She said she felt about forty-five. There was almost no unhappiness in her life—"There could be but I just won't let it." In February 1959 she was again "just fine" and reported that her husband was somewhat better. "I go to bed and get up singing about it." They sat up until midnight now and watched television, and then slept late. If her husband did not have to lie down so much, she reported, she would have loved having him at home. She said the best years of her life were from 1931 to 1941, when teen-agers were in and out of the house; the worst were from 1956 on, with her husband's illness. She felt something like a widow. In November 1959 she had dropped out of one of her clubs because it involved couples and her husband would not go. In May 1960 she reported being lonely fairly often, and said she was not satisfied with her present mode of life. In March 1961 her daughter and daughter's family had visited and decided to put the spastic child in a home. She tried to arrange an interview with the husband at this time, but the husband refused. By August 1961 she had given up Grey Ladies, but was still active in many things, especially the church. Her minister said of her, "You can always call on her to help. . . . Everyone she meets is a friend to her." In November 1961 she had fallen down the basement stairs and been "out of commission" for several weeks. She said she was "fine, I guess, but I am home a lot." She had cut down on gardening, rested more, and watched a great deal more television. The spastic grandchild had died, and she found that a relief.

This case, too, presents an interesting example of somewhat differing views of a person by three professional members of the staff. One, who was doing a series of very intensive interviews with a few of the respondents, perceived her as an overgrown adolescent. She would not talk of her daughter, but of her son-in-law, a favorite nephew, and her younger brother (when she was growing up). She was judged to have the "preoccupations and style of life of a teen-ager." (This was in September 1957, well after the onset of her husband's illness.) In May 1959 another professional staff member described her as having "persistent girlishness in the best sense." In September 1960, the clinical psychologist judged her to be a very mature person. She had had a hard time adjusting to her husband's depressive episodes and to the loss of their summer home, but she did not let anything get her down for long. She was still "involved in her social system much more fully, and it was much more essential to her, than for most people in Kansas City." A reading of all the materials collected over the five-year period would suggest that the judgment of this last person came closest to being correct.

This case well illustrated the relativity of disengagement. She used disengagement as a coping device, out of loyalty to her husband, and used it well. Even so, her life space remained larger and her involvement in it greater than for many other respondents. She was clearly autonomous-persistent, and all of her uses of action energy were rated 1.

THE LESS SUCCESSFUL AGERS

Disengaging Under Protest

This seventy-year-old respondent lived in one of the loveliest sections of Kansas City. She had been born into a family with a more than adequate income; her father had been in a supervisory position with one of the packing companies. She and her younger brother lived comfortably, and, although she could have gone to college if she had wished, she preferred the companionship of working in her father's office.

Her first husband gave her her dearest possessions—two fine sons. They had a happy life, although financially it had been quite an "up and down" one; before the youngsters were in their teens, her husband died and she was left to raise them alone. She raised them "by the book," she claimed, and they more than justified her faith and work by turning out to be morally upstanding young men, and eminent in their professions. She had kept close touch with them, a rather easy, friendly kind of relationship rather than a mothering one. But they were clearly her greatest source of pride, and she could not do enough for them financially—even though they really did not need it. Significantly, though, they accepted it.

She married for the second time at sixty-eight, for companionship, a man she had known for years. As a financial official, he was a suitable match, and she retained her good social status.

The first impression of this woman was that she was a gay, brisk, busy person, quite satisfied with her life and the outlook for the future. Her days were so filled with social and civic affairs she could hardly squeeze in time for the interviewer to call. The picture of her life space was clear. She knew over forty of her neighbors by name (her husband had moved into her old home with her), but none of these neighbors did she really consider friends. Throughout the town she had countless other people with whom she was also friendly, but not one was highly important to her. Although several of her good friends had died, she still had two very close friends, and together they attended countless luncheons and club affairs. This was an important change from her forties; in those days, when she was occupied with her boys, she had had no maid and was more tied to domestic duties, but had also had more close friends.

Her second husband did not figure in her extensive daytime activities, although they both belonged to a social club and several bridge clubs which they enjoyed a great deal. This was especially important, because she and her husband had not made plans for his retirement days; in fact, they had not even discussed it. Another change the second husband had brought about was a lessened participation in church activities. He was not the churchgoer her first husband had been, and since she found organized religion something of a chore and an imposition anyway, she did not mind lessening her attendance at formal church occasions. This did not mean that religion was not important to her; it meant a great deal, but she simply did not wish to be obligated for formal participation.

During the next two years of interviews, the respondent and her husband decided to build their own new home in a new section of the city. This made a major change in her life, even though she was not eager to admit it. It took her out of her old neighborhood at a time when she was beginning to realize that old acquaintances were more important than she had previously thought. She protested brightly that the new neighbors were wonderful and that she might have found the new neighborhood's advantages more easily if she had not suffered a heart attack just at this time. She tried to appear her old gay self, but there was a false ring to it.

Eight months later, she was beginning to settle in, and she was able to sound more convincingly buoyant again. But on questioning, she let down her guard a little and admitted she tired more quickly and was a great deal more lonely. Her husband had to work some nights, and instead of going out, she just read or watched television. However, she kept up her spirit, claiming to like her age and pronouncing her new neighborhood the best of any in Kansas City. She even said her health was better than average for her age.

The psychologist interviewed her at this period, and he reported that this bright busy life was not really a result of zest, but was hyperactivity, defensive in nature. Affectively complex, this respondent was fighting off the inevitable pressures of age in the best way she knew.

The significant others reported interestingly on her. Her husband was apparently delighted with her as a wife. Her skill as a bridge player was formidable, and together they made quite a pair. Her social roles and her relationship to others beautifully complemented what he wanted as a companion. He seemed unaware that she was slowing down, much less that she was fighting disengagement so fiercely.

One son understood her dilemma, however. "If she ever loafs, she'll die!" he said quite seriously. Her generosity to him (in thousands of dollars) was appreciated, but it also made him feel a little anxious when he did not spend all his vacations with her. This caused no real hard feelings between him and his mother—just anxiety on his part and more loneliness on hers.

The final interview showed disengagement well under way despite her protests. Her friends were dying, and she was disintegrating physically. With this physical decline went a commensurate amount of spark. Her sense of values remained stable, but she had to admit to fewer friends, fewer activities, more time at home, and more loneliness—not drastically more, but far more than she wanted.

Although not alienated or isolated, she was developing a sense of anomie because of inability to continue the type of life she valued. She had a rating of 1 on clarity of style, with a weak familism underlying it. It might have been rated a stronger familistic style if her relationships with her children had been more satisfying in and of themselves, but the picture presented by the interviewers was that her chief satisfaction came from the familistic activity, not from the sense of family closeness and shared action energy alone.

Her style of life had been and still was to live as fully as possible, but she was autonomous-precarious rather than persistent, because of the very bad state of her health and her outlook (in terms of her health) for the future. Bad health in and of itself is not sufficient grounds to describe a person as precarious, but as a person who desired to live fully (and her idea of living fully included physical stamina), she was definitely threatened. Despite her vigorous protests, aging was under way.

Don't Want to Age

This case will be presented in the same manner as "Slow and Easy" in order to bring out the sharp contrast between the two.

Life history. This woman, unlike most of the panel members, grew up in an urban environment. In fact, she had lived all her life in Kansas City. Her father had been in the saloon and restaurant business. She was the next to the youngest child in a rather large family, with three brothers and three sisters. The family had had a good deal of company, and there had been lots of people around while she was growing up. She remembered her mother as a very fine person but said she did not really know her father very well. She graduated from high school, had some college, and then taught kindergarten briefly before she was married. She married a man in the construction business, who became fairly successful. They had one daughter who had never married and was still living at home when she was in her early thirties, at the beginning of the study. The respondent was fifty-seven years old at this time. Her pattern of life remained essentially the same during the five years of the study. The daughter left home during the middle of the study, and came home for Christmas the following year.

Characteristic uses of action energy. The interviewer described the respondent as of medium build, with gray hair and a "pleasant sparkle." Her activities included many telephone calls, bridge, church on Sunday, some work for the Red Cross, and, for a time, volunteer work with a social agency. In short, she was busily, actively, and quickly "on the go" most of the time, in marked contrast to "Slow and Easy." She did not particularly like housework. The daughter did all the gardening until she left home, and then the respondent had to do it, but disliked it greatly.

The interview with the clinical psychologist brought out rather clearly that she had always been upwardly mobile and somewhat insecure about it. Friends, and sometimes lack of friends, were frequently upsetting to her. She tended to be quite outspoken and insensitive to the feelings of others. Thus, sometimes people did not return her invitations, and this was particularly upsetting to her. However, in the last regular interview, there was some evidence that the frank discussion of her problems with the clinical psychologist had given her some degree of insight. She thought of herself then as being a little more tolerant and said, "I feel it is not worth losing friends to be so outspoken. If they can play golf and bridge reasonably well, who cares about their other nasty traits?"

This respondent and "Slow and Easy" were both about the same age and were both in socioeconomic class 1. Their most marked contrast was in pace of living, but there were other important differences as well. They both showed some signs of anomie, and were rated 2 on this variable. But the source of anomie was quite different in the two cases. In his case it was associated with his tension and his relations with his wife, whereas in her case it was associated with her concerns about upward mobility, coupled with some degree of social ineptness, and her tremendous anxiety about aging. She showed some alienation, through her outspoken tendencies, whereas he had no tendency in this direction. Neither was isolated, and they both coped fairly well, but not outstandingly. He managed to achieve the style of Living Fully very clearly indeed, whereas her style was less clear.

Relations with her husband. Her husband owned his own business and had no intention of retiring. She felt that, if he did retire and were home all day, she would lose her mind. He did not read much and, except for golf at the club, their interests were rather different. She had wanted their daughter to go away to school, to marry, and to be more independent, but he had wanted the daughter to remain at home. She described her husband as "a very good person with strong character," but added, "He says I nag him. I want him to be perfect, but he doesn't change." The clinical psychologist commented that the whole subject of togetherness was not a very important part of her life, and neither the husband nor the wife made many demands on the other. During the last interview, when the husband was suffering from back trouble and not working very much, she commented, "He has a bad back anyway." Also, her husband would not eat vegetables and she wondered vaguely what was wrong with him.

In the cases both of this respondent and of "Slow and Easy," the marital relations were not the best. However, most of the time, she was just vaguely dissatisfied with some of her husband's characteristics, and, on the whole, appreciated having a financially successful and stable husband, with whom she could play golf on weekends and go to the club. It was only at the end of the study, when her husband's health became worse, that she was more outspokenly critical. She was concerned about the effects this might have on their financial situation and, even more importantly, she was reminded of aging. Our respondent, "Slow and Easy," on the other hand, had always wanted to achieve couplehood with his wife, but was unable to do so due to her vastly different mode of living. His wife's serious illness was a source of great sorrow to him, but in no way constituted a problem in coping with the aging process.

Scope of activities and interests. This respondent knew several of her neighbors, who were also upper-class people. She had no close friends, but many acquaintances. She belonged to various groups, most important of which, to her, was the country club. She engaged in some volunteer work, as something which one in her station in life should do, and she could drop it rather quickly when it was no longer convenient or to her liking. She maintained some relations with her family of orientation, but they were not close. She saw a sister in Kansas City fairly frequently and a brother, also living in Kansas City, about once a month. But she showed some ambivalence and envy concerning the brother, who was considerably more well-to-do than she was. Other siblings she saw very rarely.

This respondent's surface amplitude of activities was greater in scope than that of "Slow and Easy." This difference was largely a function of the quite different pacing of life in the two cases. A much more important difference was that one senses considerably more genuineness in his involvement than in hers.

Disengagement. Essentially no disengagement occurred during the five years of the study. The possibility of forced disengagement with aging was her core problem. At several points during the study she said very frankly that she did not look forward to growing old and being unable to play golf. She was much more afraid of becoming an invalid than of dying, an attitude found in many of the members of this panel, but found in a very pronounced way in her case. The clinical psychologist, in speaking about her anxiety over growing old, said, "This means the loss of all things meaningful in life—busyness, sports, and card playing."

Again, there is a sharp contrast with "Slow and Easy." For him, disengagement was no problem at all; he could maintain his mode of the style Living Fully on into the later years with a considerable amount of disengagement, whereas for her, this would be impossible.

Analysis. Her involvement with things familistic or having to do with the lives of couples was minimum. Her answers concerning the five most important things in life were most unfamilistic. She had many phone calls but said that phone calls with relatives were a bother and took too much time, that is, too much time away from phone calls concerning bridge and golf dates. She put her energy into building a style of Living Fully, although it was clear that she did not achieve all of her goals in this respect.

We have classified her in the middle level of the autonomous-precarious category in relation to success. Her action system was in fair balance throughout the study. The precariousness stemmed from two main sources. One was her ineptness in human relations, which was a problem to her in relation to her concerns about social class. The other, and more important, was her attitude toward aging itself. She dreaded it. When golf went, she thought, things would be bad, and when bridge went, they would be worse. In this respect, she is similar to "Disengaging Under Protest." Her manner of Living Fully required a fairly high level of energy, and, when that went, the whole way of life might collapse. If her husband lasted into this period of life, she might become highly dependent and hate it, or she might just collapse.

No Nonsense

This is another case in which the life history material is particularly rich. She spoke quite freely about various parts of it during several of the interviews. She was seen by the clinical psychologist, who, in this one instance, also interviewed the husband.

She was born in a southern state and grew up in an atmosphere of a rich and complex family tradition, surrounded by Confederate veterans of the Civil War. She was the middle one in a five-child family. The younger ones did not count for her, and she was always oriented toward the two older. There was a span of twenty years between the oldest and youngest of the five children. Her father was a gray-haired man of fifty when she was born. He had owned slaves, and even up until the time of the study he kept contact with the grandchildren and great-grandchildren of the two house servants. On the other hand, she was tutored by the sister of a Union general and traced her interest in literature to her. Several of her relatives were well-known people. The family was not wealthy, but they stuck closely together.

She had great respect for her mother, who she said was brought up in the age of enlightenment. Her mother had a great sense of justice and never allowed the respondent to think she had "arrived." When a dean commented to her mother that the respondent was the best teacher in the state, the mother reminded the respondent that there were forty-seven other states. Her father was the man all the children loved—gentle, kindly, and definitely of the old school of the south. "If my life had been left in his hands, I never would have gone to school." However, she herself insisted on going to school at the age of five. Later on the family moved to Kansas City so that she would have a better high school education. The father had to return to their original home for business reasons, but a sister stayed on in Kansas City with her and delayed her own marriage, so she could have a better schooling. The sister graduated from a professional school. The respondent returned home after high school and taught for a period. However, her mother urged that she go on to college, and the rather unheard of (for those days) decision was made for her to go to a state university. She got through the university with some interruptions to teach and earn money, and managed to get two bachelor's degrees and a master's degree.

She was married three years later, and for the next eleven years was busily and unhappily engaged in raising a family. She preferred not to say much about this period of life. When her first baby was born, it was not a happy time for her, and she thought, "My God, what a responsibility." At another point, she commented that she should have given the children more intellectual discipline and less of the other kind. At still another point, she said, "I was too strict and not a good mother with my children. They all turned out well, but I could have made life pleasant without so much dictatorship."

Her husband had followed his brother's lead in leaving home on the farm and going to a university after his second year in high school. He worked his way through the university by teaching and did extremely well as an undergraduate. He was headed for a Ph.D., but had an illness, and his marks fell from A to B. So he took a farm management job, and married shortly thereafter. This change in life plans was a bitter disappointment to him. His rosy dreams had faded, he had children, and he could not go back for graduate work. His brother did do so, and became a great success as a textbook writer. The husband then had some financial reverses and was taken in by a promoter. But he went into business for himself and did fairly well for a time.

Of the first years of marriage, he said, "My wife went along with my plans and was a helpmate." After the first eleven years of marriage, the respondent went back into teaching. Her first job was in a local college, in the town in which they were then living, so that she could be at home some of the time. But she lost this job due to rules against married women, and obtained a position in the state university, which required her to be out of town a week at a time. She also built up a lecture circuit which paid very well. During this same period, the husband went back to part-time teaching, and his work required him to travel a good deal. They did manage to keep the children, and to keep the family more or less together. She described the situation:

> My husband is a university graduate, calm, and all who have known him adore him. But we have always each had our own activities. This started of necessity because we could not hire babysitters, and each had his own professional and social engagements. Then each of us has had so many and such different activities that we have gone our separate ways.

The Depression was a particularly bad time for them because they were short on money and the children were just ready for college. However, they did manage to see that the children went through college. The husband had a series of jobs, and finally went into a business owned by his wife's brother in Kansas City, in which he did fairly well. His son was president of this concern at the time of the study.

The respondent became a university professor at the age of thirty-six, and continued in that profession up to, and through, the time of the study. At the age of sixty-one she got a position teaching in a nearby university, and at the time of the study she was seventy-five years old and still teaching in this university. Her husband had retired about four years previously, at the age of seventy-three.

During this first interview, in the summer of 1956, she expressed a strong interest in life in Kansas City, where she had spent a great many years. She had found the routine of small town life, which she had experienced in the early period of her marriage, to be "deadly." Her daily round involved teaching at the university in the mornings, playing cards in the afternoon, usually having dinner out, without her husband, who did not care about going out. The evenings were spent in studying or playing cards. She sometimes went to bed as early as midnight, but usually not until 2 A.M., and would be up the next day at 7 A.M. Teaching was what she enjoyed most, and any routine things, particularly household matters, she enjoyed least. Saturdays were spent playing cards or reading, and on Sunday, friends would come in or she would go out, generally without her husband. In the later interview with the husband, he remarked, "I go to my wife's affairs only when it would embarrass her if I didn't. At the same time, we are highly congenial in other areas."

In this first interview, and in several succeeding interviews, she expressed herself most clearly on matters relating to disengagement. She said she was freer than she had ever been—she just did not do things she did not want to do. She had fewer housekeeping tasks, many of which were done by her husband. She had dropped all of her clubs; she had belonged to many, and was president of many, but now teaching, studying, and playing cards gave her all the satisfaction she wanted. She had lots of friends, but no close ones, and her friendships formed an interesting sociological pattern: they were in nonoverlapping categories, so that the people she knew usually did not know each other. On the subject of aging she said, "I wear my age as I wear my hair, simply not a matter of concern."

It was very characteristic of her "no nonsense" orientation toward life that, in response to a question about the most unpleasant thing that had happened recently, she said, "Ike [President Eisenhower], manifesting such indolence and stupidity." The best thing that had happened was a recent trip to the Near East and Europe, where she had led a tour.

In January of 1959, she said she was fine and, in fact, she was quite proud of the fact that she had not missed a day of full activities in fifty years. She had had a pleasant Christmas vacation with the children. The disengagement theme was again expressed in relation to the best thing about being her age; it was freedom from petty conventions, freedom to accept or decline invitations, being without personal responsibility, and having her husband around the house because "it is a relief to have him do things I did when he was employed." In response to a question about wanting to see more, less, or about the same of her relatives, she said it would be selfish to wish the children and grandchildren to come and see her more, because they lived out of town.

Her daily round looked about the same in August of 1959. She said she taught eleven months of the year. She refused to give answers to the story questions on the grounds that there were not enough facts. She liked the freedom of apartment living, and she liked her age because it entailed "no responsibility and agony toward growing children." She did not feel closer to any of her friends than to others. In response to a question about the happiest time of her life, she said, "I have never been unhappy—happiness is something one seeks but never finds."

In March of 1960, parts of her value system became quite clear in relation to people she had admired or disliked. Shakespeare had had a great influence on her, in relation to the moral responsibility of intelligence. She admired Martin Luther King for his pacifist approach to the Negro problem. She would not want to be Simon Legree, Brutus, Caesar, Hamlet, Governor Faubus, Billy Graham, or Richard Nixon. And one of her attitudes toward herself was well expressed by, "I'm mad as hell because I can't go to sleep if I don't go to sleep as soon as I hit the bed. I just think, 'Well, you'll go about your business whether you sleep or not.' "

In June of 1960, the clinical psychologist described her as a tall woman, charming and captivating, and indicated that he had spent a delightful and stimulating three hours with her. In addition to teaching, she was taking a class at the university on "Politics 1960." It was clear that one of the things she disliked most was stupidity. She said of herself, "I am a rebel, but during my adult years I realized I couldn't always manifest it. Now I can't do anything wrong." She liked to play the elder statesman role to people with a variety of problems. In that same period, the psychologist found the husband to be in a mild depressive state. He had recently smashed up his car; before that he would chauffeur his wife around to various activities. But he said he managed to put in time seeing the humorous side of things. He felt that he used to have a purpose in life but now he did not. However, he felt he was successful in not being unhappy. It was noted that the name on the apartment doorbell was the wife's and not the husband's.

In November of 1961, the interviewer chatted briefly with the husband prior to interviewing the wife. The husband said the wife's work was "her meat and drink" and that she would be lost without it. Of his own family, he commented that it was a "Ripley's Believe It or Not," since all four children had married and were still living, and their spouses were still living with them.

The respondent said she was very well. Life was going on about as usual, and students came to her with all sorts of problems. She was still going to bed about 1 A.M. She was teaching two credit courses and two noncredit courses, a total of twelve hours a week, with as many as ninety students in one of her noncredit courses. Her daily round at age seventy-eight, almost seventy-nine, looked just as it had at the beginning of the study when she was seventy-four, almost seventy-five. She was still playing cards, going to the theater frequently, taking in many lectures, and reading a great deal. She pointed to ten or twelve thick volumes that had been read in the last two months. Friends came in and out frequently. She seemed to be eating dinner with her husband more frequently than she had earlier. She went to the beauty shop every Saturday morning. She liked to play cards in the evening with different kinds of people.

She had some difficulty with sleeping and occasionally took a nap when she had been awake all night. She was thinking of starting sleeping pills and wished that she never had to sleep. She said that when she finished at the university, which she thought would be about two years hence, "I will do as my mother did, sleep when I want to, day or night." She did not enjoy eating because she did not "enjoy being an animal." She claimed to have some memory loss and said, "My mind has reached the saturation point." She never entered the classroom without being fully prepared. She thought it was immoral and a disgrace to indulge or pamper one's self.

She claimed that since her husband had retired they had done more things together, but the husband, in the background, commented

sadly that when they were in college he used to be able to get a date
with the respondent. She was planning to have a Christmas party for
her great-nieces and great-nephews because she felt she should, but she
added that she did not plan to do this sort of thing often. She emphasized again that she was friends with all of her students. She no
longer belonged to a single organization, and claimed they were "useless, time-commanding, and filled with petty drives."

She had been to New Orleans on a speaking engagement the preceding week. In this context she emphasized that she had never given
up anything against her will. A little later in the interview, she mentioned that she had had to give up traveling because she got carsick,
even on the way to the airport, but then tried to make light of this.

There can be no doubt that this woman's style of life was Living
Fully, and one might add, freely. It had great amplitude in those areas
where she wanted it to have amplitude. The more problematical issue
in her case was the success category and rating. It may come as a
surprise that she has been classified among the less successful agers. We
have placed her in the autonomous-precarious category in the middle
rank. She was one of the most successful agers in this panel during her
seventies. She was in very good balance with her total, rather large,
system of relatively diffuse-neutral relationships. She was well oriented
both instrumentally and expressionally within this system. But she had
never been in balance with the smaller, more intimate system, with its
diffuse-affective and expressional requirements. When the larger system
went, she would likely be out of balance with whatever was left. Disengagement of the type frequently seen in the seventies was no problem
at all for her, but the kind of disengagement usually required in the
eighties could well be a serious problem. Perhaps she can retreat further into the life of her books and her own mind, and for this reason
she has not been placed at the bottom of the autonomous-precarious
category. She was one of several respondents in the panel for whom
one wishes it would be possible to obtain data five years after the end
of the study.

THE LEAST SUCCESSFUL AGER

The Doctor's Widow

This seventy-six-year-old woman's husband was a well-known professional man in Kansas City. When he died in the late 1920's, she took
up a service profession full time. It was an enormously satisfying career,

and she had her late husband's social status to fill her need to belong a little "higher up."

There were no children, and somewhere along the line she "discovered" religion, which filled a real emptiness in her life. She was living alone at the initial interview, and recently had retired as a result of a broken arm (and aging—although she did not care to admit it).

Much of her time was spent focusing on religion and the manners and morals of others. For example, she had most of the children on her street angry at her because she "had their safety at heart" and had repeatedly called police to keep the children from playing in the street. Her friends admired her but were also a little afraid of her because she was getting so eccentric on the subject of religion. For example, she telephoned one friend weekly to see if she had properly memorized the Bible verse for Sunday school; the friend was afraid of the respondent and wrote the verse down each week near the phone so she could be sure to read it correctly.

She had definitely disengaged from work and there was some slight slowing down of physical activity, but she went to civic and social activities as much as she was able. There was alienation evident in her antagonism toward other people's manners and behavior (also social isolation), and there was probably gradual disintegration as well.

Her last interview suggested that she was growing increasingly dependent on her friends. She was calling them constantly, ostensibly to inquire about their welfare, but it was clear that many of the calls were made to reassure herself. By antagonizing her friends and constantly communicating with them she could reassure herself that she was still involved in a complex network of personal relationships. The telephone undoubtedly plays a great part in the lives of the disengaging Living Fully types. Some use it constructively to supplement their growing physical weakness. Others, like this woman, use it as a means to clutch at fading relationships. For this reason she was classed as dependent-precarious, toward the top.

ANALYSIS

Living Fully, as a style, expresses one facet of the Christian ethic, "I am come that you might have life and that you might have it more abundantly." It is a socially approved style, and many popular programs of living arrangements and recreation for the aged are based on the assumption that this is a greatly preferred style of life. All of the most successful agers who had this style showed a lifelong pattern of competent coping with many facets of life, again something highly approved, especially in the middle and upper-middle classes. Living Fully is a particularly acceptable style for people with a ministering type of religious orientation. It is almost a glorified familism. A common phrase in religious thought refers to the "brotherhood of men." This variant of Living Fully seeks to achieve satisfaction by broad involvement in diffuse-affective relations.

Living Fully, as a style, is difficult to achieve in any state of dependence, unless the style is in transition, as it was in the case of "The Doctor's Widow." She had a clear style of Living Fully and was still caught up in it during the study. But as she became more lonely and less able physically to get around, she was moving into a dependent role and a familistic style. Her telephone calls to family and neighbors and the personal nature of these calls indicated her increased reliance on the diffuse-affective contacts of those about her. Yet, she had gotten so far away from this style of life, if indeed she had ever achieved it, that she gave little to those in her system; in fact, she mostly frightened them. Living Fully is rarely associated with dependency, and when it is, it is a precarious business.

Living Fully is particularly important in contributing to refinements in the understanding of the disengagement process. On the surface it might appear as almost the opposite of disengagement. Yet, as we have seen in several of the cases, it is by no means antithetical to disengagement. In "Forced Disengagement," the process was indeed forced, yet it was accepted and handled well. In "No Nonsense," disengagement itself was a part of Living Fully. This style well illustrates the relativity of disengagement. Some people have relatively little to disengage from, and when this is the case, disengagement as such is not likely to create problems in relation to aging. Others have much from which they can disengage. When this is the case, disengagement can be a problem. On the other hand, it is possible to disengage and still maintain the full flavor of Living Fully as a style.

Although Living Fully tends to be rather strongly associated with successful aging, it is not an absolute guarantee of it. There are two major sources of precariousness within this style. First, if the style depends heavily, sometimes almost exclusively, on maintenance of physical health and vigor, there is the great danger that when that wanes the whole system may collapse, as is illustrated by "Disengaging Under Protest" and "Don't Want to Age." Second, if the style has been developed in such a manner as to preclude the emergence of secondary styles of Familism, Couplehood, or both, the system may persist for a considerable period of time, but ultimately is in danger when the person is no longer able to keep up with the broad network of diffuse-neutral relations and transactions, as is illustrated in "No Nonsense." In the case of "Ministering to the Town," on the other hand, the respondent was involved in a broad network, but he had also been able to achieve secondary styles of Familism and Couplehood with his first wife, and of Couplehood with his second, which placed him in a much more autonomous-persistent position.

EIGHT

❧§❧

Success

and Style

In each of the six chapters on styles of life, we have been concerned with both style and success. The two themes have been interwoven in the case material. There are important relations between style and success, a matter to which we shall return in the beginning of Chapter Nine. In the present chapter we wish to focus, on the one hand, on success as such and the factors which make for it, and, on the other, on some interrelations between styles. We shall analyze two cases of the most successful agers, and two cases of the least successful agers, in some depth. Then we shall analyze two cases, each of which illustrates a fundamental relationship between styles.

THE MOST SUCCESSFUL AGERS

Golden Familism

This woman was born in 1881 in a small midwestern town. Her father was the railroad station agent, and she had one older brother. Her early life left her with good memories of shared family life. "I always loved little children. My mother and I took care of the neighbors' babies every chance we had. I loved all my dolls, too. Even now, when I see a baby, something inside me just goes out to it." Both her parents were equally important to her. They were opposites, she felt.

Mother was quick as a snap on a trigger, and more talkative, but loving and kind. She'd get mad so quick and then get over it just as quick. Father was quiet and never said much, but what he said counted. . . . Young men would come in and talk to him about their problems.

They must have been good companions as well, for when she, in her late seventies, thought of them, as she often did, it was when things came up she knew they would have been interested in. "I think how much they've missed. Even this rocket to the moon and all these airplanes flying around."

As a child she read extensively, and especially admired the self-reliance of Robinson Crusoe and the Louisa Alcott characters.

At nineteen she had finished all the schooling the local town had to offer, so she went to a nearby state to take a secretarial course and work. But her career was short. At twenty she met and married her husband, with whom she was to live fifty-seven years. On their honeymoon, she discovered her husband had smallpox. With the characteristic good humor that was to mark her life, she went with him to live in a small "pest house" set up on her uncle's farm, and there she amused herself by cutting curtains out of newspapers and otherwise making light of the situation.

For twenty-five years her husband was a traveling missionary. Then they settled down to a service business in their own home. Meanwhile, they raised a daughter and three sons. One son died in his twenties, a dreadful blow for the respondent. He had not turned out well, and she often wondered whether she was to blame, but all the other children were spectacularly successful and she gloried in their achievements. One son achieved an international reputation as an entertainer, another was successful in business, and the daughter was both a career woman and a wife.

When she was in her forties, the respondent's life space had to change to include her parents who moved in to live with them. By this time the parents were rather aged, and the respondent's mother complained of the children's noise and their friends. Exhibiting the same successful familistic approach as always, the respondent gently but firmly moved her parents to an apartment added at the rear of the house, and insisted on no further interference with the youngest generation. Things worked out well from then on, and it was a source of deep grief to her when her parents died.

As the study began, the respondent and her husband lived a quiet, secluded life. She was seventy-seven and he was eighty-four. His bad heart had forced him into total retirement. The daughter lived near enough to see them weekly, and frequent letters and tape recordings were exchanged with the sons and their families.

The relationship between husband and wife was clearly a strong and intimate one. During interviews there was much evidence of shared jokes and mutual forbearance. If either was dependent, it was he, not she. Perhaps the relationship is best implied by her answers to the question, "What has been the best time of your adult life?" This is how she answered:

> My whole life was fine—no regrets at all. There was, of course, the happiness of early married life. Each child was another happiness. We've had a few hard experiences. We've lost two children, one at two years, then a son at twenty-nine. We even spent our honeymoon in a "pest house." When things were bad I just felt I had to bear it—it's part of life, I guess.

Her three chief satisfactions in life included keeping house, just being with family, and keeping up with the news and what was going on in the world—which suggests a strong underpinning style of Living Fully. Their life space was more limited than it had been when they were in business, but she still listed five friends and neighbors, and eighty other close friends. However, she felt her husband to be her only intimate friend. Her relationship with neighbors was good, but not perfect. She was greatly annoyed by undisciplined neighbor children who came into her yard and damaged her bushes and flowers—a rather commonly expressed problem among this panel of respondents.

Although she and her husband lived quietly, at least once a year, health permitting, they went to visit the more distant children and grandchildren. She accepted this all too brief time with her family, and this was typical of her expressed attitude of accepting life. Nevertheless, she checked over half of the pessimistic statements on that rating.

By the final interview, the husband had died, and she had made a complete readjustment. She had sold the old home, moved into a small apartment, and busied herself redecorating and making a new life with church and friends, especially in the Golden Age Club. She had shifted her familism to the new friends in the club, and one could only predict a continued autonomous future for her.

"Golden Familism" was an excellent example of successful aging. This seventy-seven-year-old woman had managed her life space with deft success in a style of pure familism from childhood through girlhood to womanhood and widowhood. She had, with consistent good humor, so managed her action energy as to maintain a balance with, and most often a greater output to, her significant others, whether they were her parents, her husband, or her children. Highly important to her was the use of humor in relieving tensions created by interchange of action energy.

Another resource was her attitude toward her children. Their success was hers, and as an autonomous-persistent person, she granted them the freedom to be equally autonomous and go their own ways in terms of geographical separation and independent affective attachments. That she was not satisfied to be so separate was made quite clear in the final interview, when she reported the worst time of day to be when she said goodbye to her loved ones. Nevertheless, she was convinced of the wisdom of mutual autonomy. This attitude in a person who embraces a familistic style undoubtedly leads to greater persistence in the autonomous-persistent category. She understood the importance of the principle of insulation within familism, and could be intimate without being crushingly so.

Like Charlie Weaver

"If the next world is better than this, it is going to be a honey." Such was the response of this sixty-nine-year-old man to a question in the first round of interviews about life after death. "Be as happy as possible" was his response, at seventy-four, to a question on the main purpose in life. The best way to see this respondent is just as he was seen during the seven rounds of interviewing, with a minimum of life history material, because during these years, and probably thereafter, he clearly illustrated the characteristics of the most successful agers, as defined here.

He lived in a five-room upstairs apartment in a converted house. He had had some college education. His father had been an attorney. He was a salesman, in a line of business which required direct contact with a large number of people. He lived with his sister, age fifty, who was a school teacher. One of his hobbies was growing roses, which he was able to do in the yard below. He was a short man, tanned and of medium weight, and impressed the interviewer as having a "great sense of humor."

He had lived in Kansas City for thirty-three years, and liked it very much. He much preferred living in a large city with many different kinds of people. He said he liked children and that Kansas City was a very good place for them. He felt that things in general were better for children than they had been in his generation, and that the main problem many older people have is that they concentrate too much on themselves. By "older" he meant sixty-nine, his own age, and said most of his friends were younger.

He and his sister had a good breakfast each morning, and he then spent the rest of the day "calling on and talking to interesting people"; this was the way in which he perceived his work. In the evenings he sometimes watched television. He was more likely to listen to the radio because, as he said, "You can do something else while listening." He liked to play canasta and bridge, not with any organized groups, but with a variety of friends. When asked what part of his daily round he liked best, he said he liked it all, and added, "I'm never wildly elated or down in the dumps." By way of further explanation, he said he had lost his wife in 1921. They had been married for thirteen years and had never had a quarrel. He had lived with his sister since 1926, and they had never quarreled either.

He had one married daughter and one married son. The son lived away from Kansas City at the beginning of the study, but the respondent visited the daughter and her children quite frequently on Saturdays, or sometimes he visited his brother. He went to Sunday school and church. Other weekend activities were quite varied. He and his sister frequently read articles to each other and discussed them. He was an elder in the church and belonged to several church organizations. His son was a minister in a Protestant church.

He described his sister as a "helping teacher," and said she had this position because she was a superior teacher. He and his sister shared the household tasks and the household budget. They also shared the task of driving the car, but he said that he preferred to have his sister drive. When asked about close friends, he mentioned five, and could have gone on for some time.

He could continue with his job as long as he could walk, talk, and think. He had no boss and was on his own. He sold "cold turkey," that is, without previous contacts. His only health problem, at this time, was diabetes, and it was under control.

In March of 1957 his health was not as good. He had been suffering from rheumatism and was taking care of his business by telephone. His sister had taken over the shopping. He did not play quite as much bridge, and watched television somewhat more. Otherwise his social life and life in the church were about the same. He had his friends come in somewhat more, rather than going to see them. His son, who had a doctorate in the ministry, had moved to Kansas

City, and he saw him each week. He said that when his sister retired, which was still quite a way off, they planned to go to Florida. In response to a question about the most important thing in life, he replied, "Family."

In August of 1957 he said he was very well. He had gotten a new job and was "happy as a lark." He was still in the same line of business, but now had gotten a job in an office because his rheumatism still limited him, and he could not walk around all day long. He had lots of friends. He had a special source of supply for eggs, which he brought to his neighbors.

In November 1958, at seventy-one, he had gone into an entirely different line of selling. He had fallen and broken his pelvic bone on the preceding job, and so found it difficult to work sitting down all day and had gone back to a type of work in which he could walk around. In response to a question on the nicest things that had happened since the last interview, he said that everything had been nice, and in response to the worst things that had happened he said that it was taking a bath and having difficulty getting out of the bathtub. He added, "My whole life has been a vacation and it still is. I have never been in a bad mood." He was also particularly pleased about his present job where he could walk around and talk to interesting people all day. The grandchildren all called him by his first name. He spent a leisurely hour at breakfast each morning with his sister, and two or three evenings a week with her.

In June 1959 he was back in his original line of business and worked four or five hours a day. He spent two evenings a week going to see a widow to "make her happy." He liked being seventy-two and enjoyed being at home with his sister.

In February 1960, in response to a question about achievement of his goals, he said that he had fallen short financially, but the more important things—friends and family—were fine and he was very happy about that. He described his mother as one of the wisest women he had ever known and said his sister was just like her. His mother had taught him tolerance. He had admired his father as an upright man. He was now chairman of one of the groups at church. He said he felt very good, with no aches and pains. As to the best thing he liked on the weekend, he said it was to be with his sister with a cup of coffee and some popcorn, watching his favorite television show.

In September of 1961, five years after the start of the study, the interviewer commented that the respondent had "talked his ear off," that he was very well read, a "nice little man," and "very pleased with himself." The respondent said he was fine. There had been no major changes. He had a grandson who was going to an African country to school. He had gotten into the habit of reading editorials from the living room to his sister while she dressed in her own room. He was doing some business by telephone and considered himself semi-retired. He slept a couple of hours after lunch and then walked around visiting with the neighbors. He went out two or three evenings a week, especially to see the "pretty widow on Friday and Sunday evenings." His daughter had moved to another city in a neighboring state, and he went there to visit her occasionally. He did not regret growing old.

On Sundays, the sister was with her friends, and he was with his. He said he had very fine neighbors, "Jewish, Catholic, Methodist, Lutheran, Christians—all fine people."

He rather casually mentioned that he had had a heart attack a year and one-half previously, just shortly after the preceding interview.

He said he had sown the wild oats for the whole family. As a boy he fought every day, but he never fought now. He said, "I take it easy and rest when I want to." One of his greatest pleasures in life was "dining out with a good-looking woman." He also liked bridge and ball games. He had mild regrets that he could not run foot races with his grandsons any more, which he had done up until the age of about seventy-two, before he had his heart attack. During the time he was in the hospital, the nurse said that she had never seen a man with so many friends. He was interested in politics and did some political work at election time. Concerning his illness, he commented further that "you cannot enjoy the sunshine if there are not clouds at times," and also said he had found out how much his family and friends thought of him during that period. One other tidbit of information which he gave to the interviewer at the close of this last interview was that for twenty-five years he had gone to a Negro barber.

This respondent throws light on the sources and resources which kept his action system persistently autonomous:

1. He developed two secondary styles, Familism and Couplehood, earlier with his wife, and later with his sister, which helped to maintain his primary style of Living Fully.

2. The range and amplitude of his action system were comparatively great. That, in itself, does not guarantee successful aging in the terms used here. Much more important, the range and amplitude could change easily. His system was highly flexible.

3. His attitude toward work was an important resource. Life was just one big vacation, and work was not something apart from it. As

far as remunerative work was concerned, he could do as much or as little as he liked, and, as with some of the other very successful agers, he could pace himself in retirement.

4. Closely related to the preceding two points, disengagement was not a problematical issue for him, and he could disengage readily, while still retaining the full flavor of his style.

5. His attitude toward health was also an important resource. In spite of diabetes, rheumatism, a broken pelvis, and a heart attack, he went on living fully and happily, at whatever level he could without driving himself.

6. Success, as defined in terms of balance of action energy with the individual's social system, as we do here, and success, as defined in terms of life satisfaction, are not necessarily related. We have seen several cases of people who were successful in our terms, but dissatisfied and unhappy. In this case, the respondent was successful in both senses. When this situation occurs, it undoubtedly reinforces the persistent side of the autonomous-persistent category.

Some of this man's responses may suggest a lavish use of denial as a psychological defense mechanism. Yet the evidence from many different sources left no doubt that his system of social action was in very good balance and functioned remarkably well.

THE LEAST SUCCESSFUL AGERS

The Anxious Mother

Lack of success in aging is illustrated by the case of the anxious mother, who was becoming increasingly dependent on a relationship with her young son. This is a major reason for lack of success in aging and in life in general. When the aging person depends on another, the control of the aged one's life space is placed in the hands of another person who may or may not contribute action energy that is appropriate or acceptable from the standpoint of the ager. In this instance, the mother, by needing to give to the child, was demanding more action energy from him than he was willing or able to give as time passed. As he matured, he did not want to have her continue to give to him, and he was unwilling to respond with action energy that permitted her to give him more and more. Thus, when anyone absolutely must have a large amount of energy put into his action system to maintain him, and that energy is not forthcoming, for whatever reason, he is at once in a precarious state, which, if not remedied, may result in total personal disorganization.

Because this respondent was unusually reserved when it came to talking about herself, there were little significant life history data. She was one of six children of a midwestern farmer. Her education went through high school, and she worked at various jobs, usually white collar. She remembered her mother as gentle and kind, who corrected her for poor posture. Her father, whom she felt she resembled, was more humorous and good company. She was often saddled with baby-sitting with her younger brother, and she felt close to no one as a child.

Her marriage to an accountant, which took place in her early twenties, was childless until she was in her forties, when they adopted a child.

At the beginning of the study she, the child, and her husband lived near their rental property which she managed in addition to her household chores. She frankly stated that the child was her chief interest in life, and she was keenly ambitious for him. She wanted definite things for him in music and religion, and she hoped for the ministry for him. The most insight into this woman came from the clinical psychologist who interviewed her and reported as follows: "Her problem is that she really trusts no one and sees conflict and difficulty no matter in what direction she turns, so it is difficult for her to relate to anyone." She reported to the psychologist that she felt her husband was regressing and becoming mentally ill. They were incompatible from the start, she believed, and she said it was a mistake that they had ever married. At the same time it was disclosed that she was selling a health food because she felt it to be of such great value to her own health—a source of great concern to her.

As the study progressed, the child moved from grammar school age to adolescence. The accompanying independence manifested by him thwarted her efforts to direct his behavior. Since he was her primary object of self-satisfaction, this had become a critical problem for her by the final interview. She verbalized it by reporting to be greatly concerned about her son and the poor moral and religious training he was getting at school. She expressed a feeling of almost total loss of companionship with her husband, and also with her son, because he was becoming increasingly involved in outside activities.

This woman obviously lacked resources in relating to others. She had never been close to anyone except the boy, and when she drew close to him she felt real conflict in the relationship. Her centering of all her hopes and fears on this child was just one more effort to try to make a close relationship in her typically inadequate way. By and large, the autonomous person, although independent, is one who can relate well to others, whereas the person who is dependent is often pathetically unable to establish a really good relationship, and confuses leaning with loving.

Disengaging, Lonely, and Afraid

This rather tense fifty-seven-year-old man was a worker in a small plant and had lived in Kansas City all his life—not by choice, but just because he had. His father was a bus driver, and he had stayed in about the same social class. He flunked out of high school, worked at odd jobs, and having no economic stability, lost what little he did have during the Depression. Lack of success in everything dogged him from the beginning.

His first marriage ended in divorce when his wife accused him of running around. For some time he floundered, and then finally got into his present work at the urging of a friend. The second marriage took place in his early thirties.

At the initial interview, he appeared to the interviewer as a short, nervous little man, with a potbelly and a strained way of looking, due largely to an acute visual handicap and a hearing defect. He and his wife lived in a nice house in excellent condition, in a good, middle-class neighborhood, but they hated it because Negroes were beginning to move in on the street. As a night worker, his daytime was spent in sleep or getting in his wife's way. "She works her darn fool head off and does everything I'm supposed to do." There was no special time of the day or weekend better or worse for him. He claimed they went to social clubs just to let his wife have a little recreation, but his statements of personal loneliness that appeared not only in the first, but all subsequent interviews, suggested he needed and craved the socializing too.

On weekends they attended church and were rather active members of the congregation. They subscribed to the tenets of their faith—no smoking, no drinking, and faith healing. This was rather different from the kind of life he used to lead before this marriage, when outings with the men and a good evening at the bar were primary sources of recreation. He was helped along in his faith by the fact that he had been required to quit smoking and drinking for health reasons, and he was honest enough to say so.

By the second interview, the faith-healing doctrine had been put to a severe test and had come out second best. The wife had fallen off the porch, broken her leg, and had had to spend two weeks in a hospital getting medical healing. Their three daughters (all hers by a previous marriage) lived nearby, so she had spent fifteen weeks recuperating with them, leaving the respondent to make out alone as best he could.

At the time of this second interview, the wife was just back home, and the respondent was having to do all the housework. He was a miserable failure, and tension between them was running high. They tried to ease off some of the tension by watching a lot of television together and being as companionable as they could. But all this did was convince them both of the horrors of retirement. Would he like to retire? No! But if someone gave him plenty of money, he would "quit work in a minute and travel to all the gambling places and have fun." Work itself was no pleasure to him. He just did it because he had to make a living and stay out from underfoot. He really did not know what else to do.

Ten months later, the respondent and his wife could stand the social pressure of the incoming Negroes no longer. They sold their home and moved far away to a new, "safe" neighborhood, into a very attractive little place. It was in this new home that the interviewer found them for the third contact. Life was a bit better now. The wife was feeling much better, and both had resumed their own roles around the house—she doing all the work and he loafing. Friction was at a minimum.

Compared with his forties, his health (bad eyes and heart trouble) was much worse at the time of the study. Now that they had moved, seeing neighbors was very important—the only trouble was they were not seeing much of the new neighbors yet. His best friend was a very unusual man who was noticeably mentally deranged. "No one else can get along with him," said the respondent casually. "He'll never be any better, but I like him." His adherence to this rather strange friend was more understandable when he explained how lonely he was at the plant. He worked nights, to begin with, and he never was one to exchange confidences with other men—he did not really trust them. But it was awfully lonely not to go on coffee breaks with someone. He just was not part of the crowd. The younger men who now made up his union and controlled it did not care about the night force and cared even less about his working conditions. This made him increasingly pessimistic.

Shortly after this, the psychologist talked to him, and the respondent unloaded a wealth of fears and anxieties. He felt estranged from his friends since he had to give up drinking and partying—he knew no other way to make social contacts. His sexual potential was waning, and this was creating real panic in him. He was so withdrawn, morose, and anxious that the psychologist urged no further interviews because he felt they were stirring up such deep fears that the respondent would not be able to take the emotional strain.

There were no more interviews until the final one, and at that time the respondent expressed great relief that the interviews were all over. At this final interview he reported having had a mild heart attack, but otherwise things were about the same. As he looked back over the past five years, his health was worse, he was not sleeping as well, and he was easing off in his work. He did not go to as many social affairs, and working at hobbies at home had become more important. It took him a little more time to keep up his house and yard, but it was still important to him. He saw less of the children, although he wished he could see them more. But friends, whom he saw less of, just were not as important. Disengagement was well begun.

He said he liked best going to church, eating well, and watching television. The first he did not do, the second he could not do, and the third he appeared to do because there was nothing else to do. His ideal day would be just to loaf.

This man was definitely alienated, socially isolated, anomie-bound, and beginning to disintegrate. He was dependent-precarious and his style was one of Minimal Involvement. He was unsuccessful because he had never built up any resources for living. Aging was just one more unsuccessful venture.

RELATIONS BETWEEN STYLES OF LIFE

Among the six styles of life, we find that certain ones have an affinity for each other, or are isomorphic, in terms of their characteristic modes of orientation to interaction and types of social relationships, as defined in Chapter One. They tend to relate in two sets of three styles each in these respects.

Familism is the most characteristic style in which the orientation to interaction is primarily functionally diffuse and affective, and relationships are particularistic and contain many expressional elements. Couplehood has the same characteristics, but with a reduced social life space, heavily concentrated in a pair. Living Fully tends to have the same characteristics, expanded to a larger social life space, a sort of broadly extended Familism.

The World of Work is the most characteristic style in which the orientation to interaction is primarily functionally specific and emotionally neutral, and relationships are universalistic and instrumental. Living Alone has these same characteristics, but with a much reduced social life space. Easing Through Life With Minimal Involvement tends to have the same characteristics, but attenuated in a more amorphous social life space, due to the low level of involvement with all aspects of life.

It is convenient to name these two sets of styles, and we have chosen two German terms, frequently used in American sociological literature, which come closest to encompassing all the related characteristics. We shall call Familism, Couplehood, and Living Fully the *Gemeinschaft* set of styles, and World of Work, Living Alone, and Easing Through Life With Minimal Involvement the *Gesellschaft* set.* These two sets of characteristics are seen most clearly when the degree of clarity and saliency of style is high. In fact, it was the empirical observation that the consistency and strength of these characteristics varied which led us to the concept and definition of this variable. If the degree is high, the secondary styles, if any, will be in the same set. If it is low, they may, but not necessarily will, be in the other set. Living Fully and Minimal Involvement have a special characteristic in this respect. A person whose style is Living Fully could have a predominance of the *Gesellschaft* characteristics in his orientation to interaction and types of relationships. But if so, the degree of style is weak, and there will be a weak secondary style of Familism or Couplehood. A person whose style is Minimal Involvement could have a predominance of *Gemeinschaft* characteristics, but his style will be weak and he will have a weak secondary style of World of Work or Living Alone. Living Fully and Minimal Involvement can thus be regarded as the main bridging styles between the *Gemeinschaft* and the *Gesellschaft* sets.

Gemeinschaft cases have a high personal interaction of a diffuse, affective nature. Role activity is full and there is little alienation, iso-

* These terms were first developed in a systematic sociological sense by Ferdinand Toennies, *Gemeinschaft und Gesellschaft* (Leipzig: Fues's Verlag, 1887, and 8th ed., Leipzig: Buske, 1935). They were later used by Max Weber, Talcott Parsons (for example, in *Structure of Social Action* [New York: McGraw-Hill, 1937], pp. 686–694), and others. These terms have sometimes been translated as "community" and "society." They have some relation to the concepts of primary and secondary relationships. Here they are used to combine modes of orientation to interaction and types of social relationships.

lation, or anomie. In the cases of "Pain and Giving" and "Goodbye Miss Chips," there are two women who achieve good styles of Familism in the former, and Couplehood with underlying Familism in the latter. These warm outgoing women who devoted their lives to the profession of teaching might seem at first observation to belong to the style World of Work. But they are actually very good examples of women who work for economic necessity and who wisely chose work in which they could fulfill their basic styles. Teaching is, for women, a means of living a style of Familism when normal channels are unavailable or insufficient for the strong needs of a person whose style is Familism or Living Fully. When a woman must work because of economic necessity, her style is best fulfilled by her selection of work that carries the possibility of familistic relationships, such as teaching, social work, or nursing. Secretarial work might very well be a good outlet for a person with a strong style of Couplehood. The important thing is that such persons can appear to be devoted to the World of Work, yet they are truly cases of *Gemeinschaft.*

Gesellschaft, on the other hand, is characterized by alienation, anomie, and isolation, minimal role activity, and a few close personal relationships. In "A Dreary Life," the woman, although married and a mother, failed to find any real life satisfaction except in her work. Her social contacts at work were secondary in contrast to those of the women mentioned above. Her relationships with her alcoholic husband and her sons were superficial, and her work seemed the only bearable style she could achieve. Similarly, in "Cats and Filth," the woman showed minimal interaction even with her relatives in the same building. Her style of Living Alone had persisted in spite of four husbands and two children. "Then She Married" presents an example of Minimal Involvement as the primary style, with a weak secondary style of Living Fully, so that the two bridging styles bridged to each other and she was prevented from going anywhere else, stylewise.

In view of the emphasis found in much of sociological literature on the waning of *Gemeinschaft* in modern Western society, it is interesting to note that, in terms of style of life, one hundred ten of these respondents were in the *Gemeinschaft* set and fifty-eight in the *Gesellschaft.* We are convinced that, when one examines individual lives microscopically and over time rather than looking at grosser aspects of social structure, there is much more *Gemeinschaft* than is usually emphasized in literature. In order further to clarify these concepts we are presenting one new case to illustrate each set.

The Gesellschaft Styles—Let's Make Money

This respondent was fifty-seven years old at the beginning of the study. He lived with his wife, age fifty-six. He had one married son who lived in a nearby suburb. He was in the repair business and had a shop in his garage, but did 90 per cent of his work in people's homes.

When he was first interviewed in September 1956, he had lived in Kansas City for nine years. He did not like it because it was dirty and had bad weather, dirty politics, and labor troubles. He would prefer to live in a smaller community.

His daily round consisted of work and not doing much in the evening, although occasionally he was called out for evening repair work. Saturday was another workday, only busier. He bowled Sunday mornings and usually visited his son in the afternoon. He did not go to church. He belonged to one fraternal group but did not attend meetings. His wife belonged to such a group and did attend, but she was not very active and did not care for playing cards. He claimed he had a few friends on the west coast where he had lived until coming to Kansas City, but no friends in Kansas City.

In April 1957 his business had grown, and he had rebuilt and enlarged the garage shop. He said it was not possible to take a vacation in this business as he would lose customers. His pattern of life was essentially the same. He was not close to any relatives, except his son. His wife was closer to her relatives in a neighboring state, but they did not see them often. He still had no friends and was not well acquainted with his neighbors, although one of the neighbors talked to his wife occasionally.

He had no plans to retire. He enjoyed his work and could not stand sitting around and doing nothing. He was thinking of renting a building where he would meet more people and increase his business, and commented that in his business, "you either progress or go back." In August of 1957 we saw exactly the same picture, and it became even more clear that relating to *customers* was very important to him.

In December 1958 he had again missed his regular vacation because work was too heavy. He was pleased that his bowling team was in top place in the bowling league. He said he was never lonely and answered service calls at all hours. The last three or four years had been the best in his life because he was in business for himself, was subjected to less stress, made more money, and had his home paid for. He claimed that he circulated a lot and had many friends, but it was quite clear that he was referring on the one hand to his customers, and on the other hand to the people with whom he bowled, and with whom he had no relations other than bowling. Part of his value system was clearly expressed in answer to a question about temptations. He said he was tempted to replace good parts when the customer would not know the difference, but he knew it was unethical and resisted the temptation. He frequently emphasized that he wanted to do honest work.

In August of 1959 the picture was essentially unchanged. In response to the story question about Jones, he said that Jones took the job so that he could pay for his home and "get ahead." Of all the things the respondent did over the weekend, he enjoyed bowling the most and yard work the least.

In March of 1960 he said that he really had not had any life goals. He had just worked. He had admired his father in his youth as a good craftsman and an honest man. He had liked his mother as an intelligent woman who was good and kind to him. He also described his wife as an intelligent woman who was very good to him, and added, "I don't do much for her, but she understands."

Things were still essentially unchanged in the last interview, in September 1961. However, the interviewer commented that during the first part of the interview there were many phone interruptions and the respondent was always moving about. When he finally sat down he looked rather pathetic, seemed to be in poor health, had a troublesome back, and complained about his unpleasant neighbors. His wife had had an inheritance a few years previously and they had taken a trip to Florida. In spite of the bad back he was still in the bowling league, although he added that he did not "feel like a spring chicken." In addition to his regular work, he was developing an invention of his for a local company. He was also reading a good many technical books. He said he would like to have a place in the suburbs with a large basement where he could build things. He wished his son had been a professional man or at least in a kind of work where he could be self-employed. The least interesting thing he did on weekends was baby-sitting. He had not seen his mother, who lived on the west coast, in eight years, but he did see his son occasionally, and commented, "After all, he is my son, and we do get together." He thought that relatives did not like to be bothered, so had little or no contact with them. He stated that he did not have a really close friend.

He said he was not freer in spending money than he had been

earlier. He illustrated this attitude by saying that there was no point buying a new rug, which his wife wanted very much, when the old one would do. The most important things during the last five years for him had been getting a set of new teeth, bowling, his son's getting a divorce and marrying a nice girl, and his wife's having an inheritance. When asked about his main purpose in life twenty years ago, he said, "To make money."

This case gives us an excellent example of a completely unfamilistic man with a family he did not reject. He liked a rather large network of functionally specific relations, and avoided functionally diffuse ones, except on a basis of minimal involvement with his wife and his son. His orientation to interaction was also emotionally neutral. His relationships were universalistic and highly instrumental, even his relationships in bowling. His primary style was clearly the World of Work. He was somewhat involved with work, but not highly so, and was certainly not highly involved with any other aspect of life. Hence, he had a secondary style of Minimal Involvement, and there had been a general absence of life goals. This secondary style acted as a bridge into the family, where he almost had a style of Living Alone.

He showed some signs of anomie and a fairly high degree of alienation, especially with neighbors and with anyone who might potentially fall into the role of a friend. But he was not isolated at all, he coped very well, and he had a very clear-cut style. In terms of success, which is not the primary emphasis in this portion of the chapter, we have rated him autonomous-persistent in the bottom of the category. His total system was just barely in balance, due largely to the fact that the segments of the system relating to his wife and son were not in balance on exchange of action energy. His persistence stems from the fact that he could pace himself in relation to work and retirement, and, due to the minimal involvement, he would have no serious problems with disengagement.

The Gemeinschaft Styles—Wim, Wam, and Wigger

The three *Gemeinschaft* styles may be found in one person. This woman had held a basic underlying style of Familism all her life, and yet at times had been Living Fully and at others clearly enmeshed in Couplehood.

At seventy-two, this woman was described by the interviewer as "astonishingly lovely" with few signs of aging and a beautiful figure. Her poise and her ease of manner were most charming.

Her childhood was strongly influenced by her father, who taught her the virtues of hard work and continued effort—virtues she was to need in her life, which started with her raising two of her siblings because her parents died young. Her style of life was made most evident by her story of her marriage. When she was in her forties, she and her husband had seven children and she helped him operate a family business. However, the Depression forced them out, and the shock to the husband was so great that he "lost his mind" and had to be hospitalized. With characteristic hustle, the respondent traded on some political obligations owed her family, and secured a job as matron in a home for the aged. She became the chief breadwinner, as her husband continued to be in and out of hospitals. She maintained an active interest in both church and community throughout. When she had finally raised the children to maturity, she divorced her husband and married a man with whom she was very happy. However, he died five years later. At that time she discovered her first husband was in a hospital, seriously ill and senile. In kindness she remarried him, took him from the hospital to live with her, and made a home for him until he, too, died (during the course of the study).

She at once took up her role as grandmother and continued her active roles in church and community. She spent much of her time with friends and neighbors, and scored 95 per cent on morale when rated by an interviewer who said, "Her zest for living is expressed constantly in her speech and deeds. She always seeks the good in man and looks for the sun to shine through the clouds."

This clearly indicated the relationship of these three styles and the absence of the other three. Although employed most of her life, she listed her life's work as raising a family. She was never alone; her reaching out to others was an outstanding characteristic, and she did not know the meaning of "easing through life with minimal involvement." When asked to describe herself, she said she usually felt full of "wim, wam, and wigger."

In her style of Familism she was strongly familistic when her children needed her, and yet she was able to achieve Couplehood in relation to her two husbands. Underneath both, she maintained a style of Living Fully in relation to friends and church. She was thus able to keep on changing the focus of her style as needed to meet the changes in her life space. She was clearly autonomous-persistent at all times.

The contrast between these two cases brings out clearly the two major streams of life styles. "Wim, Wam, and Wigger" was all things to all people, and she thrived in the roles. Yet, "Let's Make Money" would have been miserably unsuccessful if he had been called on to live her life. She, on the other hand, would have found alienation and isolation truly intolerable. Further significance of these two sets of characteristics will be demonstrated in the chapter on statistical findings.

NINE

❦

Some
Related
Observations

As the analysis of the case materials was completed, our observations gave rise to a recognition of the importance of some related factors not central to the study as planned. Among these were the meaning of health and retirement as related to action theory, the rural-urban contrasts in relation to familism, and the implications of our findings for the theory of disengagement.

Although these were not included in the primary focus of our study, the rich materials dealing with these topics seemed too important to overlook. They give added meaning to Chapter Ten, which summarizes our conclusions about success and style in aging.

HEALTH AND WELL-BEING
IN THE THEORY OF ACTION

The Kansas City Study of Adult Life was not focused on health and disease in the later years. The panels were drawn to exclude persons with disabling chronic illnesses. No medical examinations were given. Yet, questions were asked about health at several points, and the interviewers generally commented on the general appearance of health, or the existence of specific symptoms, from their own observations. Thus, the data do not lend themselves to a detailed study in geriatrics, but they do provide material for suggestive insights and hypotheses concerning the relations of health and well-being to the action system of the individual in its social context. In particular, it is possible to suggest a relationship of health as a condition of action, a general sense of well-being or its lack, to style of life and successful aging, as defined here.

Several illustrations of such relations are implicit in the cases described in the chapters on styles. Among the most successful agers, "A Dreary Life" experienced a continuous and almost overwhelming sense of fatigue. "Pain and Giving" experienced years of severe pain. "Goodbye Miss Chips" had a serious illness which forced her to retire. "The Crony" became blind and had an operation with guarded prognosis (although, and here we let our objectivity go by the board, we were delighted to learn that he was beginning to see again at the end of the study). "Forced Disengagement" did not have a serious health problem of her own, but was faced with the mental illness of her husband. In each case, the respondents were able to persist, in an action sense, remarkably well. This was due to: (1) a deeply entrenched pattern of keeping their action energy in balance on the autonomous side, (2) doing so in a highly developed style, and (3) flexibility in their action systems, which provided alternative ways of expressing their styles. Most of them had a basic sense of well-being in spite of the serious problem of health. One of them, although a successful ager, was miserable.

Among the least successful agers, "The Slipping Mask" became preoccupied with his decline in physical vigor and waning sexual powers and was moving toward alcoholism. "Nightingale With Clipped Wings" became physically handicapped by arthritis of the spine and a heart condition and then slipped toward senility. "The Onset of the End" had a spinal injury, and slipped into anomie and alienation. "Rejected and Hurt" had a multitude of physical ailments coupled with personality problems. "Living With the Children" was preoccupied with a variety of less serious ills and also became anomic, alienated, and isolated. "Disengaging Under Protest" and "Don't Want to Age" had no serious problems of health, but were tremendously preoccupied with it.

In all but the last two cases, the respondents' action systems were precarious because: (1) they had failed to develop a pattern of keeping action energy in balance and easily slipped into dependency, (2) they had not developed a very clear style of life, or (3) they lacked flexibility and alternatives for expressing their styles. In the last two cases, they were barely autonomous. In one case, "Disengaging Under Protest," the style of Living Fully was quite clear, but in both cases there was a lack of flexibility and alternatives, and the style depended heavily on the maintenance of good health and physical vigor.

An interesting variant on these relations was provided by another case, "Grandma Retires." This case is also interesting in terms of a masked style. This sixty-five-year-old widow was described by the senior author in *Processes of Aging* as "The Working Grandmother."[1] Throughout the first six rounds of interviewing she lived with her daughter, son-in-law, and two grandchildren, but she interacted minimally with them and spent a busy life as manager of a department in a company. She often worked on Saturdays. Her orientation to interaction was clearly specific-neutral, and her relations were universalistic and instrumental. In the early study she was placed in the style World of Work and judged to be autonomous-precarious because of her apparently almost sole reliance on work.

Shortly after round six she suddenly retired, much to the astonishment of everyone, especially her family. After a brief period of traveling, she settled down in her room and spent most of her time in bed, reading. Between round six and round seven we also obtained life history data, especially from interviews with significant others, as she was always reluctant to give her own life history. It became apparent from her relations to her family and to work that she had always had a style of Living Alone. In fact, work was one modality of living alone, and retirement to the room in her daughter's home was another. She managed to remain autonomous in this situation, and highly persistent.

Her health, especially in the sense of physical vigor, began to wane. Essentially, it simply atrophied because it was not needed in her action system with her style of life. Once her true style emerged, it was a very clear and strong style, with flexibility.

Still another variant is illustrated in the case of "I Hold My Own." This woman, at seventy-three, was once widowed, had never had any children, and lived with her second husband in an old frame house. She appeared much younger than her years and responded ably to the interview questions. A foster daughter, who was married, lived upstairs with her family, and the respondent led a fairly typical housewifely existence. She had never worked outside the home and she reported liking all of the things she did on her daily and weekly schedule. She liked living right where she was and felt she had nice neighbors.

[1] Richard H. Williams, "Styles of Life and Successful Aging," in Richard H. Williams, Clark Tibbitts, and Wilma Donahue (eds.), *Processes of Aging*, Vol. I (New York: Atherton Press, 1963), p. 347.

On Sundays she always went to church even though her husband was not interested. Her marriage, she reported, was very happy. "No one could be any better than my husband has been to me, and I try to return the kindness." Her present age was completely satisfactory to her if she could stay well. She felt about sixty-five, not elderly, and checked all the optimistic items on that scale but one. She did not care to live life over, and if she had only six months to live, she would help others. "I never craved very much for myself." There was nothing really bad about her present age, and she felt it to the good that she had more time to do the things she wanted to do.

Two years later her husband died. Although she had lived through widowhood once before, her grief was so great that she became very ill from malnutrition. She refused to eat and could not take nourishment until hospitalized. Now she reported her age to have some bad characteristics—namely, poor health. She reported she was never bored unless she did not feel well. Babysitting made her nervous.

One year later she reported her health somewhat better and said she was happy with her age if she felt well. Two years later she still reported being very upset over her husband's death, but her pattern of life was quite full again. She liked her present age and said, "I'm happy as I am. I have my hearing, my eyesight. I can't understand why age should bring on such depression among aged. I want to hold my own and help others as long as I can. Life has been kind to me."

In her case, her single bout of poor health was a reaction to her mental and emotional state. She was generally unaware of her health unless something drastic went wrong. She was actually very fortunate in having had so few physical disabilities. As she regained control of her emotions, her general and usual state of good health returned and she continued in her accustomed cheerful state of mind. She was autonomous-persistent with a very flexible familistic style. This contrasted with some respondents, who reported with regularity a constant flow of small and large physical problems which loomed important in their awareness.

In another case, called "Responsible Aging," she was quite aware of physical health, but viewed it in terms of her religious convictions —ill health is God's will and something to be accepted with good grace. This was a fifty-eight-year old woman whose two sons were grown, and who worked as a government clerk. She and her husband lived alone, and both were very busy and active. Her over-all reaction to health was to submit to any illness with good grace. At the same time, she felt sorrow for others who had more illness than she. She reported, for example, that she saw one friend more than she did others because "she is sick and alone and needs me." Again, she said, "Life and death must be accepted. They're part of creation and in the hands of the Lord."

Her attitude was realistic, and in discussing future plans she said, "I'll find activities that are useful and geared to my energies." When her husband became alcoholic, she stayed with him and eventually he was able to regain control. She felt it morally right for her to "stick it out" during his illness.

Although suffering from anemia and a bad stomach, she reported her health as "excellent" and better than at forty-five. If her health improved, she reported it as a nice thing, but illness went unreported. When pushed to discuss the change of life, she reported having anemia, low blood pressure, nervousness, and sleeplessness, but felt she had had "as little trouble as anyone I know."

By the next round of interviews, her health problems had caught up with her, and she had been forced to retire. She did not even report the nature of the illness, and had already taken up a full life in the community. In the next interview, she reported her health had suffered when a neighbor developed an incurable disease and died, and her brother had committed suicide. "Health," in this case, seemed to be a synonym for nervous tension. In the final interview, she reported major medical care for a systemic poisoning that was still in effect. As she said, "I'm not the type of person who can ignore health entirely. [She was put on a constant diet.] Don't think I'm feeling sorry for myself because I'm on a diet. I don't have an ulcer where the diet is much worse, and there's no cancer. I'm lucky!"

With this in mind, she took up a full round of family and community activities and, as the interviews concluded, she was busily planing for an active life ahead, with physical interference held to a minimum. She was autonomous-persistent and had a well-developed, flexible style of Living Fully, with strongly supportive secondary styles of Couplehood and Familism.

Sometimes health can be nearly overwhelming, as is the case of "Grounded." No matter how hard he strived to continue his autonomy, his repeated strokes drove him toward dependency since he had little to give of affective action energy, and mostly supplied specific-neutral contributions to those around him. These were based on his work competence and his self-assurance that there was always another fortune just around the corner. When physical health prevented his active participation in work, his total sense of well-being was shaken to the core.

In many ways, senility is the extreme case in which health, as a condition of action, overwhelms the action system. And yet it, too, can be relative to the aspects of the action system with which we are concerned here. This point is well illustrated by a case we have named "Thoroughly Disengaged."

This eighty-eight-year-old woman lived with her sixty-two-year-old niece (who was also her stepdaughter). She had taught school for twenty-six years. Then, following the death of her sister, she married her sister's husband and raised the niece and a nephew. The niece also taught school.

In July 1957 she said, "We are all young people," and the niece acted as old as the aunt. Her daily round consisted of housework, television, letter writing, and naps. She had given up teaching Sunday school the previous year and had resigned from committees, one by one. She still went to church twice a week or more. When asked what religion meant to her, she said she never gave religion much thought, just grew up with it. She had a few friends, and the neighbors dropped in when she was ill. When asked what she would do if she could live her life over again, she said she never thought of things like that and added gaily, "I am in my second childhood now."

In October 1958 she was relatively well but had a cold. The best thing in life now was not having colds, and the worst, "this nasty cold." She seemed rather giddy and vague. In June 1959 she was still giggly. She walked to visit a sick friend and still went to church. She was happy she was not ill at eighty-nine, and said she had everything she wanted. In September 1959 she laughed and poked the interviewer, but had excellent memory of her childhood and her teaching days. In July 1960 the clinical psychologist said the first impression was of a pert old lady one would hardly suspect of being ninety. But her memory seemed poor. Health was the most important thing for her. She was not in the least upset, and had a happy-go-lucky attitude toward her present life.

In April 1961 the niece said her aunt could no longer be left alone. The neighbors who used to visit had moved away. They had a housekeeper, and the niece said she should try to provide more company for her aunt. The niece herself seemed very tired from teaching. That same month, a friend spoke of the original respondent's "decline" and added she should get over to see her more often. She also commented that the original respondent had been a very good school teacher. In June 1961, her minister spoke of her "remarkable memory." During the summer of 1961, a participant observer saw that "Aunt Betty," as the respondent was known, was known and loved in the neighborhood. She enjoyed having the interviewer come. She had her good and bad days, and there was a strong suggestion by the interviewer that, if the niece had not let her stay home so much, she would not have "failed" so fast. She was cheerful and very independent and jibed the niece about men. Her independence was a source of some irritation to the niece.

In January 1962, at the age of ninety-two, we had a somewhat different picture. In the intermediate interviews she had appeared essentially senile. Here, the interviewer found the respondent alone at home for the first time. She gave quite relevant answers. She said growing old did not bother her one bit. One can hazard the guess that there was less tendency to "play the senile" when her niece or other "keeper" was not present.

Her style of life had always been to live fully. She was still living fully, in her own way, and was thoroughly disengaged. Disengagement had come gradually and easily. There may have been a true senile disease process with occasional remission. However, much of her behavior could be readily interpreted as disengagement within her action system. She remained autonomous and persistent, with flexible ways of living fully. When the significant others in her system attempted to constrict her, she simply disengaged further and acted senile.

Attitudes Toward Death

Most of the respondents admitted thinking of death, but most denied fear of death. Their beliefs about life after death varied with religious affiliation and degree of commitment to a religion, but most were somewhat skeptical and only a few believed they would recognize and relate to their loved ones. The striking thing, however, in relation to this question, and sometimes others, was that again and again respondents *volunteered* that they dreaded crippling accidents or chronic disease. Immobilization of the action system, rather than death, was the great source of anxiety among the aging. As "Then She Married" put it, "I'm not afraid of death—but the way I might die."

RETIREMENT AND THE THEORY OF ACTION

Retirement, like health, has frequently been considered a major problem of aging. It can be a major crisis of transition and present special problems for coping. The same cluster of factors which influences the way in which a person copes with problems of health and disease is also closely related to the way in which he copes with retirement, but with some modifications in its internal relationships.

Among the most successful agers, "Beyond the World of Work" was able to cope with retirement partly because he had not developed the style clearly and had achieved flexibility in this way. He was a rather unusual case in that he had a latent secondary style of Living Fully, which falls in the *Gemeinschaft* rather than the *Gesellschaft* set, and acts as a bridging style. It is possible to have a very clear style of World of Work and cope with retirement well, as will be illustrated in another case, below. In this case, the respondent also maintained an activist orientation in retirement, together with some disengagement, a posture which seems to fit the style of World of Work well.

"Goodbye Miss Chips" and "The Crony" coped with retirement just as they did with problems of health. Their action energy was firmly in balance and their styles, quite different in the two cases, permitted great flexibility.

Among the less and least successful agers, "Grounded" and "Nightingale With Clipped Wings," both with a style of World of Work, had the same problems in coping with retirement that they did in coping with health. They had developed a constricted and somewhat exaggerated style of World of Work, with little flexibility. When the real world of remunerative work was no longer available to them, there was little left by way of support, and their action systems became precarious. "Don't Want No Friends" lived in a world of semiskilled labor all his life, but failed to develop a strong style of World of Work. For him, work was the only aspect of reality which could give any form and substance to his action system. When it was gone, he had no idea how to "spend his time." After retirement he slipped into the style of Living Alone in an anomic, alienated, and isolated mode, in a precarious position and dependent on his common-law wife to keep him going.

Sometimes people have problems with their social system when in retirement, but these problems are not related to retirement as such. In the case of "Living With the Children," the life history strongly suggests that he had wanted the world to think he had a style of Couplehood, but actually had a weak style of World of Work, in a dependent mode. When his wife died, six months prior to the beginning of the study, he achieved a flimsy autonomy for a while, from about age seventy-eight to eighty, and a temporary style of Living Alone. He kept "busy" in restricted, personal real estate transactions and house repairs, and had a controlled, minimal social system with his son and his son's family. But it proved too much for him, and he slipped into the style of Minimal Involvement, in a dependent-precarious position, which was the only thing preventing complete breakdown.

Not Enough Responsibility

The World of Work as a style is more likely than any of the other styles to make retirement a problematical issue. One can, however, cope with retirement successfully in various ways within this style. At the beginning of the study in July 1958, this respondent was seventy-five years old and had been retired for ten years. He still resented the idea of compulsory retirement, and, at this time, did a small amount of work on his own in his skilled trade. He lived with his wife, who was the same age, and an unmarried defective son. One of his three daughters lived in a house next door, which he owned. His daily round consisted of gardening, which he enjoyed, puttering, and listening to ball games and fights. He had worked at his trade in the same company for forty-six years and commented, "I would be working now if they let me." He agreed with the notion that most women did not like retired husbands around the house. His relations with his wife seemed to be fairly good, but he preferred to go at his own fairly rapid pace, and did not like waiting around for her, or spending much time visiting.

He got into some difficulty with his wife after the first interview because he had not said enough good things about her, and refused to be interviewed on the next round. He was brought back into the study in early 1961, and consented only because he felt it had something to do with retirement and he had a hatred of compulsory retirement. At this time he had built up a considerable amount of work for himself, so that at seventy-eight his daily round looked considerably more active, especially workwise, than it had at seventy-five. He still spent some time driving his wife to church and chauffeuring her to other places. He spent most of his weekends working around the house and commented, "I like to keep busy." The thing he liked least on weekends was church and "carting" his wife around. He expressed attitudes of business before pleasure. There was a strong denial of boredom and anger, but his wife said, "Everything and everybody bothers him." He claimed, "I never get *that* angry," but the wife said to the interviewer, "You're on a touchy subject."

During the course of these interviews, all in early 1961, it became clear that he had managed to make an arrangement with a man who owned many houses to do repair work, and he was constantly on call. In November 1961, the daily round looked just as it had during the rest of that year. When asked about the best things in life in recent times, he referred to the chance to work and earn extra money. When asked about the worst things, he said, "I do not have enough responsibilities."

This man's style was remarkably clear. He was rather bored and restless when not working. He coped with this situation by keeping busy in doing as much part-time work as he could get. His persistence in this fashion was remarkable. He would probably go on this way until he died rather suddenly without an illness. On the autonomy-dependency side, his action energy was barely in balance, and he was classified in the third level of the autonomous-persistent category. He showed some signs of anomie, alienation, and isolation, and was rated 2 on these variables. But he was rated clearly 1 on coping and style. He did not have the kind of flexibility which would permit him to fall back on one or more secondary styles, but he had one very important kind of flexibility for those whose style is World of Work. Although he had been faced with compulsory retirement, he was able to pace himself reasonably well after retirement. The importance of this factor in successful aging was also very well illustrated in the case of the "Contented Salesman," described in the chapter on the World of Work.

A Long Retirement

Retirement is less likely to be a problem of Couplehood than of the World of Work. This seventy-eight-year-old man had lived in Kansas City all his life. He remembered his mother as "a real mother" who spent the last year of her life in his home. His father, a skilled worker, was just and upright and would never steal or lie. The respondent left school after the sixth grade and took a job as a messenger boy at age fourteen. Later he held various managerial jobs. But he had always wanted to "retire and loaf," and had started saving for retirement very early. During his younger years he traveled a good deal. He disliked politicians because of their dishonesty, but he was an alderman in his late thirties and at one time was asked to run for mayor, which he did not do.

He did not marry until the age of forty-one. His wife had a ten-year-old daughter at the time of their marriage. He moved easily into the style of Couplehood. He and his wife were always together, and he was very devoted to the stepdaughter and later to her children, one of whom obtained his M.D. degree during the course of the study, and of whom the respondent was very proud. He had had a stroke the year before the study began, but as late as 1959, at age seventy-seven, he still mowed the grass. He achieved one of his major goals—an early retirement—and had been retired for twenty years at the time of the beginning of the study. He spent a rather "meandering" day, all of which he thoroughly enjoyed. In fact, he described himself as always having enjoyed life and being very satisfied. If he had his life to live over he would not change it. In response to the story questions, Jones did not take the job, because he would not wish to be away from his wife, and Mrs. Birch did marry over the daughter's protests.

He had a few friends, none of them close. He visited with the neighbors, but not extensively. He participated somewhat in church life. But the focal point of his social life space was his wife. They were always together and she was unquestionably the most important person in his life.

At the time of the last interview, in November of 1961, he and his wife were living in the exquisitely furnished home of the step-daughter. They had not wished to leave their own home, but he had had another stroke and required constant care. He was too ill to be interviewed, but his wife very graciously offered to be interviewed in his place. She said that her husband knew he was failing rapidly. He sometimes managed to play a little bridge with the family. Throughout the illness he had remained pleasant, alert, and sharp. At the end of the interview, his wife said, "My husband and I have always been very close."

Clearly, retirement was no problem for this respondent. In fact, he had lived for retirement, and achieved a very long and happy one. Even with constant physical care, which he required after his second stroke, he gave a great deal to those around him and remained autonomous-persistent to the end.

Successful Retirement

Familism with a strong underpinning of Couplehood greatly reduces the problematical aspects of retirement. This seventy-two-year-old man came from a farm background. His parents "came over from the old country" and raised nine children. He admired his parents all through life. Everyone in the family had a job to do, and "we did it without hollering." He had a fifth-grade education. When he was in his early twenties, he and five of his brothers came to Kansas City and set up a business together which they ran successfully and very harmoniously for many years. He married at the age of thirty, but his wife died three years later. He then remarried at the age of thirty-five. He and his second wife had two children; they lived in the same house in Kansas City from the time of their marriage and had been there thirty-seven years at the beginning of the study. When he was in his early sixties, three of his brothers had died. He and the remaining brothers decided that the business was too much for them, and they easily and happily sold out. He had been retired ever since and thoroughly enjoyed it.

With characteristic good humor, he described his day by saying, "I get up and do nothing and go to bed with nothing done." His wife, who was present during many of the interviews, wanted the interviewer to be sure to know that her husband actually took care of all the widows in the neighborhood, some eight or nine of them, cutting their grass, and doing repairs for them. He was very proud of the fact that he had come through three Depressions without committing suicide as some of his business acquaintances had done. He could never think of anything unpleasant that had happened, nor any especially good time in his life, because he had enjoyed it all. In response to a question about loneliness, he said he was lonely only "when the old lady goes to town or plays bridge, because then I have no one to fight with." The wife was again present, and the interviewer commented on their mutual enjoyment of each other's company. In response to a question about boredom, he replied, "That's a silly question, how can I get bored?" He said he got angry more often at age forty-five than now, although not very much then, and then proceeded to describe a recent incident. One morning he was carrying out some trash on an icy side-walk. He managed to get the trash out and then when he turned around to come back, he slipped and broke his arm. He thought that was a rather ridiculous thing to do. However, he seemed to take the whole thing pretty much as a joke. In relation to a question about temptation, he replied, "The devil thinks I'm not even worth trying to tempt." If he suddenly inherited $25,000, he would "say 'hot-doggie,' and get myself a bottle of liquor and then I would see how many people and churches I could help."

He saw the two remaining brothers and his two sons frequently. Also, he frequently saw a dozen nephews. One of the sons had a chronic disease and had had a pretty rough life. The other boy was doing very well. The respondent had several friends and a lot of inter- action with neighbors, particularly the widows whom he helped. At one point, he bragged that he had been able to shovel snow for seven widows on the block. He felt very close to his grandchildren and saw them frequently. In commenting on his parents, he said, "I am a family man like they were." If he could do anything he wanted on an ideal day, he would take his wife to Switzerland because that was where she wanted to go.

This respondent had worked consistently in the same business for many years, and he enjoyed his work more than did "A Long Retire- ment." It was a harmoniously run family business, but there had al- ways been much more important things in his life than work, and when he and his brothers felt that to continue in the business would endanger their health, they sold out without hesitation. He was a highly successful ager and was placed in the autonomous-persistent category, with a rank of 1. He received much from and gave much to his wife, children, grandchildren, and neighbors. He was also given ratings of 1 on anomie, alienation, isolation, coping, and style.

RURAL-URBAN CONTRASTS IN RELATION TO FAMILISM

The majority of the respondents in this panel came to Kansas City from rural and small-town backgrounds. We have also seen that Familism is the most frequent of the six styles of life for this group. These two phenomena are undoubtedly related. The focus of our study has not been a systematic analysis of rural-urban migration, nor of organization and functioning of the family. However, the material does lend itself to some suggestive insights concerning relations between rural backgrounds and Familism when rural-urban migration occurs. They are best indicated, from this material, by two contrasting cases.

Rural Familism Transplanted

In December 1956 this fifty-one-year-old man lived with his wife, age forty-one, and teen-age daughter. He was a semiskilled worker and his wife did some minor selling. He had been in Kansas City for eighteen years, but he said, "I don't like none of it. I don't like no city. It's too crowded. I would like to be on a farm." His father, eighty- two, and his seventy-two-year-old mother lived on a farm in a nearby state. Four of his brothers had also come to Kansas City, and only the youngest had remained on the farm. He mentioned liking to hunt on weekends. They sometimes had company Saturday evenings, and were mostly home on Sunday. They did not go to church.

In May of 1957 he had developed arthritis of the hip, which was very painful. However, he answered all the questions cheerfully, and gave a good deal of thought to each one. He said he had an aunt in Kansas City—he knew her maiden name but not her married name, and he asked the interviewer how to go about finding her. His father had died, following a stroke. He had bought a new car for his daughter for her graduation from high school. His wife had tried to get him to go to church the previous Sunday, but could not drive him out of the house. He had been doing a good deal of visiting, especially with family. He saw his mother on the farm every two months, and his brothers in Kansas City frequently. He also kept in touch with his sisters. His mother had also raised four nieces, and he saw them about once a year. He had seventy-five or eighty cousins, some of whom he saw and some of whom he did not; he commented, "'There is one bunch of cousins that I don't remember seeing." He said he knew six neighbors with whom he talked over the fence. If he had his life to live over, he would not leave home for eight months and fail to let his parents know where he was; he had gotten mad at his father. When asked about the most important thing in his life at that time, he said it was his daughter, but he was getting a little disgusted with her because she did not seem to know what to do after finishing high school. He had worked at various kinds of jobs after leaving the farm but still wanted to quit and go back to farming. He thought he might do that once it was settled what his daughter was going to do.

In April 1958 he spoke again of his daughter. She had just been to a wedding, and he commented that she was the only one of her friends who had not married. He also had a stepson to whom he felt quite close. This stepson had recently moved to a distant state, and the respondent was rather upset because he did not know when he would see him again. When asked about the difference between friends and strangers, he said, "In the Word of God, there ain't no stranger." He complained of feeling older than he really was, and said he had "lots of aches and pains."

In January 1959 he said he had been fine and had had fairly steady work all year. His wife had undergone an operation but had gotten over it well. He did express some concern that he was no longer able to keep up with the younger men at work. The best time in his entire life had been between the ages of eighteen and thirty, when he was still on the farm and had led a rather gay life going to dances.

The worst time in his life was during the Depression. His sister had been killed, and he had had no money with which to bury her. The next year there was a fairly good crop on the farm and he moved to town to work for wages, and had never managed to get back to the farm. His major temptation was drinking beer.

In January 1960 a nephew came to live with them temporarily. The daughter was still with them and employed as an office worker. His daily round was the same as it was at the beginning of the study. In response to the story questions, Jones would not take the job, Franklin would give the boy the money, as "all fathers would do," and Mrs. Birch would marry.

In July 1960 he said he considered his life work to be farming. He had done that for thirty years of his working life and he still hoped to go back to it. The most important person in his life when he was growing up was his mother, who was all that a mother should be, and he had minded her. His father was stern. Now the most important people were his mother and his wife. Of his wife he said she was easy to get along with, a good wife, and a hard worker. If he had his life to live over he would never work as a wage earner again. He would marry young and have all the children he could. The thing he enjoyed most on weekends was feeding and "fooling around" with three cats.

In June of 1961 he was visited by one of the students in the participant observation study. Things had been rather bad. He had been unemployed most of the year. His wife had taken a factory job as an unskilled worker. He had had eighteen days of work in another city in a neighboring state, and hoped to have a temporary job in a still more distant city, which would keep him away from home for long periods. He had been doing some hunting, which also kept him away from home. His daughter had married a skilled worker in the meantime. He said he went to the nearby state to visit his mother on the farm eight or ten times a year. He mentioned liking to drink and said he did drink a good deal in his younger days, but was no longer able to. His wife no longer went to church, and he commented that she "bellyaches a good deal." The observer saw him again in November 1961. He had had various jobs, all outside of Kansas City and in various states, and he did a good deal of traveling when he was not working, in the form of hunting trips. He was caring for the daughter's baby at the time of this visit, and he offered the observer a "shot of moonshine."

In the final interview, that same month, he had visited his stepson in a distant state. He was not feeling very well. He had gotten cold and wet on a hunting trip. His daily round was quite variable, depending on sporadic work. He was beginning to feel that family gatherings were not particularly important, because too many relatives got together at one time. He said, "I am not against them, I just don't care for them." His answers to questions on reactions of other people to his behavior, on responsibility, and on attitudes toward spending money indicated that disengagement had begun. The greatest sorrows in his life were the deaths of two sisters, one of whom had been killed by her husband and the other of whom had committed suicide.

This respondent has been classified as autonomous-precarious and given a rank of 3 within that category. One has to see him over the five and one-half year period to get this picture, because in the early interviews he appeared autonomous and persistent. Toward the end of the study, his action system was just barely in balance and he was near the point of dependency, especially in relation to his wife. He showed no special problem in relation to disengagement, but aging as such did bother him a great deal. He was rated 3 on anomie, with a sagging level of action energy, a strong dislike of city life, and long periods of either complete inactivity or wandering around. He was still coping, but not particularly well, and was rated 2 on that variable. He still showed no signs of alienation or isolation.

His style of life was Familistic. He had a rather gay early rural adulthood and then was finally married at the age of thirty-five to a woman with a fifteen-year-old son. He came from a very familistic background and transplanted his rural familism to the city. Several other members of the family came too. However, the familism wore somewhat thin in the urban environment. He was given a rating of 3 on clarity and saliency of style. His hope to return to the farm and start life over again was probably a forlorn one, and he did not have sufficient action energy left to do so successfully.

Familism Returned to the Country

In September 1956 this sixty-four-year-old man lived with his third wife, the previous two having died, and had a job doing very hard manual labor. He had lived in Kansas City for about twenty years, a similar length of time to the preceding case. Like "Rural Familism Transplanted," he said that Kansas City "doesn't suit me at all." He would prefer a smaller community with a lower cost of living, where people were more friendly, and where there was less noise. He also preferred a place where people are similar. He felt much better in old clothes and did not not like to dress up. He felt that the city was not a fit place in which to raise children. He planned to remain in the city just one more year, until he went on social security.

He went to work every morning at 3 A.M., and worked until 11. Then he took naps and went to bed early. It was very hard work, but he had been working at the same job for the past four years and had worked there three times previously. Weekends were largely spent visiting friends and kinfolk in the country.

In April 1957 his wife's mother had come to live with them. She had a serious illness but was too old for an operation. He had had a bad hip injury and was sorry to say that he had had to miss two days at work. He talked about a big family reunion the preceding summer. He told the interviewer that he had had a problem of alcoholism at one time but had taken a cure and had had no further problems of that kind.

In August of 1957 he was beginning to wonder about retirement. He wanted to see more of his relatives and said that he saw more of and felt closer to the relatives on his wife's side of the family. He wanted to leave his present job but felt that he must work as long as he was able. His family had had ten children. He was the third from the oldest and there were a lot of people around, including large groups of friends. He still wanted very much to get back to that type of living.

In December 1958 he had retired but was having difficulty in selling his house. He mentioned the late teens as the best time in his life, and the worst time was after his second wife died. He said, "The more friends you have, the better off you are," and he missed this kind of friendship pattern in Kansas City.

In June of 1959 he had managed to achieve his goal of moving back to the country. The mother-in-law was still living with them. He spent much of his time visiting and said that there had been a big family reunion the preceding Sunday, with sixty or seventy people. He did odd jobs on various farms to supplement his social security. He was especially pleased because some close friends had fixed a good dinner for his birthday. He talked a great deal about his early life in the country. He had had no schooling, which he regretted somewhat. He had been raised to take what came. His mother and father were both fine people. When he was old enough to farm, his father died. He had an uncle who was a lot like his father, kind and always helping somebody, and his uncle's house was the gathering place of the countryside. "There were seven of us boys, and none of us ever went to prison." When asked what he would have done if he had his life to live over again, he said, "Maybe I would not have went to the city when my wife died."

In January 1962 the mother-in-law was still living with them, at age ninety and in spite of the chronic illness. The interviewer commented that the respondent looked about sixty, although he was actually sixty-nine. He was described as a friendly, husky, jovial farmer type. By this time he had been living in this rural environment for three years and liked it very much. He knew all the people around, continued to do many odd jobs, and now owned his house. He said he had grown up in a log cabin with no conveniences and that his present home was very comfortable by contrast. He did a little hunting and fishing and mostly did as he pleased and liked it. He enjoyed yard work and odd jobs that helped with the upkeep of the house. He still expressed more than average sorrow over the death of his first two wives, but was very happy with his third wife. He said the main purpose in life was to be as happy as possible.

This respondent was clearly oriented toward diffuse-affective and expressional relations, with a broad network of family and friends, typical of a rural way of life. He was quite unhappy within an urban environment and worked only because he had to. However, unlike the preceding case, he always kept his action system firmly in balance and achieved the kind of life he really wanted in his late sixties. He is a good example both of success in the sense defined here and success in terms of life satisfaction. He has been placed in the autonomous-persistent category, with a rank of 1. He showed no signs of anomie, alienation, or isolation, and was rated 1 on each of those variables, as well as on coping. On clarity and saliency of style he was rated 2 because his style was a somewhat more general rural way of life than a highly developed Familism, as such. However, a considerable amount of familism was inherent in this way of life.

In the over-all picture of conflict between rural and urban life, we do not mean to imply that it is impossible to transplant rural familism to an urban setting without creating difficulties. Several of the most successful agers with a familistic style came from rural farm backgrounds. On the other hand, a rural background is not a guarantee of successful coping with the aging process and may become a fairly serious problem. It can lead to precariousness by fading and failing to provide sufficient support for waning action energy, or it can aid successful coping if the person returns to the original farm environment.

IMPLICATIONS FOR THE PROCESS OF DISENGAGEMENT

After an intensive examination of the lives of one hundred sixty-eight people over the age of fifty, during approximately a five-year span, and to some extent, over their entire life spans, we are convinced that disengagement is a characteristic process faced by the majority of people within the predominant pattern of American, and probably western European, culture, and a problematical one for many. If the actor is not himself disengaging, some of the persons in his social system most probably are, and hence, disengagement is almost inevitably an issue. The relation of disengagement to successful aging, as we have defined it, is not that to age successfully the actor must disengage, but rather that he must cope with disengagement to the extent to which it does arise as an issue. To cope successfully with disengagement requires flexibility in the action system which, in turn, has four main aspects, of varying importance depending on style of life: (1) self-pacing, (2) development of a secondary style or styles, (3) ability to give things up and still retain the style, and (4) ability to cope with the problematical aspects of health and retirement.

We are also convinced that, for the majority, disengagement is inherent in the aging process of the individual's action system, and is conditioned by the aging process of his biological system in varying degrees. However, disengagement can be forced upon the action system of the individual. When it is forced it must be coped with to age successfully. "The Onset of the End," who failed to cope with disengagement, and "Forced Disengagement," who consciously used disengagement as a coping device for serious problems created by the mental illness of her husband, make a sharp contrast in this respect. When disengagement is resisted, it can be a source of precariousness, as illustrated in "Disengaging Under Protest" and "Don't Want to Age."

Disengagement can come at various chronological ages, and at least one case has been documented in which it still had not occurred between ages eighty-two and eighty-six. Biological aging had occurred, but apparently minimally, suggesting some, to be expected, relation between biological aging and aging of the action system, yet some independence between them. In general, it is our strong impression that, if preparation for disengagement is not laid between the ages of fifty and sixty-five, the probability of unsuccessful aging is significantly increased. A few cases of intrinsic disengagement can be found in the early fifties. The late sixties and the seventies are the periods when the issue of disengagement becomes most prominent.

Disengagement occurs in all styles of life. It is affected by style of life and is a relative matter. Those whose style of life is Living Fully tend to be fairly highly engaged when they are 50 per cent or more disengaged, and those whose style is Living Alone tend to have a low level of engagement before they disengage. The World of Work presents the most problems of disengagement. Familism and Couplehood affect the style of disengagement, but appear to have no relation to its amount or timing.

Television is an important medium of disengagement. Although we do not have precise numerical figures, we are strongly convinced that the great majority of respondents watched increasingly more television over the five-year period, and did so at a rate which was higher than the rate for the general population between 1956 and 1961. A few of the respondents commented on this apologetically, but most of them expressed the attitude that watching television was something they just seemed to enjoy more as they grew older.

Disengagement creates something of a methodological problem. In the seventies, in particular, respondents tend to be resistant to being probed. They have lived their lives, and they do not want either to look back or to analyze their present situation. In the eighties, after disengagement has been pretty well worked through, the resistance is less.

TEN

֍

Statistical

Analysis

and Conclusions

THE DISTRIBUTION BY SUCCESS AND STYLE

We have been studying a group which is predominantly successful in terms of balance of their energies with their social systems, and also in terms of their persistence or stability. Table 3 indicates that two-thirds were autonomous-persistent, and only one-tenth were dependent-precarious; 80 per cent were autonomous and 20 per cent were dependent; three-quarters were persistent and one-quarter precarious. Certain groups who might be expected to age less successfully in these terms, notably the grossly underprivileged and the chronically ill, were eliminated from the original Kansas City Study by the method of selecting the panel (see Appendix One). Also, persons who had already become unsuccessful agers by being public charges in the community or by being placed in an institution were not included. Nevertheless, the degree of success in this group is impressive. Thirty per cent fell in the first rank in twelve possible rank orders of success, autonomous-persistent 1. The senior author has indicated elsewhere how the matrix of American culture makes aging a problematical issue to which much research is currently devoted and for which many programs of action are developing.[1] He has also suggested that the great majority of

[1] Richard H. Williams, "The Changing Matrix of American Culture and Problems of Aging," in Clark Tibbitts (ed.), *Aging and Social Health in the United States and Europe* (Ann Arbor: University of Michigan Press, 1959), pp. 156–166.

TABLE 3. DISTRIBUTION OF SUCCESS CATEGORIES

Success Category		Number	Per Cent
Autonomous-Persistent	1	51	30
	2	29	17
	3	28	17
Total		108	64
Antonomous-Precarious	1	8	5
	2	9	6
	3	8	5
Total		25	16
Dependent-Persistent	1	8	5
	2	5	3
	3	5	3
Total		18	11
Dependent-Precarious	1	10	6
	2	4	2
	3	3	1
Total		17	9
Total Cases		168	100

people in this culture actually do age quite successfully, but that a small minority with a cumulative tendency to deviance absorb a disproportionate amount of the energies of others and have a negative influence on the mental health of those around them.[2] The findings on distribution of success in this panel tend to confirm this view.

The distribution of style suggests that, when one takes a microsociological approach and intensively studies the lives of people over time, there is more Familism and more *Gemeinschaft,* in general, in our culture than is usually recognized in the sociological literature. As is indicated in Table 4, nearly one-third of the cases have a familistic style, and the cases in the *Gemeinschaft* set outnumber the cases in the *Gesellschaft* set two to one. Again, we cannot be sure that this finding would apply to American society as a whole, but we strongly suspect, on the basis of this experience, that there is a quite significant

[2] Richard H. Williams, "Changing Status, Roles and Relationships," in Clark Tibbitts (ed.), *Handbook of Social Gerontology* (Chicago: University of Chicago Press, 1960), pp. 261–297.

TABLE 4. DISTRIBUTION OF STYLES

Style	Number	Per Cent of Total	Autonomous	Dependent
World of Work	25	14.9	23 (92%)	2 (8%)
Familism	55	32.8	44 (80%)	11 (20%)
Living Alone	21	12.5	16 (76%)	5 (24%)
Couplehood	33	19.6	24 (72%)	9 (28%)
Minimal Involvement	12	7.1	5 (42%)	7 (58%)
Living Fully	22	13.1	21 (95%)	1 (5%)

TABLE 5. SUCCESS CATEGORY AND STYLE

(in per cent)

Success Category	Total Cases	World of Work	Familism	Living Alone	Couple-hood	Minimal Involve-ment	Living Fully
Auton-Persist	64.3	60.0	65.5	61.9	69.7	33.3	77.3
Auton-Precar	14.9	32.0	14.5	14.3	3.0	8.3	18.2
Dep-Persist	10.7	0.0	10.9	9.5	18.2	33.3	0.0
Dep-Precar	10.1	8.0	9.1	14.3	9.1	25.0	4.5

amount of *Gemeinschaft* throughout our culture. The cases that exhibited the *Gemeinschaft* set were impressive in quality as well as in quantity. Such people often gave full, delightful interviews if they were in the successful group. And even in a case such as "Familism Persistent in Hardship," the essential warmth of the individual came through.

When style and broad success categories are combined, we find that a noticeably high percentage of persons whose style is Living Fully or World of Work fall in the autonomous categories, whereas Easing Through Life With Minimal Involvement has noticeably fewer. When we look only at the subcategory autonomous-persistent in Table 5, Living Fully still is noticeably high, and Minimal Involvement quite low, but World of Work drops below the rest. In Minimal Involvement, 58 per cent of the cases are dependent, as contrasted with 8 per cent in the World of Work and 4.5 per cent (one case) in Living Fully. Familism, which accounts for one-third of the total cases, also accounts for about one-third of each of the four success categories. When we look at the highest of the twelve ranks of success, with fifty-one cases in all, in Table 6, Familism comes out high with 43 per cent.

TABLE 6. STYLES OF LIFE IN AUTONOMOUS-PERSISTENT 1

Styles	Number	Per Cent
World of Work	6	12
Familism	22	43
Living Alone	2	4
Couplehood	7	13
Minimal Involvement	2	4
Living Fully	12	24

It is noticeably ahead of Living Fully, with 24 per cent. Minimal Involvement and Living Alone are quite low, with only two cases, or 4 per cent, each.

There are no dependent-persistent cases in the World of Work or Living Fully. However, in spite of some general relations between style as such and success, we wish to emphasize that there are some most successful agers, some less successful, and some least successful, in each style. Although some styles favor success more than others, no style precludes it. The more important relation between success and style, to be analyzed later in this chapter, is that each style presents its own special problems which must be met to age successfully, and its own supports which favor success.

STATISTICAL FINDINGS IN RELATION TO STYLE

After all of the cases had been analyzed, described, given their rankings on success, and ratings made on anomie, alienation, isolation, coping, and style, the authors then inspected various ratings, other statistical measures, and classification by personality type made by members of the Committee on Human Development of The University of Chicago. These measures were not used in making the authors' classification and analyses of cases; in fact, the data were not available to them until after this was done. Age and sex were, of course, known, but were essentially bracketed in making the analyses.

Analysis of the statistics relating to style indicates that, although the individual styles had significance in relation to some of the variables, the most consistent patterns appeared when the styles were grouped into the two major sets of styles, *Gemeinschaft* and *Gesellschaft*.

The comparison with the University of Chicago material showed the following: Total role activity scores were consistently higher for the three *Gemeinschaft* styles than for the three *Gesellschaft* ones. The scores for the former were 45.2, 43.2, and 42.9, while the latter were 39.6, 36.5, and 28.3, the last (Living Alone) being a full standard deviation (11.8) below the mean of 41.1.

For total role investment, the same relationship held, with scores of 36.5, 36.1, and 31.0 for *Gemeinschaft* and 30.3, 22.4, and 20.3 for *Gesellschaft*. Living Alone was again a standard deviation (11.3) below the mean of 31.5. Four other measures of role activity (family and community) and of involvement in these roles showed the same characteristic patterning with only one overlap (total family roles) on the part of scores for Living Fully and Minimal Involvement, which fits the discussion of these two styles as bridging styles which occasionally demonstrated characteristics of the other groupings.

With regard to measures of leisure-time use, the same relationship appeared, and Living Fully was a full standard deviation above and Minimal Involvement was almost a full standard deviation below the mean.

The interaction index, which rates the amount of each day spent with others, followed the same pattern. World of Work appeared to have a higher interaction index at the time of the second round of interviews; however, by the seventh interview, the measures showed the pattern was the same as before, with no overlapping between *Gemeinschaft* and *Gesellschaft* cases.

A measure of decline in physical vigor over the past ten years did not bear any relationship to style groups. Living Fully people were somewhat below the mean, Minimal Involvement were slightly above, but all the styles were generally clustered right on the mean.

Life satisfaction was measured at two separate times, the first at the end of the fourth interivew and the second at the end of the seventh. At Time 1, the *Gemeinschaft* cases were higher on life satisfaction than the *Gesellschaft* ones, but at Time 2, the World of Work cases overlapped slightly with the others. The outstanding extreme was the style Living Fully, which was more than a standard deviation above the mean. Living Alone was close to a standard deviation below the mean.

The average age of respondents was 70.2 at the end of the study. Most of the styles were clustered at the mean except for Living Alone and Living Fully, which averaged five years older than the other styles. The average social class was 2.1. Living Fully, however, was more noticeably upper class.

Further analysis was made by noting relationships that appeared from the authors' findings, ratings, and rankings. Marital status seemed to have little relation to style except that no divorced people held the style of Couplehood. This was the only category in all the styles, as related to marital status, that was totally lacking in cases.

Regarding ratings of anomie, the *Gemeinschaft* style had percentages of 58, 33, and 9 for degrees 1, 2, and 3 of anomie, respectively, as opposed to 38, 36, and 26 per cent for the *Gesellschaft* cases. The former are clearly more adequate in action energy usage regarding this aspect of their social system than are the latter cases.

The same pattern of good action energy usage held even more strongly for alienation. These percentages, in the same order as before, were 67, 30, and 3 for *Gemeinschaft*, and 33, 38, and 29 for *Gesellschaft*. This same relationship held well for isolation, with percentages of 71, 28, and 1 for *Gemeinschaft*, and 24, 54, and 22 for *Gesellschaft*.

Coping showed approximately the same relationship, but with not quite such a difference between groups. The *Gemeinschaft* cases were effective in coping generally, but so were the *Gesellschaft*, even though slightly less so; over-all coping percentages were 68, 30, and 2 for *Gemeinschaft*, and 53, 38, and 9 for *Gesellschaft*.

Clarity and saliency of style showed no relation to style of life except in the World of Work, where 88 per cent of the cases were given a rating of 1. No other style had more than 55 per cent of its cases in this category. Minimal Involvement had the most classed as

3, or weak in style (33 per cent). This suggests that work as a style of life is not lightly held. Either it is dominant or it is not very important at all.

The sex distribution by style groups indicates that in the *Gemeinschaft* set the females outnumber the males slightly less than 2 to 1 (72 to 38), and in the *Gesellschaft* set the males outnumber the females slightly more than 2 to 1 (41 to 17). Any differences related to sex were considered to be due to different social expectations for the sexes rather than to biological differences. Nevertheless, it is useful to look at the style groupings by sex, as there were approximately the same number of males in each set of styles (41 and 38). This breakdown permitted emphasizing even more strongly the divergent characteristics of the style groups when male sex was held constant.

Some of the variations seemed particularly sex-linked. On the ratings of anomie, Table 7, it appeared that males who had a *Gemeinschaft* style had a lower percentage (7.9) than did *Gemeinschaft* females (9.7) in the most anomic rating, number 3. The reverse was

TABLE 7.   ANOMIE BY SEX AND SET OF STYLES

| | Gemeinschaft | | | | Gesellschaft | | | |
| | Male | | Female | | Male | | Female | |
Rating	No.	%	No.	%	No.	%	No.	%
1	26	68.4	40	55.6	17	41.4	5	29.4
2	9	23.7	25	34.7	12	29.3	9	53.0
3	3	7.9	7	9.7	12	29.3	3	17.6

true for *Gesellschaft;* females had 17.6 per cent and males 29.3 per cent in the lowest rating. Alienation, Table 8, showed the same pattern

TABLE 8.   ALIENATION BY SEX AND SET OF STYLES

| | Gemeinschaft | | | | Gesellschaft | | | |
| | Male | | Female | | Male | | Female | |
Rating	No.	%	No.	%	No.	%	No.	%
1	29	76.3	44	61.1	16	39.1	3	17.6
2	9	23.7	24	33.3	11	26.8	11	64.8
3	0	0.0	4	5.6	14	34.1	3	17.6

even more dramatically. *Gemeinschaft* males had 0 per cent in the extremely poor rating, as opposed to 5.6 per cent for females, and *Gesellschaft* females had 17.6 per cent against 34.1 per cent for males. Coping, Table 9, also repeated the pattern and showed *Gemeinschaft*

TABLE 9. COPING BY SEX AND SET OF STYLES

	Gemeinschaft				*Gesellschaft*			
	Male		Female		Male		Female	
Rating	No.	%	No.	%	No.	%	No.	%
1	27	71.1	47	65.3	21	51.2	10	58.8
2	11	28.9	22	30.5	16	39.0	6	35.3
3	0	0.0	3	4.2	4	9.8	1	5.9

percentages of 0 per cent for males and 4.2 per cent for females. For *Gesellschafts,* it was 5.9 per cent for females and 9.8 per cent for males. Thus, when persons develop a style somewhat at variance with cultural expectations for their sex, they tend to be well integrated in the dimensions measured by anomie, alienation, and coping.

Isolation showed no special pattern other than the previously mentioned greater isolation for all *Gesellschaft* than for *Gemeinschaft* cases, regardless of sex. The relatively high percentage of female extreme isolates (35.3) in the *Gesellschaft* group suggested that females who went against cultural expectation perhaps were penalized by a degree of social ostracism.

Clarity of style showed no pattern in relation to style, and sex appeared distributed rather evenly.

STATISTICAL FINDINGS IN RELATION TO SUCCESS

Analysis of success by these same variables showed less dramatic trends generally.

On total roles there was a slight downward trend with the chief difference being between autonomous people and dependent ones. The same held for total role investment. For family roles and family role investment, the dependent-precarious people were a little below all the others.

The dependent cases were again slightly lower than the autonomous ones in total community roles. In community role investment, the dependent-persistent were much lower. Leisure-time use was also low for dependent-persistent people.

The dependent people showed a slightly greater decline in physical vigor and a much lower degree of life satisfaction than the autonomous ones. The autonomous cases were right on the mean at Time 2, but the dependent ones were not quite a standard deviation below. This suggests that highly unsatisfactory agers have less life satisfaction, but that successful agers do not necessarily have a high life satisfaction (mean, 35.6, standard deviation, 6.6, dependent, 30.7).

Marital status and success showed some interesting relationships. Eight out of the nine people (88.9 per cent) who were divorced at the end of the study were in the most successful of the four categories, whereas only 58.5 per cent of the married (55 out of 94 cases) were in this category. The greatest percentage of dependent-precarious were single people who had 14.3 per cent of their number in this class.

Taking the success categories separately, certain relationships to anomie appear, Table 10. In the autonomous-persistent category, 75 per cent of the cases were rated anomie 1, and 2.8 per cent were rated 3, while in dependent-precarious, 0 cases were rated 1, and 58.8 per cent were rated 3.

This same pattern held generally for alienation and isolation, although dependent-precarious people were less isolated proportionately; 53.0 per cent of the cases fall in category 2, and only 29.4 per cent were rated as 3. Coping showed the same pattern. Dependent-precarious people were the poorest in coping, with 35.3 per cent falling in rating 3.

Clarity of style is generally unrelated to success in this statistical sense, but has an important functional relation to how success is achieved, as will be indicated below.

COMBINATIONS OF VARIABLES

Because the analysis showed the significant success groupings to be the general groupings of autonomous and dependent, further analysis was made by taking the cases in autonomous-persistent 1 (51 cases) and comparing them with all the dependent cases (35) on such variables as role participation, life satisfaction, and the like. There were no statistically significant findings. However, the means of the autonomous cases were always above the dependent cases in any success type ratings, and the autonomous cases followed a pattern of high role participation and interaction as opposed to low by the dependent cases. When compared with our own ratings, Table 11, certain relationships were very strong. For anomie, 88.2 per cent of the autonomous-persistent cases were rated as anomie 1, while only 5.7 per cent of the dependent cases were anomie 1. Similarly, 90.2 per cent of the autonomous were rated as alienation 1, and only 11.4 per cent of the dependent were rated as highly. Further, 80.4 per cent of the autonomous were isolation 1, and only 20.0 per cent of the dependent were

TABLE 10. CATEGORIES OF SUCCESS BY VARIABLES

Success Category	Total Number	Anomie			Alienation			Isolation		
		1	2	3	1	2	3	1	2	3
Auton-Persist	108									
Number		81	24	3	82	22	4	73	28	7
Per Cent		75.0	22.2	2.8	75.9	20.4	3.7	67.6	25.9	6.5
Auton-Precar	25									
Number		5	13	7	5	15	5	12	12	1
Per Cent		20.0	52.0	28.0	20.0	60.0	20.0	48.0	48.0	4.0
Dep-Persist	18									
Number		2	11	5	4	10	4	4	12	2
Per Cent		11.1	61.1	27.8	22.2	55.6	22.2	22.2	66.7	11.1
Dep-Precar	17									
Number		0	7	10	0	8	9	3	9	5
Per Cent		0.0	41.2	58.8	0.0	47.1	52.9	17.6	53.0	29.4
Total	168									
Number		88	55	25	91	55	22	92	61	15
Per Cent		52.4	32.7	14.9	54.2	32.7	13.1	54.8	36.3	8.9

TABLE 11. EXTREMES OF SUCCESS BY VARIABLES (in per cent)

Success Category	Sex		Marital Status				Age			
	M	F	M	W	S	D	50's	60's	70's	80's
Auton-Persist 1	47.1	52.9	51.0	37.3	7.8	3.9	25.5	31.4	33.3	9.8
Dependent	42.9	57.1	57.1	25.7	14.3	2.9	45.7	14.3	31.4	8.6

	Anomie			Alienation		
	1	2	3	1	2	3
Auton-Persist 1	88.2	9.8	2.0	90.2	9.8	0.0
Dependent	5.7	51.4	42.9	11.4	51.5	37.1

	Isolation			Coping			Clarity of Style		
	1	2	3	1	2	3	1	2	3
Auton-Persist 1	80.4	15.7	3.9	96.1	3.9	0.0	72.5	25.5	2.0
Dependent	20.0	60.0	20.0	8.6	71.4	20.0	42.8	28.6	28.6

isolation 1. Clarity of style seemed similarly related, if not as strongly, with 72.5 per cent of the autonomous being rated 1, and 42.8 per cent of the dependent being so rated.

Marital status showed little relationship, with the exception of single people. Of the autonomous group, only 7.8 per cent were single; of the dependent group, 14.3 per cent were single.

Further analysis was made by looking at individual styles of life in each of the success categories. Although numbers of cases in each were small, some suggestive findings were made. In the autonomous-persistent category, which had the largest number of cases, total role activity showed Living Alone to be almost a standard deviation low. Total role investment for Living Alone was also almost a standard deviation low. Under community investment in roles, Living Fully was about a standard deviation high, and this style was also about a standard deviation high in leisure time total use. Living Fully was slightly more than a standard deviation high in life satisfaction rating. Of the successful agers, the Living Fully were the oldest, with an average age of 74.6, and World of Work were youngest, at 68.6 years. Social class for the group was consistent at slightly over 2, except for Living Fully, who were distinctly more upper class, with an average of 1.4.

Under the remaining categories of less successful agers, cases in each category, though small, showed patterns quite consistent with our analysis. For World of Work, both autonomous-precarious and dependent-precarious were well over a standard deviation low in leisure time total. The eight less successful agers who were Living Alone were all well over a standard deviation low in roles and role investment, whether total, family, or community. The dependent Living Alone cases (5) were a standard deviation low in leisure time total, as well as a standard deviation low in the interaction index, as might be expected. The dependent Minimal Involvement cases (7) were generally low in role totals and investment, and were a standard deviation low in community role totals, suggesting that, as stated in the analysis of cases, Minimal Involvement people simply do not use their action energy any more than necessary and involvement outside self and family is almost unthinkable!

Living Fully, regardless of success, continued significantly a standard deviation high in leisure time total and life satisfaction, except for the single dependent-precarious case which was a standard deviation low in leisure time total, but remained quite high in life satisfaction.

The oldest single category was composed of three autonomous-precarious people with a style of Living Alone, who averaged 85.7

years of age at the end of the study. The youngest category was composed of five Familism autonomous-precarious cases with an average age of 63.3 years.

Minimal Involvement, dependent-persistent (4 cases), and Living Alone, dependent-precarious (3 cases), both averaged a low social class of 3.0. The highest social class, with the exception of a single case at 1.0 in Living Fully, dependent-precarious, was Living Fully, autonomous-precarious (4 cases).

PERSONALITY AND PATTERNS

Although personality ratings were not made by The University of Chicago on all the cases used in this study, comparison was made on the sixty-three cases rated by William Crotty on the basis of a life history interview, and fifty-eight cases rated by Gutmann on the basis of TAT material. Table 12 indicates that the mature personalities, as judged by Crotty, and the active-mastery type, as judged by Gutmann, fall heavily in the autonomous-persistent success types. However, there is an appreciable number of passive-mastery types in this category. The fact that six of the ten autonomous-precarious types are judged to be passive-mastery, only one to be active-mastery, and only three to be mature, is suggestive of a relationship there. Also, it should be noted that there are instances of people judged to be defective or constricted in personality in the autonomous-persistent group. Inspection of the data does not reveal any relation between personality type and style of life; as far as we can judge, there are examples of almost all of the personality types in all of the styles.

Tobin, in Chicago, classified forty-nine cases between ages seventy and eighty into eight general patterns: General Engagement, Focused Engagement, Holding On, Happy Disengagement, Succorant Seeking, Passive Apathy, Constricted, and Disorganized.

Living Fully is clearly related to General Engagement and Focused Engagement; seven of the eight cases were in those two categories. Five of the ten Living Alone cases were classed as Disorganized, and all three of the Minimal Involvement cases were Passive Apathy.

By success, the only significance was that seven out of the nine cases of dependence were Passive Apathy or Disorganized.

SUMMARY OF STATISTICAL FINDINGS

Summarizing the statistical findings, the most outstanding concept is the consistently significant pattern showing life styles of *Gemein-*

TABLE 12. SUCCESS TYPES AND PERSONALITY TYPES[a]

Total Cases in Study = 63	Success Types	Crotty[b] Total Cases Rated Mature	Gutmann[c] Personality Types				
			Active-Mastery	Passive-Mastery	Constricted	Magical-Mastery or Defective	Gutmann Total
41	Auton-Persist	20 (of 38 rated)	18	11	2	3	34
12	Auton-Precar	2 (of 10 rated)	1	6	2	1	10
2	Dep-Persist		1			1	2
8	Dep-Precar	1 (of 8 rated)	1	1	1	3	6

[a] The Gutmann assessment is for the end of the study. A few cases refused to do the TAT a second time. Ratings were unavailable on 5 cases, but fortunately each of the 5 fell into a different success-style of life category.
[b] Based on personal interviews.
[c] Based on TAT.

schaft and *Gesellschaft* to be related to variables of interaction, numbers of roles, role investment, leisure time use, anomie, alienation, and coping. These two groups showed patterns of relationship highly consistent with the case analyses, not only for the larger group but in general for the specific life styles as well.

The success variables were less striking in the findings, but the findings were consonant with the case analyses, and the trends were in the expected direction. Personality ratings were particularly consistent with success. Although the cases were too few for adequate comparison, the suggestive relationship that appeared between these variables and Tobin's disengagement types lends further validity to the combination of these approaches in describing successful aging.

CONCLUSIONS

In Chapter One, we indicated several theories of aging and successful aging which have been developed in connection with the Kansas City Study of Adult Life. We raised the question as to whether these theories can be combined into a more general theory, especially in relation to successful aging. Now, at the conclusion of our own study, we are convinced that it is possible to develop such a theory of optimal aging, starting with our definitions of success as a base. This theory was reached only after we had made all of our other analyses. It was certainly not explicitly in our minds at the time we read our cases, and we are convinced that it is not an artifact of our particular mode of operation.

We begin with the exclusive bases which we used for judging success, namely autonomy and dependency, persistence and precariousness. We do so partly for the practical implications of this approach. We believe that, like the people in this panel, the majority of people in the dominant American culture who are age fifty and over will be found to be relatively successful agers. As indicated elsewhere by the senior author, the highly unsuccessful agers constitute a small minority, but one which absorbs a greatly disproportionate amount of energies and resources of others.[3] How much of our scarce resources in mental health and welfare services must, or can, be used to maintain older people on any level? In addition, if one looks more theoretically at the broader social system, to maintain it requires avoidance of entropy in action energy. If there were more dependent than autonomous persons in the total system, it would run down. Similarly, if there were

[3] Williams, "The Changing Matrix of American Culture. . . ," *op. cit.*

more precarious people than persistent ones in the system as a whole, it would begin to crack at the seams.

There are varying degrees of success deriving from the combination of these two sets of variables. We have been able to distinguish twelve ranks of success with high reliability. But then, on the basis of our empirical observations, we have found that certain factors tend to push in the direction of, or reinforce, successful aging; their absence or weakness tends to push in the direction of unsuccessful aging. They do so in varying degrees of importance. If a person is autonomous and persistent and has a high degree of clarity of style, successful aging is reinforced. If he has these three characteristics and, in addition, the characteristic uses of his action energy are on the good side, that is, rated 1, success is still further reinforced. Then, it is further reinforced by flexibility of the action system in relation to self-pacing, secondary styles, ability to give things up and still maintain the style, and ability to cope with problematical aspects of health and retirement. If the person has a high degree of all these characteristics and, in addition, there is a high degree of life satisfaction, successful aging is still further reinforced. Finally, in some instances, and particularly if the style is World of Work, successful aging can be reinforced by keeping active.

If a person has the fifth of these characteristics to a significant extent, he will most probably be able to cope with disengagement, and if he has both the fourth and fifth, he most probably has a mature and integrated personality. The relation between these variables and concepts is diagrammed in Chart 2.

This over-all view of optimal aging has been derived empirically from greater and greater familiarity with all one hundred sixty-eight cases. Some of the factors have been rated. Clarity of style does tend statistically to be greater for the most successful agers, autonomous-persistent 1, and characteristic uses of action energy also have a strong tendency to be rated 1 in this group. There is a less strong tendency for life satisfaction to be high in this group, and an even less strong tendency for its members to be active. Flexibility was not rated. We are not maintaining that these factors intercorrelate perfectly, or that they must all be present for optimal aging. Also, it is possible to find persons who are medium, or perhaps even low, on the first two factors, our definition of successful aging, and are high on some or all of the others. But we do maintain that these factors are functionally related in the sense that, in the order given, if a person is high on one factor, optimal aging is reinforced by the addition of being high on the next

CHART 2. FACTORS IN OPTIMAL AGING
IN ORDER OF PRIORITY

1. Autonomy

2. Persistence

3. Clarity and saliency
   of style

4. Characteristic uses of action
   energy on the "good" side

5. Flexibility

   a. self-pacing
   b. development of secondary
      style
   c. able to give things up
      and maintain style
   d. coping with health and
      retirement

   able to cope with disengagement

   Mature and Integrated Personality

6. Life satisfaction

7. Keeping active

one, and so on down the list. This theory emerged at the end, from the study as a whole. A new study could be designed to test it further.

It will be noted that disengagement and mature and integrated personality have not been treated as factors in optimal aging in this general theory. Rather, they are considered as emergent properties associated with optimal aging.

It will also be noted that life satisfaction has been placed fairly far down on the list of priorities of variables. As indicated above, there is some slight relation between life satisfaction, on the one hand, and autonomy and persistence, on the other. However, it was quite clear that successful aging, as originally conceived in this study, and even as expanded above to include the other elements, is not always a source of satisfaction to the individual, and one can be successful though miserable. There is, however, another kind of relation between success and life satisfaction of which we became more and more aware as we analyzed our cases. Although in some instances success may not be a source of satisfaction to the individual actor, it usually is a source of great satisfaction to anyone else whose life space includes this actor as an important person. "We are so proud of her (or him)" was a remark often made by offspring of a really successful ager. Such genuine pride was not based entirely on the selfish aspects of not having to be so responsible for a successful ager, although this is certainly an important factor in life satisfaction for these significant others. It also included a feeling of genuine pleasure based on the joy of seeing anyone complete a life's pattern in a constructive and contributing fashion. It was interesting to note that not only the original interviewers but also the authors and the secretaries occasionally began to feel genuine annoyance at some of the more unpleasant and unsuccessful agers, and became quite enthusiastic about some of the successful ones. We do not mean to imply that all of the significant others of the successful agers have a high degree of life satisfaction, which was clearly not the case in the actual study of these significant others. We do imply that the significant others are more satisfied than they would have been if the original respondents had been further down the line toward unsuccessful aging.

Our concern throughout the study has been not only with success but also with style, and with the relations between success and style. As we have seen above, there are a few general statistical relations between amount of success and type of style. On the other hand, as we have emphasized throughout, there can be successful and unsuccessful agers in all six styles. The important relation between success and style, to be particularly emphasized, is that each style has its own, and somewhat different, prerequisites for success.

In the World of Work, self-pacing and maintenance of a fair amount of activity are especially important. In the case of Familism, a social system which is more open than closed (contrast "I Want to Retire" with "Faded Familism"), ability to maintain appropriate relations, especially with offspring (as was very clear in "American Familism in Pure Culture" and in "Golden Familism"), and having some familism in the background while growing up (compare "From Orphan to Aloneness" with "Familism Persistent in Hardship") are important in relation to successful aging.

In the case of Living Alone, to age successfully is associated with, but not guaranteed by, a low degree of anomie and a high degree of coping. Then, in turn, it is made possible but not guaranteed by having a minimal social system and minimal energy exchange, so that a balance can be maintained at this low level. It is a somewhat deviant style, suitable to persons with tendencies toward alienation and isolation, who might otherwise be unable to maintain their mental health. In the case of Couplehood, the same principle obtains as in Familism, concerning an open rather than a closed system, with amplitude and alternative focuses for the style. Success in this style is facilitated if it is a first choice as a style, as can be seen by comparing "Trapped in

Couplehood" and "Rejected and Hurt," on the one hand, with "Good-bye Miss Chips" and "Couplehood Though Alone," on the other hand. Success is also reinforced when both parties have this same style.

Easing Through Life With Minimal Involvement is a difficult style to achieve, and even more difficult to achieve successfully. Success is facilitated because disengagement is no problem, due to the low level of engagement. It is also facilitated by having a network of diffuse-neutral relations, in which one can play the role of "crony." "The Crony" did so, and "Keep on Living" did so to a lesser extent in the neighborhood store. "Then She Married" might do so, but was somewhat precarious because she might not. "Nearly Styleless" did so weakly, within the narrow confines of his family. "A Life That Was Not Lived" and "Living With the Children" were unable to do so and became unsuccessful agers. When aging is less or least successful, this style, more than any of the others, protects against complete breakdown of the action system in mental illness. Living Alone has some of this same characteristic.

Living Fully tends to have a greater, though by no means complete, tendency to be associated with successful aging than any of the other styles. Disengagement is not antithetical to the style, but presents a somewhat greater issue to cope with and still maintain the style than is true in the case of other styles. Success in this style implies a life-long pattern of competent coping with many facets of life. Without this amplitude, within which it is possible to disengage and still maintain the style, this style is associated with precariousness, as is particularly well illustrated by "Don't Want to Age." Similarly, success in this style is reinforced if there is a development of a secondary style for additional support.

The general theory of optimal aging which emerges from this analysis will, we hope, provide some suggestive leads for people who plan and direct service programs for older persons, and, especially, for people who are concerned with the reduction of the entropic tendencies of aging, and hence with prevention of these tendencies. We do not suggest that this view of aging leads to a recipe for any particular program. On the contrary, it should lead to: (1) perspectives which might suggest modifications of existing programs, and (2) a recognition of the need for varied programs. Of these two possible results in application, the second is the more important and would contribute to the first.

We have analyzed one hundred sixty-eight lives in their later years. These lives were found in a panel which differs from the full range of the population of the United States and other countries of western

European culture in being a rather homogeneous sector in relation to class, ethnic origin, and health. And yet, within this relatively homogeneous group, all midwestern during the Study and mostly of midwestern origin, there were different styles of life, degrees of success in maintaining themselves in the aging process, and degrees of optimal aging for themselves and others. Most were successful, the largest single category in twelve ratings being very successful. For them, the scarce mental health and welfare resources should not be diverted except as they may benefit indirectly from preventive and consultation programs.[4] None was completely unsuccessful, by our definition, although a few were on the brink. For them, a variety of programs and certainly not one oriented to a particular view of aging should be provided. People whose styles are in the *Gemeinschaft* set need quite different supports from those in the *Gesellschaft* set.

For a few with a *Gesellschaft* orientation, especially with a style of World of Work, a program focused on keeping active, with a "program director" or "social director" can be useful. But, as the senior author has stated elsewhere, with regard to them and to all aging persons,

> Keeping people "employed" into the later years will not, of itself, solve the basic problems either. It is the meaningfulness of activities and relationships which are important, rather than their volume. Some of the current emphases on "staying active" may actually prove to be misplaced and to be largely a reflection of the value system of the "youth culture." The development of more "mature" and "autonomous" values may be important for older persons and may, in turn, enrich the culture as a whole.[5]

It may also be suggested that influencing the general situation so that persons can maintain their styles of life as they grow older, yet at the same time cope with the process of disengagement, may be more important and affect more people than direct intervention. This approach should be developed in the earlier years of life so that persons become deeply entrenched in autonomy, develop a clear style, use their action energy in optimal ways, and learn to be flexible. Then, in old age, they will be much more likely to remain autonomous and to follow the motto, "To thine own style be true."

---

[4] Richard H. Williams, "Trends in Community Psychiatry: Indirect Services and the Problem of Balance in Mental Health Programs," in Leopold Bellak (ed.), *Handbook of Community Psychiatry and Community Mental Health* (New York: Grune & Stratton, 1964), pp. 343–356.

[5] Williams, "The Changing Matrix of American Culture . . . ," p. 166.

Appendix

ONE

❦

General Perspectives of the Kansas City Study of Adult Life

The present study is based on the findings of the Kansas City Study of Adult Life, a collaborative project of the National Institute of Mental Health and The University of Chicago. Several staff members of the Committee on Human Development of The University of Chicago participated in the study, and the senior author of this book represented the National Institute of Mental Health. The study has produced numerous articles and one previous book, and two other books are in preparation.[1]

[1] The following publications have come from the Kansas City Study of Adult Life: Elaine Cumming, Lois R. Dean, and David S. Newell, "Measuring Successful Aging—A Validity Problem," *Human Development Bulletin,* 1958, 22–32; Elaine Cumming, Lois R. Dean, and David S. Newell, "What is Morale?—A Case History of the Validity Problem," *Human Organization,* 17, 2, 1958, 3–8; Elaine Cumming, Lois R. Dean, David S. Newell, and Isabel McCaffrey, "Disengagement—A Tentative Theory of Aging," *Sociometry,* 23, 1, 1960, 23–25; Elaine Cumming and William E. Henry, *Growing Old* (New York: Basic Books, 1961); Elaine Cumming and David H. Schneider, "Sibling Solidarity: A Feature of American Kinship," *American Anthropologist,* 63, June 1961, 498–507; Lois R. Dean, "Aging and the Decline of Instrumentality," *Journal of Gerontology,* 15, 4, 1960, 403; Lois R. Dean, "The Pattern Variables: Some Empirical Operations," *American Sociological Review,* 26, 1, 1961, 80–90; Dan C. Lortie, "Middle-Aged Men and Their Work: An Exploration of Meanings," *Human Development Bulletin,* 1956, 1–7; Robert J. Havighurst, "Successfully Aging," in Richard H. Williams, Clark Tibbitts, and Wilma Donahue (eds.), *Processes of Aging,*

The Kansas City Study consisted of a panel of subjects, from ages forty-nine to ninety, who were studied by intensive interviewing over a five and one-half year period. The main body of the study consisted of seven rounds of such interviews. Fifteen members of the panel, well distributed by age, sex, and social class, underwent two sessions of intensive interviews by a senior member of the field staff fairly early in the study; these interviews obtained life history data as part of an effort to define the concept of morale. Ten members of the panel, including most of these fifteen, were seen by another member of the field staff in a special study of kinship. Ninety-one members, including most of the fifteen, were seen by a clinical psychologist just after round six. He, too, obtained life history data, this time in relation to development and refinement of the concept of life satisfaction. In sixty-three cases, all of whom were also seen by the clinical psychologist, there was a study of significant others, between round six and round seven. Approximately five other people, ranging from most primary and intimate relations to the more secondary and instrumental, who were significant in the lives of the original respondent, were interviewed about themselves and their relations to the respondent. At about this same time, twenty-four subjects were part of a special study of holidays and rituals. There were numerous brief contacts with many of the panel members about various matters between the regular interviews. Finally, just prior to round seven, nineteen panel members were studied by two graduate students, using the method of participant observation, with frequent informal contacts over a period of up to six months.

The data obtained concerned many aspects of life. The main areas, in which data were obtained during at least two points in time, were:

1. General welfare and well-being, including attitudes toward the respondent's own health.

Vol. I (New York: Atherton Press, 1963), pp. 299–320; Robert J. Havighurst, Bernice L. Neugarten, and Sheldon S. Tobin, *Patterns of Aging* (in preparation); William E. Henry and Elaine Cumming, "Personality Development in Adulthood and Old Age," *Journal of Projective Techniques, 23,* 1959, 383–390; Bernice L. Neugarten, "Personality and the Aging Process," in *Processes of Aging,* Vol. I, pp. 321–334; Bernice L. Neugarten, *Personality in Middle and Late Life* (New York: Atherton Press, 1964); Jacqueline L. Rosen and Bernice L. Neugarten, "Ego Functions in the Middle and Later Years: A Thematic Apperception Study of Normal Adults," *Journal of Gerontology, 15,* 1, 1960, 62–67; Richard H. Williams, "Styles of Life and Successful Aging," in *Processes of Aging,* Vol. I, pp. 335–371.

2. Various measures of life satisfaction.
3. The network of social relations, kin, neighbors and friends, and group affiliations—that is, the structural properties of the social life space of each individual respondent.
4. The daily round of activities—the overt behavior in this social life space.
5. General attitudes about life, the world, and modern society.
6. Attitudes toward the self and others, ego ideals and self-images.
7. Orientations to interaction (to be defined below).
8. Decision-making.
9. Affect and impulse control, projection and introjection, and other aspects of personality.
10. Much of the above over the life history.

The total body of data is thus unusually rich, and lends itself to many kinds of analyses, both qualitative and quantitative, and to the exploration of different theoretical interests. Several main theoretical plot lines have emerged. It was from a part of these data that Elaine Cumming developed the hypothesis of disengagement, which was then elaborated by Cumming and Henry in *Growing Old*.[2] Henry, Neugarten, Gutmann, and Crotty—all on the staff of the Committee on Human Development—have been particularly interested in explorations of personality and personality change with age. Havighurst has been interested in the development of measurements of life satisfaction as one approach to a concept of successful aging. Havighurst, Neugarten, and Tobin have been developing an analysis of patterns of aging relating the dimensions of life satisfaction, social interaction, and personality.

The Populations Studied

The characteristics of the original panels, and the way they were drawn, are described in detail by Cumming and Henry.[3] The main panel was a representative sample of the urbanized area of Greater Kansas City, between the ages of forty-nine and seventy-one, and stratified by age, sex, and social class. At the end of the first year of study, the staff was convinced that seventy-one was too young a cut-off point to catch the more important changes with age, and two

[2] Cumming and Henry, *Growing Old, op. cit.*
[3] *Ibid.,* Chapter III and Appendix I.

quasi panels of persons in their seventies and eighties, reasonably well distributed by age, sex, and social class, were added to the study.

There were two hundred eighty-one respondents who completed round one or round three special (the seventies and eighties, which included key material from rounds one and two for the original panel). Their distribution by age, sex, and social class is given in Table 13.

TABLE 13. DISTRIBUTION BY AGE, SEX, AND SOCIAL CLASS
(at Round 1)

Social Class	50's M	50's F	60's M	60's F	70's M	70's F	80's M	80's F
Upper Middle	14	12	11	9	1	9	2	4
Lower Middle	18	19	8	16	14	15	7	9
Upper Lower	22	14	15	16	19	16	7	4
Totals = 281	54	45	34	41	34	40	16	17
Total by Age	99		75		74		33	

This distribution for respondents who completed round seven, the respondents used in the present study, is given in Table 14. There was,

TABLE 14. DISTRIBUTION BY AGE, SEX, AND SOCIAL CLASS
(at Round 7)

Social Class	50's M	50's F	60's M	60's F	70's M	70's F	80's M	80's F
Upper Middle	11	8	7	8	1	7	1	2
Lower Middle	14	9	4	6	6	11	2	5
Upper Lower	13	11	10	9	9	11	1	2
Totals = 168	38	28	21	23	16	29	4	9
Total by Age	66		44		45		13	

obviously, attrition; 63 per cent of respondents who were interviewed in round one completed round seven. Although there are no closely similar studies with which to compare its attrition rates, those who participated in the study were not surprised by this rate. In addition to the usual losses by deaths and moves, some panel members simply were worn out by so much interviewing. One respondent was contacted twenty-five times, many twelve or thirteen times, and most eight or nine. The characteristics of attrition by age, sex, and social class are given in Tables 15 and 16. Attrition rates for females were somewhat

TABLE 15. CHARACTERISTICS OF ATTRITION

Sex, Age, and Social Class	Interview Round							Per Cent of Round 1 Who Completed Round 7	Number of Dropouts
	1	2	3	4	5	6	7		
Males	88	80	74	69	65	66	59	67	29
Females	86	77	69	65	61	58	51	59	35
49–59 years	99	88	82	77	73	72	66	67	33
60–71 years	75	69	61	57	53	52	44	59	31
Upper Middle	46	42	42	39	37	37	34	74	12
Lower Middle	61	52	47	43	39	37	32	52	29
Upper Lower	67	63	54	52	50	50	44	66	23
Totals	174	157	143	134	126	124	110	63	64

TABLE 16. CHARACTERISTICS OF ATTRITION
(Rounds 3–7)

Sex, Age, and Social Class	3	Interview Round 4	5	6	7	Per Cent of Round 3 Who Completed Round 7	Number of Dropouts
Males	50	39	31	32	20	40	30
Females	57	51	48	47	38	67	19
69–79 years	74	63	54	55	45	61	29
80 and over	33	27	25	24	13	39	20
Upper Middle	16	13	14	14	11	69	5
Lower Middle	45	36	31	33	24	53	21
Upper Lower	46	41	34	32	23	50	23
Totals	107	90	79	79	58	54	49

higher than for males for the panel as a whole, but higher for the males in the seventies and eighties. Rates for the lower-middle class were somewhat higher than for the other two classes for females. In spite of this attrition, the one hundred sixty-eight cases used in this study were 47 per cent males and 53 per cent females.

Cumming and Henry speculate:

> It is our impression from interviewing some of the respondents ourselves that there is a survival principle involved and that it is connected with narcissism. In short, those people who like to talk about themselves to outsiders remain, while those who find this distasteful fall out, and this difference may be related to some of our findings. Some of the latter do, however, remain out of a sense of duty or because they gave us their word, but it cannot be overlooked that some personality factor is probably at work in selecting the continuing members of each wave.[4]

We do not really know what effect the dropout rate may have had on our study. It is possible that it produced a picture of greater success in aging than would have been true of the original panel as a whole. However, as we are defining success here, we doubt that the effect was great, if it existed at all. We believe it is even less likely that the relations we have analyzed between success, style, disengagement, and other variables were affected by attrition.

Finally, the population in the significant others study, the group for which we have the greatest volume of data, is given in Table 17. It is reasonably distributed by age, sex, and social class.

TABLE 17. SIGNIFICANT OTHERS

Social Class	50's		60's		70's		80's	
	M	F	M	F	M	F	M	F
Upper Middle	6	5	4	7	0	4	0	2
Lower Middle	6	6	3	3	4	2	2	2
Upper Lower	5	7	1	6	1	1	0	0
Totals = 77	17	18	8	16	5	7	2	4
Totals by Age	35		24		12		6	

Cumming and Henry have called attention to certain character-

4 *Ibid.*, p. 34.

istics of this panel which should be borne in mind to give proper perspective to the findings of any study using these data. They say:

> We decided to minimize heterogeneity in the panel itself because we were concerned mainly with making new formulations about the aging process through intensive interviews with a relatively small group of people. Therefore, the panel was restricted to white respondents of the working and middle classes as determined by a modified Index of Status Characteristics (78). The sample deviates further from the general population by being equally divided among the upper-middle, lower-middle, and working classes. We attempted to get equal numbers of men and women, for while this does not reflect the population composition, it facilitates analysis. We ended with slightly more men than women, unlike the general population.[5] [And again] In summary, the majority of our panel members belonged to stable working- and middle-class families; they were relatively affluent, had no chronic illnesses, and lived in small household units. They had a history of mobility, for almost all of them had come to Kansas City from somewhere else. On the whole they appeared to conform quite closely to the stereotype of Middle Westerner.[6] [And, finally] Any sample which is less than national in scope is certain to have regional biases. The population we used, although representative of the metropolitan area of Kansas City (within the limits described), is by no means representative of the United States. The ethnic composition of the area is markedly more Anglo-Saxon than that of many of the urban parts of the country. Nor do we have more than a sprinkling of second-generation Americans, let alone immigrants. Negroes were excluded and so was the very important lower class. All of these limitations lead to caution in generalizing too widely from our findings and reduce the generality of our theory.[7]

On the other hand, we are convinced that the general relations between variables which we have analyzed have wide applicability beyond the population of Kansas City. The senior author has read several cases in the large study of geriatric mental illness at the Langley Porter Neuropsychiatric Institute in San Francisco, in which he also partici-

[5] *Ibid.,* p. 28.
[6] *Ibid.,* p. 33.
[7] *Ibid.,* pp. 35–36.

pated, and the relations seem to hold well in them. We believe that regional variation would be minimal. Ethnic and racial differences may be greater, and we hope that studies of this general type will eventually be done with groups quite different in these respects.

Appendix
TWO

❧

Rank Order of Successful Aging by Style

WORLD OF WORK

Autonomous-Persistent (Top)

1. *School Is My Life—Female, Age 62.** This woman was distinguished by her devotion to her chosen profession of teaching. Her teaching was her life. Even her widowed mother, with whom she lived, came secondary. She took physical ills in stride and yielded to them only when necessary. Her only friends were other, equally devoted, teachers. At sixty-two she had not yet had to face the reality of retirement and perhaps she would not seem so stable when she did. But at the conclusion of the study her style was clearly World of Work 1. She was autonomous-persistent, at the top, and except for a 2 in alienation, based on her preoccupation with her work, she had a 1 in all other ratings.

2. *From Retirement to a New Career—Male, Age 64.* During the study this man retired from a semiskilled job he had held for many years, and became a minister. He was classified autonomous-precarious then, although it was noted that he was especially difficult to classify on the persistent-precarious continuum. It appeared his ministerial

* Ages given on the first, identifying line, are ages at the end of the study. Text in this appendix is given only for those cases not more fully described in the preceding chapters.

226

activities were wearing him out, and that he would have to retire a second time soon and would not have much to sustain him. However, when his social system was seen through the eyes of his significant others, and he himself was seen in round seven about a year and one-half later, it was clear he was now really a minister, and a successful one. In fact, from this material alone one would scarcely suspect that he had ever been anything else. His relations with his wife looked far better, and he had inner resources to sustain him. He was then classified autonomous-persistent, at the top. His style of life, as well as other characteristic uses of action energy, was rated 1.

3. *I Fell Into the Business—Male, Age 61.* This respondent owned and operated a small shop which he had inherited from his father. He was living with his second wife. He had one stepson, who moved in with them during the course of the study. He had a few relatives and friends who did not seem to be especially important in his life.

At the beginning of the study he expressed a lot of interest in going out at night, usually alone. He would come home from work, sleep until about nine o'clock and then go out. This pattern faded away during the course of the study. At about the middle of the study he made the following comment, "I am a drunkard but not a good one. I thought I was the champion worst husband, but my wife has found some in our neighborhood that are worse, so I am not even best at that."

During the first six rounds of interviewing, it appeared that he did not have much interest in his shop. His father had let it run down, and he had had a good deal of difficulty in building it up. On the basis of this evidence alone, he would have been given a rating of 3 on degree of clarity of style. One got a rather different picture the seventh round, five years after the start of the study. The respondent was full of life, said that he enjoyed people, and his one big complaint was that his wife was not companionable and was a perpetual complainer. He expressed a great deal of interest in his work and said he was getting very interesting jobs to do in the shop, all of which he enjoyed. He had slowed down ten years before but had not slowed down a bit since. Thus, through most of the study, he appeared as a man dominated by the World of Work, but a playboy and traveler at heart. In the last interview he was very enthusiastic about work and expressed many sentiments about moderation. He could not imagine himself retired, except as somewhat more time off for travel. His level of involvement in his social network was low, but he put more into it than he took out, and he would be able to go on this way indefinitely. He would probably be able to retire gradually, and perhaps never completely. He was rated 1 on alienation and coping, but 2 on style, anomie, and isolation.

4. *The Contented Salesman—Male, Age 65.*
5. *A Dreary Life—Female, Age 65.*
6. *Beyond the World of Work—Male, Age 85.*

Autonomous-Persistent (Middle)

7. *The Meticulously Functionally Specific—Male, Age 55.* At the beginning of the study this man, a responsible businessman, had recently separated from his wife. He had a son in whom he was rather disappointed.

This respondent liked to discuss things in abstract and general terms and seemed unable to reveal anything of his personal life. For his childhood period, his mother was mentioned as the most admired person because she was a good homemaker, but this, too, was said as something of an abstraction. His father was "all right," but should "have been more ambitious." As a young man he "supposed" his mother was still the most admired, but mentioned his admiration for doctors and lawyers as a group. It is clear that his college days were very important, and he frequently returned for reunions. He knew some "intellectuals" then, and had wistfully tried to reach beyond his ego boundaries ever since. He did not marry until the age of forty, and his only child was born when he was forty-one. Three years later he was divorced; he said he had "hated to do it." This first wife, when seen accidentally at the time of the first interview, had complained that he was very meticulous and hypercritical of her and of their son. From various clues he appeared more ashamed than sorry about the divorce. A year later he had remarried, to a woman of secretarial background.

This man was clearly oriented to the World of Work in a highly functionally specific way. He showed no signs of alienation, anomie, or personal disintegration, and was not greatly isolated. He had not started to disengage. He was autonomous-persistent now, in the middle group. He put little into his social system, but he took very little from it to keep him going. One might well wonder what would happen when the supports for this life style disappeared—esteem, prestige, and success associated with work. He might have done fairly well as an organization man in church or other secondary groups, or he might have become an "angry old man." He was in the World of Work and rated 1 on style. He was rated 1 on all action energy expressions except for a 2 on isolation.

8. *Unremitting Labor—Male, Age 57.* One interviewer succinctly summed up this case. "If indeed man expiates original sin through unremitting labor, then Mr. X is my candidate for the right hand of God." There is little that needs to be added to round out the picture of this foreign-born man. He was raised in extreme poverty and taught by observation and example that hard work was the only means to a successful life. According to his own life story, he had been a compulsive worker since he was thirteen and he still valued work over education—one of the few respondents to do so.

He was a very meticulous man, and in his contacts with the interviewers he gave lengthy anwers to all questions. Specific neutral behavior characterized most of his social situations. He was not cold or unfriendly, but all human intercourse, to be legitimate with him, had to have a productive purpose.

He, together with his wife and son, operated the family business, but on his wife's death he retired. Nevertheless, he continued to expend great amounts of action energy and maintained his life style to the last contact.

Obviously, his style was rated 1, and he was listed as autonomous-persistent in the middle. Other ratings were 1 for anomie and coping, and 2 for alienation and isolation.

9. *Slightly Overworked—Male, Age 60.* This man lived in a household with his wife. He had one stepson who lived with him for a while at the beginning of the interview period, but left, returned, and then left again to get married. The respondent was engaged in maintenance and repair work, the nature of which was so exacting that he worked six days a week (seven in the summer) with occasional days off and a brief paid vacation each year. He had a few friends and some relatives, including a father, in the area, with whom he interacted as much as time permitted. He faced mandatory retirement at the age of sixty-five. He was placed in the middle of the autonomous-persistent group. He was rated 1 in everything but isolation, which was a 2.

10. *Deaths in the Family—Male, Age 80.* This partially retired salesman had found it necessary to adjust throughout his life to an incredible series of deaths which included, by the end of the study, ten of his twelve children, his wife, son-in-law, parents, two sisters, and three brothers. He worked away at survival in spite of all this

and, despite his age, he was considering remarriage to a woman he had met at the weekly dances he felt vigorous enough to attend. He was in the middle of the success category, and rated 1 in all characteristic uses of action energy.

Autonomous-Persistent (Bottom)

11. *I Was Saved and Life Became Earnest—Male, Age 65.* This busy man who lived with his wife was sixty-five at the end of the study. As a professional man in the field of religion, his work was the central theme of his life. Because his work involved living fully, he was involved in many lives deeply, but his own action system was built around work itself. He was quite anxious about himself, and his aging and gradual disengagement troubled him greatly. He paid much more attention to himself and his health than he had in younger years.

Because of his work-centered life, his style was World of Work 1. He was autonomous-persistent, at the bottom, but rated 1 on all the other ratings.

12. *Let's Make Money—Male, Age 62.*

13. *From the World of Music: An Old Refrainer—Male, Age 74.* This music teacher enjoyed looking back over his past as a boy in Europe and his manhood as an immigrant. Music had been his life and, although he now held a respected position in the community, had a lovely daughter who was quite dear to him, and had countless acquaintances, nothing was as important to him as his music. He was aware that age was creeping up but he did not let it bother him at all. He was at the bottom of the autonomous-persistent category and was rated 1 in anomie, alienation, and coping. His isolation and style were rated 2.

14. *No Ambition—Just Worked—Female, Age 73.* This shy woman, whose style of World of Work persisted into her aging years, had always been aware of a pull to the style of Living Alone. Orphaned at an early age, she was unable to form any really close, warm, affective bonds with anyone. She reported the happiest time of her life to have been her marriage, which lasted only six years and had concluded forty years ago with her husband's death. She had worked ever since until her forced retirement at age sixty-five. At sixty-eight, when first interviewed by the study, her sole employment was the care of an invalid neighbor. She worked hard at this and provided well for the neighbor, but there was no indication of her doing this as a way of maintaining a style of Familism. On the other hand, it was clearly just one more job. She missed working regularly, and she in-

tended to keep on doing "one thing and another" as long as she could. She withdrew increasingly into her own resources and, except for this one neighbor, saw almost no one. She was at the bottom of the autonomous-persistent group; her use of action energy gave her a 1 on style and coping, for she managed to work on in her style despite enormous disengagement, but she also rated a 2 on anomie and alienation and 3 on isolation.

15. *Not Enough Responsibility—Male, Age 78.*

Autonomous-Precarious (*Top*)

16. *Mr. Almost Average—Male, Age 62.* This insurance salesman lived with his somewhat younger wife. He had one son, whom he saw on Sundays. He did not have to retire and planned to stay at work as long as he was able. Things went along about the same way over the five-year period. He was put in the precarious category because his life and his emotional poise were so thoroughly involved in work and not much else. He was rated 2 on alienation, anomie, and coping, with a 1 on isolation and style.

17. *The Protestant Ethic—Male, Age 75.* This long-time businessman inadvertently retired himself by selling his business, as he was unable to find other employment, and so gradually moved into a rather anomic kind of life. His life space suddenly became much more constricted. He was beginning to disengage and in the process became more dependent on his wife without giving her much in return. He was at the top of the autonomous-precarious group, and his style was 1. He was given 2 on all other ratings.

Autonomous-Precarious (*Middle*)

18. *Out on an Intellectual Limb—Male, Age 64.* This music teacher was a tall, aesthetic-looking man, the stereotype of the "arty" person, and his strange behavior, his remoteness from his children by his previous marriage, and his detachment from society did not fit the pattern of the typical person in the upper middle class to which he belonged.

He and his ill wife and ten-year-old daughter lived in a large rundown home surrounded by an unkempt yard. His day was divided into the time he taught and the time he spent at home—which was all the rest of the day, except for attending various musical functions. He did all his work at home and did not especially enjoy or dislike any part of it. He claimed to do some of all the tasks around the house except for cleaning clothes and the heavy housework, which was provided for commercially. Because of the illness of his wife he had to operate the home in large part. He attended church on weekends, but solely because he conducted the choir; religion meant little to him. His daughter made it clear that she did *not* go to the same church as her father; she wanted to go to hers. All other organizations in which he participated were associated with music.

The psychologist found him to be a man who so intellectualized all his emotional behavior that he was very difficult to get to know, much less to analyze.

He was definitely alienated—by his own choice, because there were many in the community who liked his music and would have been most willing to be friends. He was, in fact, as much a social isolate as he dared to be.

From early childhood, nothing, with the exception of his mother, meant much to him but his music, so he was judged to be in the World of Work. Further judgment made him autonomous-precarious. The autonomous aspect of his life was quite clear, but he was judged precarious because of the extremely intellectualized handling of his emotions which led to speculation of possible collapse under pressure. He was rated 2 in anomie, 3 in alienation, and 2 in isolation. He was rated 1 in style and coping.

19. *Work, Work, Work—Male, Age 57.* This hard-drinking, unskilled laborer and his wife had no children. They both worked. He and his wife seemed to provide each other with the minimal emotional satisfaction they required. This man's value system was one of accepting the inevitability of work. He never had any great ambition to get ahead. There were elements of precariousness in his life. Should anything happen to his wife or sister, who were his sole sources of stability, he would be thrown out of emotional balance quite readily. Consequently, he was placed in the middle of the autonomous-precarious group and rated 1 on style and anomie and 2 on everything else.

20. *No Hobby Except My Work—Female, Age 73.*

Autonomous-Precarious (Bottom)

21. *Brink of Disaster—Male, Age 55.* Had this man not held a style of World of Work, it is doubtful he would have been able to avoid a complete mental breakdown.

He was the owner of a small business. During the time of the study, his wife committed suicide and he had to try to re-establish the family stability for his two teen-age children. He was tremendously upset by the event and was unable to do much more for the children than provide them food and shelter. They were left to their own resources and little action energy was exchanged between father and children.

To avoid facing social contact, he retreated into theoretical mathematics as a hobby and absorbed himself in his work by day.

He exhibited a great emotional disturbance throughout the study and was not greatly improved at the end. Consequently, he was rated as autonomous-precarious at the bottom. His style was clear and, therefore, rated 1. Anomie and alienation were profound and were rated 3, while isolation and coping were rated 2.

22. *Grounded—Male, Age 61.*

23. *Never Underestimate the Power of a Woman—Male, Age 61.* This man had had two previous divorces and, until he met his present wife, had been caught up in wild living and aimless job drifting. This wife helped him become a trusted city employee, a role he valued greatly, and an active worker in the church. He was quite dependent on his wife emotionally, even though he played an active role in their marriage. Therefore, if his wife's health became very bad, his situation would become precarious. In the bottom group of autonomous-precarious, he was rated 2 on style, with a strong underlying style of Couplehood. He was also rated 2 on coping and isolation but 1 on alienation and anomie.

There were no World of Work cases ranked dependent-persistent, nor were there any in the top rank of dependent-precarious.

Dependent-Precarious (Middle)

24. *The Slipping Mask—Male, Age 56.*

Dependent-Precarious (Bottom)

25. *Nightingale With Clipped Wings—Female, Age 80.*

FAMILISM

Autonomous-Persistent (Top)

26. *I Want to Retire—Male, Age 64.* This man, who worked in a small business, although divorced and living alone, had a clear style of Familism 1 due to his preoccupation with his mother, his daughter,

and his siblings. His chief regret in life was that he had not had more children. He also wished he had not been divorced. His family depended on him for many things, both material and emotional. Consequently, he was autonomous-persistent, at the top. Because he felt some alienation due to his divorce, his ratings were 1 on anomie, isolation, and coping, but 2 on alienation.

27. *The Schmaltzes—Female, Age 66.* One interviewer described this woman as "just plain schmaltzy." She was a good example of Familism, and well adjusted. At sixty-six she lived with her husband, a retired salesman, and they both doted on their married son and his family.

She had survived a mixed religion marriage and acute illness without losing her faith in her family, herself, or her church.

She had a style of Familism 1 and was autonomous-persistent, at the top, with ratings of 1 in all other categories.

28. *Pain and Giving—Female, Age 72.*

29. *American Familism in Pure Culture—Female, Age 55.*

30. *Small-Scale Familism—Male, Age 64.* This man was one of only three foreign-born respondents in the panel. He came to Kansas City at the age of fifteen and had lived there ever since, working for one of the large industries as a semiskilled laborer. He lived with his wife, five years younger than he, and his thirty-four-year-old son who had never married and who had a skilled trade. On Saturdays he did a great deal of work around the house and garden. Sundays, he fished with his son and some friends. His wife indicated that he would never have a problem with retirement because there were so many things he liked to do around the home. His wife became crippled during the course of the study, and he was much concerned about her. He spoke of her as a wonderful person and a good housekeeper, wife, and mother, and he tried to help her as much as possible. He always considered her opinions. He was quite angry at one point when a neighbor had burned his fence and "a lovely rosebush." He had not spoken to the neighbor since, but the neighbor would pay for the new fence, and, he said, "We will send them a Christmas card." At the age of forty-five, he said, he would have fought the neighbor—illustrating a general tendency for easing off with age.

By the end of the study the wife had undergone an amputation and was learning to use an artificial leg. They were looking forward to the retirement of the respondent in two months, and the wife thought she would be able to use the artificial leg with his help. He was still fishing with his son on Sundays. When asked about the worst things in life, about all he could think of was, "I don't like wash dishes for one t'ing. I tell truth!" He said he liked to be out in the sun where he always felt better and when he retired he would like to move out on some lake. He said he never napped, and commented, "I enjoy the eatin' part, but I don't see how they enjoy the sleepin' part if they got anyt'ing to do." There was some interaction with a few cousins on holidays. His bills were all paid up. He and his wife were both the last of their families. He was afraid to go overseas when members of his family of orientation died because of the wars, the Nazis, and the Communists; he was afraid he might be held as a spy. The best thing in life was his change of hours from the night shift to the day shift, and his imminent retirement. The worst thing in life was the amputation of his wife's leg.

This is a case of Familism on a very small scale, with a strong underpinning of Couplehood. The smallness of the scale is partly due to circumstances, as he was the only member of his family of orientation to come over from the old country. The world of hard work had occupied much of his life but it did not become his style. He regretted being the last of his family and also regretted that his son had not married by the time he reached his late thirties. He was about as autonomous-persistent as one can get. He had done as much for his wife as she had done for him—even the dishes, which he hated doing. He looked forward to retirement, and disengagement was no problem at all. He was 1 in anomie, isolation, alienation, and coping and had a style of 2.

31. *Motherly Independence—Female, Age 64.* This widow kept house for one son and maintained close but not smothering ties with her other son and an adopted daughter. Besides them, she was close to an indigent family who also needed her, she felt. She liked keeping house, being with family, and doing church work. In response to the story questions, she was "sure" Jones would not take the job, because he preferred his family. She reported herself to be very content with aging, and her only unbalanced dependence was a financial one. Her son supported her, but she took this as her due, and there was no emotional disturbance. Her life was centered in an affective, mature, mothering role to anyone who was lucky enough to be in her social system.

Her strong sense of Familism (rating 1) in such diffuse directions enabled her to age most successfully. The ratings were easily arrived at. She was classed as autonomous-persistent at the top, with complementary ratings of 1 on anomie, alienation, isolation, and coping.

32. *The Ministering Barber—Male, Age 71.* Some people live for their own selfish goals, but some live to share the best of life with all who come into their social system. This man fell in the latter class.

He lived with his wife near their two grown daughters, and ran a one-man barbershop in town. His wife worked, and their schedules were rather independent. But he was clearly fond of her, even though they saw little of each other.

He spoke as if life was a careless existence to him. For example, he said religion was unimportant to him and that the most important things were eating and sleeping. Nevertheless, beneath this tough exterior, the interviewers found a warm, gentle person, ever sensitive to the needs of others. The indigent got free haircuts, his close friend was waited on hand and foot in his last illness, and his son-in-law's debts became his own. Home was really the focal point in his busy life. Repeatedly he tried to convince the interviewers of his hard nature and tough ways, but he had to admit that a perfect day for him was doing just as he was doing.

Thus, he was classed as Familism, with a rating of 1, and autonomous-persistent at the top. Because of his superficial hard way, he was rated 2 on alienation, but 1 on anomie, isolation, and coping.

33. *Family, Friends, and Fishing—Male, Age 56.* This man presents a good example of American working-class Familism, with the interesting variant of having had one child rather late in life. At the beginning of the study, this man, at fifty-one, was living with his wife, a son of nineteen, another son of seven, and a daughter, age three. He was a skilled worker who had his own shop near his home. The oldest son was studying to be a professional man. They were living in a new house which they had built themselves and of which they were very proud. They lived in a small working-class suburb and liked to be among working-class people and to live outside of the city proper. He thought it was a very good place for children. They liked their neighbors and commented that the neighbors took care of older people. He, himself, did work for old people and did not charge them for it. He enjoyed watching television but had very little time for it because he worked some evenings and the family usually had friends in on the others. He enjoyed fishing on vacations. His son helped out in the shop on Saturdays; otherwise he worked alone. He was proud that he had been his own boss since the age of forty-five. He and his wife were the sole owners of the business, and she helped out with the bookkeeping. He named eight friends and said he had many more. The closest ones were a couple of fishing buddies.

He had no plans for retirement, but was able to pace himself and expected to slow down gradually. In fact, he claimed that he had already slowed up considerably, although he was still working full-time, some evenings, and on Saturdays. His father had been an easygoing sort who had managed to retire at the age of fifty to go fishing. He stated that the most important thing in his life was raising the family.

His son graduated from the professional school during the course of the study, and was teaching part-time. The respondent was very proud of his son. Fishing, and some hunting, were frequently mentioned during the course of the interviews. He said all times of his life had been good, and, in fact, he had been able to get a job and hold it during the Depression. It was just after the Second World War that he had started in business for himself, and friends had helped him to do it.

By the end of the study, at the age of fifty-six, he talked even more about fishing and hunting and said that he managed to have more time for recreation now. His eldest son had married, and he saw him about once a week. He also saw his lodge brothers and many old friends frequently, and helped his neighbors and friends with various chores. He had more money, but he spent more, particularly on better fishing and hunting equipment, eating out with his wife, and paying his lodge dues.

There is no doubt at all that he should be classed as autonomous-persistent at the top. His characteristic modes of use of action energy were all rated 1. This case is very similar to the one described in Chapter Three, "American Familism in Pure Culture." Although the content of the action system is somewhat different in the two cases, the structural and functional properties of the action systems of the individuals in question, one a man, the other a woman, are very similar. Although technically they fall into different social class groups, one in the lower middle and the other in upper lower, one senses very little difference in ethos. "American Familism in Pure Culture" had an ISC (Index of Social Class) rating of 64 and "Family, Friends, and Fishing" a rating of 52, but it can be seen that there can be very little difference in ethos within this range of the scale.

34. *Solidly Familistic—Female, Age 63.* This was the case of a woman living with her husband in a comfortable but not elegant home surrounded by a large yard and beautiful garden. Her husband was a skilled worker of foreign background. They were Catholic. They had two daughters and one son, all living in Kansas City.

Her health was reasonably good, and she was not preoccupied

with health problems. The family was financially solvent. She obviously got a great deal of emotional satisfaction from and gave emotional satisfaction to her family, which included the grown children and grandchildren. Her characteristic modes of use of action energy were all rated 1.

35. *Familism Returned to the Country—Male, Age 69.*

36. *Wim, Wam, and Wigger—Female, Age 73.*

37. *Familism Persistent in Hardship—Female, Age 70.* This respondent showed true persistence in style as her name indicates. At the beginning of the study she lived with her mechanic husband, her daughter, son-in-law, and two grandchildren. She and her husband, who were never prosperous at best, had been foster parents to over twenty-five children over the years, in addition to their own. It was a great source of pleasure to her. Now, in her later years, as she looked back, she saw her life's work to have been caring for her family.

At the end of the study her husband was dying of cancer and she focused all her wifely and motherly energy on him. The two of them had moved into their own apartment next door to the daughter so they could be more independent. Her health was rather bad, too, but she still showed her well-balanced exchange of action energy. This rated her as autonomous-persistent at the top, and her style was distinctly Familism 1. She was rated 2 on anomie. All her other ratings were 1.

38. *Aging Well in Widowhood—Female, Age 74.* At the beginning of the study this woman had been widowed for six years and said that she was used to it. She had lived in Kansas City all of her life and, in fact, had been born on the same block where she was still living. She had had one son and one daughter. The son took her grocery shopping on Saturdays. She liked to have the children and grandchildren in frequently. She had one brother in Kansas City to whom she felt very close. She saw her son almost every day and her daughter once every two months. She wrote to a sister about once a week and saw another sister in Kansas City about once every two weeks. In the course of the study she took a trip to New York to see the new "grandbaby" of another sister and brother-in-law. She came from a strongly Familistic background, with a lot of people around when she was growing up. She looked back at the best time of her life as when her children were little and her husband was alive. The worst time was during the Depression, but they did own their own home and managed to save it. Her answers to the story questions were all strongly Familistic. She persisted in this general pattern throughout the study. She was rated 1 on all her characteristic uses of action energy.

39. *Regretfully Aging—Female, Age 77.* At the beginning of the study this woman, at age seventy-four, was a widow, living with her unmarried daughter and close to her son and his family. Her husband had been a buyer for a firm, and they had had a good, happy life in Kansas City. When the study first encountered her, she was very busy keeping house for her daughter, visiting with her grandsons, and visiting neighbors. But, as was so often the case, the time of the study was long enough that she was observed becoming more isolated as the grandchildren grew up and went out on their own, and her friends died. Her daughter became ill, and she had additional home chores which isolated her still more. She regretted aging, but she disengaged gracefully and managed to be a real source of emotional strength for her family. In contrast to some mothers, she was not, in her own words, "an ambitious mother." Therefore, she was clearly autonomous-persistent, at the top, with a pure style of Familism 1, tending to be of a closed-system type, and rated 1 on all but isolation, which was 2.

40. *Golden Familism—Female, Age 80.*

41. *I Raised a Good Family—Female, Age 76.* This respondent had been widowed twice. She had had five sons and one daughter. There were twelve grandchildren and six great-grandchildren. She came from a farm background. She lived in Kansas City for fifty-two years and liked it very much because she had raised her family there and felt it was a good place for that. At the time of the study she was living in a low-rent housing project. At the beginning of the study her second husband, eighty years old, was alive. She spoke of him as a fine man with a good disposition, and said they were always together, and that she even went fishing with him. All her children had turned out well. She felt closest to one daughter, but very close to the rest. Two of the sons had had problems with drinking and she did not approve of that but did not reject them. She said she felt about sixty years old. If she had her life to live over she would get more education and do more studying of the Bible. However, she would still like to raise a large family. Her health became a little worse during the course of the study but this did not bother her particularly. Her second husband died at about the middle of the study. She found her weekends to be the hardest, but neighbors did occasionally visit. As her own health began to fail even more toward the end of the study, her children rallied around. She is another good example of strong Familism, together with a high degree of success in life, and has been rated 1 on all her characteristic uses of action energy.

42. *Widowed Early—Female, Age 77.* This woman was widowed during the flu epidemic in 1917. She then went to work and raised her two sons and one daughter. She lived alone at the time of the study. She is a particularly clear case of Familism with a rating of 2, again illustrating that the clarity of style and the clarity with which the judgment can be made are two different matters. She had enjoyed work and did not like retirement at first, but then became used to it. Her answers to the story questions were quite characteristic. Jones would not take the job *if* he were a family man. Franklin probably gave the money to save his son but it would do no good. Mrs. Birch was foolish to want to remarry.

The respondent reported that she missed her husband, and was very close to her daughter and a small group of fairly intimate friends. Her success category was quite clear—she had always been well in balance. Disengagement would be no problem for her. She was rated 1 on anomie, isolation, and coping, but 2 on alienation. This, too, presents an interesting situation in terms of the relation between alienation and isolation. She was alienated from the dominant value system, since she tended very strongly toward the value systems of the hate groups. These were her true values at heart, and she thought that the whole society was going to the dogs. But, in general, she managed not to express these values when it would alienate others from her, and hence, did not become isolated. Had she let others become alienated from her, she would have been rated 3 on alienation. As it was, she was rated 2.

43. *Successful Disengagement—Male, Age 73.*

44. *Successful Retirement—Male, Age 75.*

45. *I Hold My Own—Female, Age 76.*

46. *Devoutly Religious—Female, Age 75.* This respondent had been widowed for three years at the beginning of the study. She had had four sons and four daughters. There were thirty-three grandchildren and twenty-nine great-grandchildren. She lived alone in a low-rent housing project during the study. She came from a farm background, and had always been a housewife. The eight children ranged from twenty-eight to fifty-four years of age. Her daily round consisted of housework, Bible reading, and occasional visits to sick friends. She had no interest in television. She said she was never bored or tired, and when she felt a little that way she turned to the Bible. Saturdays were spent shopping and preparing for her Sunday school lesson. Sundays were occupied with church and Sunday school. She thought of her husband as a wonderful Christian man and "daddy."

They had had a happy life, worked hard together, and had not minded working hard. The children did not all belong to her church, a conservative Protestant sect, but she did not like them to smoke. However, they were all very kind to her. Most of the sons were laborers, although one was in office work. This pattern persisted through the four years that she was seen. She was strongly Familistic and spread her familism to church and friends. At the very end of the study her health began to fail but this did not change her basic action system at all, nor was she preoccupied with it. She was rated 1 on all characteristic uses of action energy.

47. *Mother and Daughter—Female, Age 90.* This respondent was born on a farm, as was the case with many of the very old respondents in this panel. She had first been widowed toward the end of the nineteenth century and again in the late 1930's. She had had two sons and one daughter, and there were several grandchildren and great-grandchildren. She lived with the daughter, age fifty-two, who was a school teacher. She had lived for twenty-eight years in a suburb of Kansas City and liked it very much. She would not like to live in the city proper, nor in a smaller community. She said that, until she was seventy-five or seventy-six years old, she could do all she wanted to and had an excellent appetite. At the time of the study she napped two hours, on doctor's orders. She watched television in the evenings. The preceding evening she had gone to the country to see her brother. She said she was by herself a good deal of the time because her daughter was away teaching and had her own clubs and friends. However, she very much enjoyed having company in the evening, which she indicated was her daughter's company. She had not been to regular church services in the last six or seven years; however, she did attend some church activities and read the Bible. She had two brothers and two sisters in Missouri and two sons in Missouri, all of whom she saw fairly frequently. However, she rarely saw the grandchildren or great-grandchildren. She knew all the people in the apartment house in which she lived and did some visiting. Two years later she said she had not felt quite so well the preceding summer. She hurt somewhat, and her head "felt funny." She refused to answer the question about the most unpleasant thing that had happened recently, but let the interviewer understand that it had something to do with her daughter, and the interviewer knew that the daughter had been dating recently. The best things were that she was still up and around and could read. She said the worst thing about her life at that time was being somewhat crippled and being unable to get out very much. She did

not like being told what to do. She described having been the oldest in a large family and having to act like a mother to the younger children. Later that same year she mentioned not liking to be alone, especially when the daughter's boyfriend took her away on Sunday.

The following spring she described her life's work as having been her family. It had been a long-standing ambition and she was very proud of it. A year and one-half later, the picture looked about the same. Whenever her daughter's bridge club came she stayed up and enjoyed watching. She said she was not old in spirit.

On the surface, this woman might appear to be "dependent" on her daughter. She had, in fact, organized her action system in a way which depended on the presence of the daughter, and was somewhat upset by any potential threats to this arrangement, such as a boyfriend. However, in terms of balance of action energy, she was still autonomous, and the daughter derived a great deal of satisfaction from doing things for her mother. She was rated 1 on anomie, alienation, and coping, but 2 on isolation. That rating is due to the fact that she would have liked to have had much more company. She was clearly Familistic but has been rated 2 on clarity of style because she was not quite as distinctly Familistic as some of the other respondents.

Autonomous-Persistent (Middle)

48. *Early Retirement—Male, Age 57.* This prosperous Jewish businessman, a life-long resident of the city, found it convenient to retire in his early fifties. He cherished the thought of taking up a career in art to fill up the hours not occupied by family, civic, social, and religious obligations. But his art was not well received by the critics, and he was forced to abandon his dream. However, there was work to be done in the community, and since he had the time to do it, he devoted himself to fufilling his moral obligation to serve and to encouraging his only son's checkered career. This man was in the middle of the autonomous-persistent group and was rated 1 on everything, including style.

49. *Well Worth Trying Again—Female, Age 55.* This teacher and her husband never had children, but she greatly enjoyed her two stepdaughters who, because of their ages at the time of her marriage, were more like sisters to her. Her first husband died and she had loved him a great deal, but was mature enough to make a happy second marriage. She was greatly contented with her way of life. Her work interested her, but was not a primary concern—it was just something she drifted into. She actively helped others around her and showed

herself to be generally autonomous-persistent. She was placed in the middle of this class. Her style was Familism 3, and her other ratings were all 1.

50. *Tolerant But Firm—Male, Age 67.* This small-time professional man and his wife had three grown children, all living away from home. Nevertheless, his family was the chief concern of his busy, intense life. He was very active in his church, and it represented for him a still larger family of concern.

He was generally stable and in good health, although quite anxious about what retirement might mean to him. He seemed unable to cope with this idea very well. Since he was a family man, the frequent visits of his children and grandchildren were very important to him.

His style was one of Familism 2, largely due to his underlying style of World of Work. He was autonomous-persistent in the middle, and rated 1 on other ratings, but 2 on coping.

51. *Let's Plan—Female, Age 69.* This woman lived with her husband, who was a skilled worker. She would have liked to plan the lives of her son and his family who lived in the east, but she settled for an active social and civic life for herself and her husband. She and her husband spent a good deal of their time remodeling their house. She was rated 2 in style and alienation and 1 in everything else.

52. *Snail's Pace—Male, Age 68.* This man lived with his wife, and together they ran a small apartment and rooming house which they owned. They had a number of friends who dropped in on them, but, he said, "We don't go anyplace." He thought lodges were a stabilizing influence and his father had been an Odd Fellow, but, he said, "I didn't need this. I stabilized myself." They frequently left the apartment house to take rides in their car. Their daughter and son-in-law lived with them. He said he was always together with his wife; "She's a darn good worker." He could not name any close friends. He was very fond of playing solitaire. A nephew came around frequently for meals. He had a brother living in Kansas City with whom he was in touch by phone a few times a year. He saw another brother in a nearby town a few times a year. His life went on essentially the same way during the five years of the study. He commented that he was "never much of a fellow to circulate" and liked "to watch people go by." He said he had never had any life's work—"After you are married, that's your central interest." His daily round looked the same at the end of the study as it did at the beginning, and he commented, "I do things when I feel like it." A favorite aphorism of his was, "A snail's pace, if organized, will get you somewhere."

He was in balance at a very slow pace. There was no issue at all on disengagement, and he could go on this way indefinitely. He is a good example of a very mild Familism. None of the other styles apply, but this one does, mildly. He was somewhat isolated, but that was entirely of his own choosing. He was rated 3 on style.

53. *Driving Independence—Female, Age 69.* Although predominantly Familistic in style, this woman had an uncommon underlying style of World of Work. She had four grown children and spent a great deal of activist World of Work type energy, not only in caring for her retired husband's needs, but also in sewing for grandchildren, refinishing furniture, and the like. Her first husband died when her children were babies and this was the worst time of her life, but she rallied with characteristic energy and actually regretted she had not made better use of her talents when younger.

She responded interestingly to the story of Jones by saying Jones did not want to take the job, but Jones' wife thought he should take it to provide more necessities and luxuries for the family.

At the end of the study her husband had died, and she was consumed with doing things for the family to prove her independence. Disengagement was minimal and unwelcome.

Her style might have appeared to be pure Familism, however, her attitude was not so much that she enjoyed doing for the children as that doing for the children was something to do. She would have been an excellent career woman, and she even stated how happy she was when her children finally grew up and were less demanding of her. She was autonomous-persistent in the middle—not at the top—because she was driving so hard there seemed to be some measure of protest in the extent of her activity. Nevertheless, she was generally so successful and well balanced in her social and personal life that ratings of 1 in anomie, alienation, and coping were justified, but she rated a 2 in isolation because of her increasing tendency to bury herself in her work.

54. *My Dream Was Over—Female, Age 76.* A former public health nurse, this widow kept house and did most of the chores for her retired brother and sister with whom she lived. Her heart was not in the kind of life she led—her dreams had died with her husband, she said—but being strongly Familistic and very succoring, she made the best of it. Her siblings were almost totally dependent on her, which she accepted grudgingly but with grace.

She was definitely disengaging, and it worried her. She also had a growing sense of alienation as her career work was farther and farther behind her and her life became more and more interrelated with her siblings. Her style was Familism 2, which accounts for the anomie 2 and alienation 2; she would have had less feelings of separation if she had been a pure Familism type. Her closeness with siblings gave her an isolation rating of 1, and her over-all efficiency in time of trouble rated her 1 in coping. She was autonomous-persistent in the middle range.

Autonomous-Persistent (Bottom)

55. *I Wished Upon a Star But Now It's Too Late—Female, Age 57.* Even the significant others knew this fine, pleasant, hard-working woman wished with all her heart that she could have been a wife and mother. She illustrated well how a person can be familistic even without having family in the conventional sense.

At the beginning of the study she was fifty-two and held down a responsible job as a school administrator. She fell into the job quite by accident—she had been teaching most of her life—but by hard work and quiet perseverance she made a success of her work.

Her days were devoted to her job and her nights and weekends to social and professional organizations. She chatted with her neighbors, but had no special friends among them. In fact, she had only five fairly close friends, although she contacted many others on a friendly basis in connection with her work.

She was a rather shy person until she relaxed, and then was quite gracious and charming. Her real closeness was with her sister and her mother. The sister was everything the respondent was not (and in many ways wished she were). She was outgoing, married, and had a family. The respondent was very fond of the sister and her family and spent much of her emotional energy planning and thinking about them. She lacked the fulfillment of husband and family (which she mentioned often), and felt the weight of her years, even at fifty-two. She looked forward to retirement because her work was not her chief interest. This woman was a good example of a person who was a very hard-working, capable, and conscientious employee, who behaved in this manner because of her personal character and personality—not because she loved the work. Upon retirement she planned to devote herself to hobbies and to the care of her mother.

She admitted she had less desire to go to social and cultural events and had fewer friends in. She showed a slight trend toward social isolation but no real alienation or disintegration, and was rated 1 on all but isolation. She was judged as autonomous-persistent, at the bottom, based on her need to give to her mother, her sister, and her work, but she was not work oriented. She was distinctly Familism 1 in style.

56. *When the Kids Were Home—Male, Age 63.* This businessman had two married daughters and lived in a nice house with his wife, a part-time teacher. He shared jobs with his wife and enjoyed most the time spent with her. Active in religion, he felt a great need for it, especially when he became faced with a serious illness that threatened his whole life pattern. Nevertheless he persevered in independent action and met his handicaps head-on. He coped unusually well, but his life satisfactions were decreased noticeably.

Because of the continued major physical threat to his life pattern and the obvious life dissatisfaction this brought on, he was placed in the bottom category of autonomous-persistent. But, despite his fears, his coping behavior enabled him to be put in the rating of 1 in anomie, alienation, isolation, and, certainly, coping.

His style of life was Familism 1, with a good strong underpinning of Living Fully. This enabled him to relax into the family when he was forced to by ill health and yet continue to cope by using his drive for living fully.

57. *A Nice Little World—Male, Age 65.* This railroad engineer lived with his wife, and worked various shifts during the course of the study. He loved his work, where he was highly respected by workmates, and he loved his family, wife, children, and grandchildren. He went through the Depression and suffered a good deal but came out well. There was little evidence of change over the five-year period, and he was clearly autonomous-persistent, in the bottom group. He was given a 1 on all ratings.

58. *Job's Descendant—Female, Age 69.* This woman taught school and cared for her old mother. Her husband was a guard at an industrial plant, and they had a twenty-four-year-old son. During the study her mother died about the time the son married and moved away, so she began to care for her husband's father even though her husband had a heart attack. Next, her husband died, and she developed a severe diabetic condition. Finally, the father-in-law died, leaving her alone. Surprisingly she weathered all this with courage and was even brightly anticipating her second grandchild at the close of the study. At the bottom of the autonomous-persistent group, she rated 1 on everything but isolation, which was 2.

59. *The Breadwinner—Female, Age 56.* This woman lived with her husband, a semiskilled worker who had been out of work for some

time, and worked only sporadically during the study. She had been working for three years, six days a week, and continued to do so during the course of the study. She had managed to take a trip to the west coast, went bowling regularly with her married daughter, saw other members of her family, and helped her children through divorces and other emotional crises. At the bottom of her success category, she received a 1 in all ratings.

60. *A Good Friend—Female, Age 66*. As a widow, this woman's life revolved around her married son, daughter, and grandchildren. She worked with the school system. She was very active in her church and went square dancing weekly. If her family were to move away, she would probably change her style of life to Living Fully. At the bottom of the success category, she was 1 in all ratings.

61. *My Terrible Neighbors—Female, Age 74*. One interviewer described this woman as a "miserable, selfish, critical woman who feels superior to her friends and environment."

With her husband, a former salesman, dead, and no job interest of her own, all she had to do was spy on the neighbors and collect the gossip of the housing project in which she lived. The one bright spot in her life was her married daughter, and although there were no grandchildren, she still enjoyed spending time with the daughter when the daughter's husband was not at home. She considered the son-in-law a selfish and thoughtless man. She saw a few friends—but rarely. Because of her rugged independence and her determination to live on her own, away from the daughter, she was classed as autonomous-persistent, at the bottom, and her style was a rather impure Familism 3. She was also rated 3 on alienation and 2 on all the others.

Autonomous-Precarious (*Top*)

62. *Passive Parenthood Fading Away—Male, Age 54*. This optical worker headed a household of five children. He had seen three other children leave home already. Retirement attracted him, but he could not afford it. He had worked steadily at being a good father but was getting tired of the routine. His family was still most important to him but he just did not feel like giving out as much any more. He was at the top of the autonomous-precarious group. He rated a 1 in style, alienation, and isolation, but a 2 in coping and anomie.

63. *God Gave Us Children—Female, Age 60*. At the beginning of the study this respondent was living with her husband, who was not very well and had been unable to work for a few months. She had

raised seven children, the youngest of whom, a boy, was still at home and in high school. In the earliest interviews she seemed to have Familism as a rather weak style and to be generally frustrated. Her husband was just around the house and was not interested in doing very much, and had been this way even before he became ill. Later on she took a part-time job, from nine to three, and perked up considerably. She almost seemed to have a frustrated style of World of Work. About the middle of the study her husband died, and she took over very strongly to see that her youngest son got through school. Also, it became apparent that her relations with her other children were rather close. The most important thing in life to her then became raising the boy. She was rather worried about him and felt he was not turning out quite as she wished. Toward the end of the study she expressed her Familism very clearly indeed. She felt very close to two of her daughters and one of the sons, not the one living at home. When asked about her life's work, she said, without hesitation, that it was raising a family. And she added, "God just gave them to us." At the very end of the study she was "seeing a gentleman who is awful good to the kids, and we go there a lot." He was a caller for square dancing and she considered her hobby to be square dancing, which she had never been able to do with her husband who had no interest in it. It became increasingly clear that she took her Familism for granted and thus did not emphasize it as much as others might have done.

She also expressed a certain amount of loneliness toward the end of the study. She derived a great deal of satisfaction in working in a rather Familistic environment. If she had to stop working and if she lost the boyfriend, she might become quite dependent on one or more of her children, but in the dependent position she would probably be persistent. She showed some signs of anomie, alienation, and isolation, and her style was rated 2. On coping, however, she was clearly rated 1.

Autonomous-Precarious (Middle)

    64. *Frustrated Familism—Female, Age 62.*

    65. *What's Left?—Female, Age 79.* This woman had just lost her husband and brother as the study began. She lived at home with one unmarried daughter and worked nights as a cleaning woman. She hated to admit she was aging and still did a great deal for her five children. They were her primary focus. Toward the end of the study she retired and found herself growing increasingly "blue" staying home

all day. Her growing dependence on her children was an added source of dissatisfaction. She was judged to be in the middle of the autonomous-precarious group and was given a 2 in all ratings.

Autonomous-Precarious (Bottom)

66. *Rural Familism Transplanted—Male, Age 56.*

67. *Family First—Female, Age 61.* This woman and her truckdriver husband had seen their four children grow up, marry, and leave home. She feared retirement for her husband, feeling that it would mean complete deterioration for him. She was a nervous, tired woman, beginning to disengage and fearful of her mental stability. She was at the bottom of the autonomous-precarious group and rated 1 on style but 2 in all the other ratings.

68. *The Heavy Loser—Female, Age 55.* This respondent had two strikes against her—a speech defect, and female disorders which resulted in a hysterectomy in her early twenties. When only twelve, she had begun work as a mother's helper, and she had worked ever since. By hard effort she got her nurse's training and had made this her life's profession. When still comparatively young, she met her husband and helped him get through a mechanics training school. She continued nursing. As the years rolled by she ate more and more, despite her doctor's warnings, so that at fifty she weighed at least 300 pounds and was having to give up a great deal of her nursing career. They lived in a working-class neighborhood and the family included an adopted daughter, of whom the respondent was extremely fond. This daughter and food seemed to be the only things that really appealed to this woman, although she was very happy with her husband (ten years her junior—to her delight) and was proud of his accomplishments.

Her style of life was Familism, even though conflicts with her siblings were acute. She was autonomous-precarious, at the bottom, because the one thing she had given her family all her life had been her nursing services, and she would soon be physically unable to do this. She rated 1 in style and 2 in all other ratings.

69. *Hopelessly Confused—Female, 72.* This woman lived all alone and supported herself as a kitchen maid. She was discharged from her job but married a persistent suitor. She found marriage to him difficult because he was bored and restless. This did not trouble her long, however, because he died a year after the marriage. She went back to work and took into her home her divorced daughter and family, but

it was an unhappy arrangement and she was chronically depressed and confused. At the bottom of the autonomous-precarious group, she rated 1 in isolation and 3 in all the other ratings.

Dependent-Persistent (*Top*)

70. *Not Quite With It—Female, Age 61.*

71. *Compulsive Familism—Female, Age 57.* Some people carried their styles to excess as far as their significant others were concerned. This woman's style became such a directive for her action energies that she was afraid even to try to function in any other style.

As she was among the younger panelists, she still had three teen-age children at home and a two-year-old grandson by one of the children, besides her skilled laborer husband. These gave her a lot of subjects on which to use her familism.

She had lived in Kansas City over half of her life and liked it very much. Right from the first interview, her style was made clear. She said, "It's ridiculous the way they talk about teen-agers now. The problem lies with both parents working." Her own schedule for family care began with getting up at six to fix her husband's breakfast. Then one child got up at seven, another at seven-thirty, and another later yet. She fixed a separate breakfast for each one and helped each one off for the day. She did all the laundry, sewing, and ironing for each, as well as taking care of the grandson's needs. She urged the children to bring home flocks of their friends after school and after dinner helped the children with homework and finished household chores. It was nearly midnight before she got to bed. She rarely saw any television.

The children were not expected to do any real part of the chores and the older girl, who was working since her marriage had broken up, was not contributing financially to the household either.

Her weekends were spent pampering the children in a similar fashion. She went to church or to amusements only if there was "room in the car" or she had finished all the chores for the children. She expressed a great desire to go out riding and get away from home occasionally. The hectic weekends she disliked most of all. Still, her style was so compulsive she could rarely fit her own wishes in.

Her style was evidenced in even more ways. At a later interview, when asked about the nicest thing she had experienced recently, she reported it to be receiving such good Mother's Day presents from her children, and even one from one of her children's friends.

Of her own friends, she listed five, but all but one were much younger than she, and she clearly played a big-sister role to her friends. She also considered many of her neighbors as personal friends.

Most interestingly, she reported she had wanted to be a doctor, but her family had talked her out of it. She said if she had her life to live over she would get more education and travel more before marriage. She also would have bought many pretty things before children came along. She said she started to feel old in her forties.

Toward the final interviews the compulsive quality of her style and the reason for it became more evident. She revealed she was deeply dissatisfied with her marriage and reported her husband was most uncooperative in family ventures. (One of the psychologists said he had probably been greatly neglected by the wife in favor of the children.) She already was dreading her husband's retirement and having him around all day, and she was fed up with her cares for the children, but could not seem to find any way to stop it.

On the story question about Jones she reported, "They gave it quite a bit of thought and Jones took the job. It left the wife more time for hobbies or something like that."

At the last she was still buying extravagant clothes for her daughter and wearing the daughter's cast-off clothes. She was also caring for four grandchildren now that her own children were out and married. She still worked slavishly for them, even doing the income tax for the grown son and daughter. In conclusion, she said, "I wonder if I'll ever be able to put my family out of my life."

This woman had compelled herself to live a style of Familism when her original style was probably World of Work. She had been sold the idea of Familism and she was unable to depart from it. Her relationships with people were a mockery of true, warm Familism, yet her style was carried out in every detail of her life. Consequently, she was classed as Familism 1, but dependent-persistent, toward the top, because of her compulsive dependence on the style. She was given a rating of 2 on alienation, anomie, and coping, but a 1 on isolation because she compulsively surrounded herself with people as part of her style.

72. *Too Old and Sick to Have Goals—Female, Age 80*. This respondent had been widowed three times. She had two sons and five daughters. She lived alone at the time of the study. Her day was spent mostly in "sitting around," with occasional visits from others. A sister came to visit her frequently and a granddaughter took her for rides. A church person came over and read from the Bible. The children were all nearby and she saw them a few times a month and phoned them

more frequently. She spoke of all three husbands as good men, at the first interview, although at the last interview she mentioned that her second husband drank. Her eyesight was failing and she could not read. On her general pattern of life she commented, "I had a big family and worked very hard." When asked about goals in life she said she was too old and sick to have them. At the end of the study, one son, who was divorced, was staying with her nights. During that interview the apartment looked rather disorderly because the granddaughter had not been in to clean it up. She spoke of one of her sons as being "a mess" because he drank too much. She complained that she could not visit her daughters in their homes any more, although the preceding February she had managed to visit a daughter in Texas for two months, and the daughter took her places every night. The interviewer, however, commented that she did not seem despondent or bitter.

We have another clear case of Familism with a rating of 2 on clarity of style. Her life had been a matter of hard work over a long period of not very easy family situations. She probably was autonomous up into the late seventies, just before the study started, although there is some evidence of tendency toward dependency in the early phases of life. Her very clear dependency during the course of the study was related to her health, but the judgment was based on her preoccupation with health and on the way she used her health problems in relating to others. Also, she protested too much that she did not really like to be dependent. The lack of despondency noted by the interviewer is probably an expression of some satisfaction in dependency. She was rated 2 on anomie, isolation, coping, and style, although 1 on alienation, since she managed through all this to share in the values of others and not to alienate them from her. The 2 rating on isolation was due to a latent tendency for her to alienate others, due to the marked dependency. She could have had a somewhat richer social system had she been somewhat more autonomous.

73. *Raising a Girl Was Fun—Female, Age 76.* It was a question whether to rate this woman as autonomous or dependent because of her close interdependence with her family, which consisted of her husband and thirty-nine-year-old daughter.

At the beginning of the study she was retired from her former employment as a clerk. She loved retirement and could hardly wait for her husband to retire so he could be around all the time, too. She liked her age because she was freer, her own boss. The worst features were her increasing physical disabilities. She felt her life's work had been raising her daughter and being a good wife and mother. Her outside work had been solely a way of helping the family out of the Depression years. Her daydreams centered about her family, and she worried about what her husband would do without her.

She also stated she would not be enjoying her life nearly as much if her daughter had moved out. All in all, she made it clear she resented any interference that kept her husband and daughter from being closely dependent on her.

This woman's style was obviously Familism, but a good example of a closed system. She saw little of others outside the family and tended to alienate them. She was happy, rather well adjusted, and would have been a successful ager except for her acute dependence on her immediate family as a source of gratification for her emotional needs. Consequently, she was dependent-persistent, at the top. Her other ratings were 1 on anomie, isolation, and coping, with 2 on alienation. Her style was clearly 1, pure Familism, with no other style evident.

74. *Aging Is Pitiful—Female, Age 80.* This respondent makes an interesting contrast with the preceding one. She, too, lived with her daughter, but the daughter had recently married, late in life. The son-in-law was a farmer whose farm was near a small town a considerable distance away. She worried a great deal that the daughter and son-in-law would move there; she hated the thought of the possibility of losing her home and worried a great deal about living alone. However, the daughter worked in Kansas City, and an arrangement was made whereby the daughter and her husband spent alternate weekends in Kansas City and on the farm. During the week the respondent got up at five o'clock every morning to get the daughter off to work. She attended church regularly, prayer meetings on Wednesdays, and all church suppers. She mentioned four friends, and a brother and sister, neither of whom lived in Kansas City. She was having a great deal of trouble with her eyesight and could read only with a reading glass. A year and one-half after the beginning of the study she complained again about her eyes. She said that she had had a nice Christmas, with family visiting. She again emphasized that she did not like to be alone. She wished that she had had grandchildren. The best time of her life had been her married life. She had taught Sunday school classes, and her husband was an assistant pastor. The worst time of her life had been after seventy, when her husband died, and she began to go blind, and her daughter was divorced and later remarried.

Six months later, the daughter was living at home much less and was generally on the farm on weekends. Six months after that she emphasized that church and family go together and that they had been her life's work. She had been raised in a house of prayer. It was during this interview that she particularly stressed that "old age is pitiful." Toward the end of the study she mentioned a celebration for her eightieth birthday to which her brother and all his family had come. The daughter and her husband were again taking turns on weekends on the farm and in Kansas City. She described her daily round, however, as if the daughter were at home. She had found a lady who would come in once a week to read and talk all evening with her. One of the church members came to drive her around in his ambulance. She said she would die if she did not get out. Once in a long while she would go to the farm with her daughter. It was apparent from some of her remarks that actually many friends came in to take care of her. Her last comment to the interviewer was, "My daughter got married the year after my husband died, and I had thought I would have her to lean on."

Her success rating of dependent-persistent, at the top, is due to the fact that she certainly gets more from others than she gives. On the other hand, she did not completely block the daughter's marriage and went along with the arrangement fairly well. She had a rating of 1 for alienation and coping and 2 for anomie, isolation, and clarity of style.

Dependent-Persistent (Middle)

75. *Sick All My Life—Female, Age 87.* This respondent had been widowed for about twenty years. She lived with her sister, a little younger, in a house owned by the sister. She had never done any work outside of family matters, and had had no children. From the beginning of the study she complained of various kinds of ailments such as dizzy spells, poor eyesight, arthritis, poor appetite, being unable to sleep, and so forth. She dwelt frequently on problems of the aged, prominent among which were medical problems and finding someone to *help* you. Her daily round consisted of little jobs and doing what she pleased. The sister did most of the household chores. She had two brothers and four sisters in the Kansas City area, all of whom she visited quite frequently. All five of the sisters, including herself, were widowed. She knew most of the neighbors, and was in and out of their homes all of the time. The most important thing in life was being close to her folks so she could be taken care of. She described herself at one point as being "just ornery because of my arthritis." She could not afford to see the doctor to have her teeth out or get her ear-

ache attended to. When asked about the nicest things in life she could not think of any. "I just have everything wrong and have been living on borrowed time since my cancer operation seventeen years ago." The worst thing about life was not being able to do anything and just sitting. But she insisted that she was not lonely or despondent. She mentioned a time when she had had seven operations in one year. Both she and her husband had spent a lot of time in hospitals. They had had a business which failed, and had given up farming because of sickness. She said her sister was sick most of the time, too. At one point of the study the interviewer was unable to find either the respondent or the sister at home, and a neighbor said that they both often went out visiting in the evening. When asked about her life work, she replied, "Doctors and hospitals."

On the last round of interviews, the interviewer commented that the sister, then eighty-four, was amazingly active and was still driving a new car quite a bit. She also commented that they lived in a nice little home and that the sister was well loved in the neighborhood. The interviewer thought that the respondent felt completely inferior because of the sister's strong personality. The respondent at this time did not wish to be interviewed, but the interviewer was able to set a date two days later and found the respondent looking rather changed. She had curled her hair, was wearing a neat dress, and was quite animated and bright. At the end of the interview, the respondent made the interviewer promise that she would come back and visit. The content of the interview, however, was about as usual. The respondent said she was not well at all. She had been in a terrible wreck. The sister had been driving the new car, and she did not think her sister would live. Her daily round looked about the same. She would do odd chores here and there and sit and rock, and the neighbors were always dropping in. Saturday was spent in shopping. Sunday she listened to sermons on television. Then somebody, always family, would come by and take her to his or her home for dinner. If she had a daughter she would want her to be herself and not a comic—"They always said I was that." She claimed she had lost all hobbies a long time ago.

This respondent undoubtedly had had a number of physical ailments during the course of her life. On the other hand, from age eighty-three to eighty-seven, the interviewers constantly commented on how well she looked for her age. It was also clear that she got out a good deal. Essentially it was her action system that was somewhat ill, and she had made a long career of being sick, a point which she herself recognized to some degree by describing her life's work as being "doctors and hospitals." Her style of life, though familistic, was a very weak Familism, almost verging on Easing Through Life With Minimal Involvement, one of the two bridging styles. Again we have a very good illustration of the point that, in terms of the action system, it is not physical illness as such which is important, but rather the way in which physical illness is used in relation to one's mode of living. She was rated 2 on anomie, alienation, and coping. The fact that she could be rated 1 on isolation in spite of the 2 rating on alienation was due essentially to her sister's popularity, which resulted in there being lots of people around, rather than to her own behavior. Also, her alienation was not so great as to alienate family members from her.

Dependent-Persistent (Bottom)

None of the cases in the study fell into this category.

Dependent-Precarious (Top)

76. *Second Struggle—Female, Age 61.* If the respondent had not been so tired and despondent, her current marriage would have ended as her previous one had. As it was, she found herself at fifty-five, at the beginning of the study, dependent on a fireman husband, ten years her junior, who was a drinking, argumentative crank.

Although she had business-college education, she supplemented their income by selling in a department store. About her only pleasure was occasional visits with her three married daughters of the previous marriage. She rated no better than 3 on alienation and coping and 2 on anomie and isolation. Her style was only a 2 because it was weak, with an underlying style—also weak—of Living Alone.

77. *Faded Familism—Male, Age 63.*

Dependent-Precarious (Middle)

78. *Will I Make it With Aging?—Female, Age 69.* This rather neurotic woman was approaching seventy and still running from herself. She blamed herself for her divorce and ultimately her husband's death. In a desperate search for some stability, she moved from job to job in such fields as hotel work and clerking. She feared her own death desperately and, even more, she feared ending her days dependent and in a nursing home. She worried incessantly about whether she would be a burden on her children. Because of her anxious worrying and ceaseless searching through others for her own happiness, she was classed as dependent-precarious, in the middle, with a style of

Familism 3. She received a 2 on anomie, 3 on alienation and isolation, and 2 on coping.

Dependent-Precarious (*Bottom*)

79. *The Onset of the End—Female, Age 83.*

80. *So Lonely—Female, Age 84.* Life was just one tragedy after another for this old woman who had lost her husband, parents, and one child. Her other daughter, with whom she lived, was often ill, and the respondent was nearly deaf and blind. She was also nearly senile and reduced to galling inactivity and isolation—totally dependent on her daughter. Her rating was clearly dependent-precarious, at the bottom, and her style was Familism 1. She was given a 2 on anomie and coping, and a 3 on alienation and isolation.

LIVING ALONE

Autonomous-Persistent (*Top*)

81. *Into Retirement and Becoming a Widower—Male, Age 77.* This was a man who retired and whose wife died fairly early in the study. He continued the familistic pattern with his children for some time after his wife's death. But by round seven, his style of life had changed markedly. He still saw his children and grandchildren, but much less frequently, and they were no longer important to him. One son had had an unstable career, and there was evidence of alcoholism. He was not interviewed. The other son played a cat-and-mouse game of breaking appointments for interviews, and was not interviewed either. The original respondent's style of life had clearly become Living Alone, but he remained autonomous-persistent, at the top. He rated 1 on anomie, alienation, and coping and a 2 on isolation and style.

82. *Fiercely Independent—Female, Age 72.* This was another rural transplant who retained all her rural values and standards—despite twenty-five years in Kansas City. She still liked gardening and canning for recreation, and got up at six in the morning, regardless of anything. The worst aspect of her living situation was that she could not see the sunrise from the porch.

She was living alone when interviewed, had never had children, and did not seem to regret it. She had worked for ten years in a factory, and retired at sixty-five, with no regrets for her career. Her life was not enjoyable, but she did not give the idea she had ever expected it to be. In her own words, "Religion means a whole lot." She felt she could not have taken the death of her husband without it. She only admitted to one close friend and she did not know her first name. Her relatives were seen only occasionally.

Work for this woman was a way of life—a style she had embraced almost simultaneously with Living Alone. Age brought the second style into greater focus. She never had any goal in her work; she just did not know what else to do with her life. She was given a style rating of 2 and listed as autonomous-persistent, at the top, with ratings of 1 on anomie and coping and 2 on alienation and isolation.

Autonomous-Persistent (Middle)

83. *Let's Look at Antiques—Male, Age 61.* Some people live alone in a world of their own, finding the characters of their mind and memories to be the significant others in life. Such a person was this government worker, who lived in a museum-like apartment with his sister. He collected antiques and classical knowledge. His values stemmed from his family heritage, and he continued to live mentally in the carriage days of his youth. In contrast to the case, "The Good Old Days," this man was not even faintly senile. He simply preferred the values of the past to the values of the present and deliberately cut out of his social system anyone who did not meet the social standards he maintained. His greatest frustration was having to work to maintain his income.

There was little change evidenced in his life during the course of the study. He was classed as Living Alone, a rating of 1 in style. He was given a rating of 1 on anomie and alienation, and a 2 on isolation and coping.

84. *A Minimal Social System—Male, Age 64.*
85. *Grandma Retires—Female, Age 71.*
86. *From Orphan to Aloneness—Female, Age 70.*

Autonomous-Persistent (Bottom)

87. *Living Alone Well and Hating It—Female, Age 55.* This woman was divorced shortly before the study began. She had taken a job as a stenographer, at the age of forty-three, to prepare for the time when the children left home, which they had done by the beginning of the study. She was unhappy and somewhat bewildered by the divorce, initiated by her husband, and very preoccupied with the problems of living alone. She did it well, but frankly said the worst thing

in life was living alone and feeling so well. She looked about thirty-five and would have liked to live fully if circumstances had permitted. She was rated 2 on all ratings except for 1 in style.

88. *The Daily Grind—Female, Age 59.* From the beginning of the study, this divorced woman, who worked as a practical nurse, gave hints of unspoken bitterness, disappointment, resignation, and loneliness. At the very beginning of the study she was temporarily living with a daughter, son-in-law, and grandson, but she usually lived in an apartment in the city. Throughout the study she gave the impression of a dreary life of work, seven days a week, and in response to questions about the best and worst things, she said frankly, "Nothing nice or not nice has happened." She hoped she would not be living after retirement, and felt she could not stand it because it would be too monotonous. Early in life she had wanted to be a registered nurse, but her father had opposed this. She said that her marriage had been much less happy than most. At another point in the study she said, "Life is nothing but get up, go to work, and come back." In response to the story question about Jones, she said he would not take the job, but her reason was a variant from most—he would not take it "in order to tinker around in his workshop." She thought of her life's work as bringing up the kids, which was "just something you were supposed to do." At the end of the study she again said, "My life is very dull." Her biggest sorrow in life had been when her husband left her, but she had just made the best of it.

This respondent represents something of a variant on the style of Living Alone, in that she was more or less forced into it by marital adversities. She was reluctant to talk much about her past, but some glimpses of it suggest that she may have had a tendency toward living alone even when the family was growing up. By the time of the study she had certainly developed this style, but not strongly, and she was rated 3 on clarity of style. Her system was in balance on a minimal level of interaction and she could probably keep going this way for some time. There was perhaps some ultimate danger of suicide, but the evidence was not sufficiently strong to move her over into the precarious category. She was rated 2 on anomie, 2 on alienation, and clearly 3 on isolation. Again, in spite of all these characteristics, she coped very well and was rated 1 on that variable.

89. *Take It As It Comes—Male, Age 74.* This man worked part time as an usher since his retirement as a carpenter. He had no special friends or neighbors but enjoyed his casual contacts with celebrities. It pleased him to do small favors for people, especially his children and

grandchildren, but essentially he was oriented to Living Alone and aging without protest. He was rated 1 on isolation and coping, 2 on anomie and alienation, and 3 on style.

90. *Pessimistically Disengaging—Female, Age 73.* The daily schedule of this woman helped to classify her as Living Alone. Up at six or seven in the morning, she had her breakfast, then cleaned, crocheted, sewed, or read until lunch. After lunch she sewed, washed, and ironed until her supper at five or six. Then there was television, and bed at nine-thirty. She liked mornings because she felt energetic, but at night she felt dark, quiet, and lonesome. People weren't prominent in her day's activities.

She had been a sales clerk for forty years. Married and divorced twice, she had never had any children of her own but had raised her sister's son somewhere along the way. She saw none of her relatives regularly—not even this foster son—and she did not really care.

Her description of her husband made it clear there had been little exchange of action energy between them. She had a few friends and neighbors who kept her from being isolated. She had actually maintained a style of World of Work most of her life, with a secondary style of Living Alone. In her disappointment at retirement, she found her secondary style an easy solution to her disengagement.

It was not a pure style of Living Alone, because she still cared about having close relations with her friends and neighbors. In fact, she really would have preferred her World of Work style. Therefore, she was classed as autonomous-persistent, at the bottom, with a style of Living Alone and a style rating of 3. She was given a 1 in anomie and coping and a 2 in alienation and isolation.

91. *Loneliness—Male, Age 77.* This man was a retired machine worker living entirely alone in a cluttered, gloomy apartment in a low-rent housing project. He had two sons and two daughters and ten grandchildren, but he did not know their ages because he was not in touch with them. He stopped work when he was sixty because it got too heavy for him, and lived on his savings from sixty to sixty-five. Now he lived on Social Security and a pension. When he was forty-five years old, he had been vice-president and chief instructor in an auto mechanic school and had made an excellent income.

He got out very little. He walked around occasionally, enjoyed cutting grass, and was acquainted with his neighbors, whom he liked to help out, particularly with their cars. He was Catholic and went to church regularly. He occasionally visited his stepchildren who lived in Kansas City. He claimed that he liked visiting, but added, "I am old now, and people are not interested." He also said, "I like to hunt and fish, but there's no place to go." He admitted that he was lonely. His parents were Methodist, but he had become a Catholic. He described both his wives as fine, good Catholics, and both marriages as perfect. The children were doing all right, but he rarely saw them.

He clearly fit one stereotype of the "plight of older people" and expressed this explicitly. For example, he said, "When one is younger, one doesn't realize how lonely old people are—not enough people care about old people, because they don't believe in God enough." If it were not for television, he would have had no pleasure at all.

He left home when he was fourteen, when his mother died, and worked his way through school studying "steam." He was forty-eight when his first wife died, and he married again at fifty-two. His second wife died when he was seventy-one. His father lived to be ninety-eight years old and died when the respondent was forty-eight. His father had been a veterinarian, and the respondent had frequently helped him with money in his later years. He thought of his father as a wonderful man.

For a time a girl who looked like his daughter lived in his apartment with him. He prayed that she would convert to Catholicism, and he gave her money and clothes, but she was "kind of wild." He had great admiration for a number of Catholic figures. His health was reasonably good, and he did not seem especially preoccupied with it. He recovered from two hernia operations with little difficulty and had minor complaints about having to take pills. He had grown accustomed to his small income. He got few satisfactions from life, but prominent among them was helping other people, such as the neighbors. He was lonely and somewhat unhappy, but not depressed in the clinical sense. He had reconciled himself to his way of life.

He was a particularly good example of the fact that people do not have to be satisfied, active, or living in a network of close relationships in order to age successfully, according to the definition of successful aging in this analysis. He rated 1 on style, 2 on alienation and coping, and 3 on anomie and isolation.

92. *The Lonely World of the Mind—Male, Age 81.* This man filled his somewhat lonely life with his work—skilled carpentry and amateur anthropology. His travels had been extensive and his self-education, tremendous. However, the death of the son who had been his confidant caused him to begin to feel his age, and final interviews found him traveling less and disengaging slowly. He could never understand why others around him were not fascinated by the unusual an-

thropological artifacts he had discovered. He was rated 2 on style, anomie, isolation, and coping, but 3 on alienation.

93. *Don't Take Nuthin' From Nobody—Female, Age 80*. This widow lived with her employer, also a widow who worked full time, and the employer's mentally retarded daughter. They lived in a very small house with three tiny rooms on the outskirts of Kansas City. The respondent's job was to take care of the mentally retarded daughter and to do all of the housework. She had broken her hip four years previously and had a pin in it but was able to get around quite well. She went away most weekends unless the employer and the handicapped daughter also went away. The employer always wanted her to go along with them but she strongly resisted this. She visited a few relatives. She described her life's work as being a housekeeper. She had no education but thought she had done all right. She had never gotten fired. She had been on her present job for eighteen years. She described her husband as having been a good man who did not have much to say, like herself. She was always her own boss. The best time in her life was around the age of twenty, when she found the man who loved her and married him.

She liked to be home alone on weekends and "not be dragged along with them." The employer tried to drag her up to her brother's on weekends, but the brother treated her very meanly, and all she did was to clean the house for him. She liked her present job, however, because no one bossed her, and she could take the child and go where she pleased. She was quite hostile during the first interviews but later on became more friendly.

She denied having any great interest in her family, but one son in California sent her money. She and her employer had many fights but she felt quite secure in her job. She would rather have been alone, but she was forced to live during the week in the cramped quarters with her employer. She was tired of hearing her employer talk, and said, "She talks just like the TV and never stops." Also, "She always wants to go with me; I don't want her to—my friends and I like to talk and not have her and the handicapped daughter around—when I am angry I get mad and have it over." Her husband had died several years previously and had spent some time in the state hospital before that. He became mentally ill during the Depression.

She said, "I'd rather be by myself and have always liked to be by myself." And her characteristic description of herself was, "I don't take nuthin' from nobody." This had been a lifelong pattern. For example, she said, "If my husband didn't want me to go, I'd wait until he went to the cornfield and then I'd go and not get back until suppertime. I did as I pleased." She was paying for her own tombstone, in order not to have to depend on anybody for it, but at the same time she claimed that she never thought about death. She was still living the same way at the end of the study and at the same place, which the interviewer described as very depressing. She said, "I always liked to work out in the yard and fields and can't do that any more. I just sit and I can't stand that any more." She did not like television. She had not been able to work for several months, but her employer allowed her to continue to live there.

This is an interesting variant on the style of Living Alone. She married her husband so she could have this style. She would rather have lived physically alone but was unable to do so. Her attitudes toward others were those characteristic of the style Living Alone. She had a minimal system, but it was in balance, especially through her few friends. She was quite strongly anomic and alienated, and was rated 2 on isolation, coping, and style.

Autonomous-Precarious (*Top*)

94. *The Almighty Dollar—Male, Age 81.*

Autonomous-Precarious (*Middle*)

95. *How Little I Do—Female, Age 81.*

Autonomous-Precarious (*Bottom*)

96. *Getting Old Now—Female, Age 91.* A weak type of Living Alone was her style at this age, but it was preferable to dependence. This woman had strongly held a style of World of Work all her life. She had lately become senile, deaf, and increasingly feeble, so the style was no longer physically or mentally possible. She lacked family and wanted none to care for her. She dreaded dependence and would have preferred death. She still showed her old world of work activist energy by continuing to cope with her circumstances singlehandedly. For this she was rated 1 on coping, an unusual rating under these circumstances, generally. Similarly, she was classed as autonomous, but the rating had to be precarious because physically and mentally she would be unable to cope singlehandedly much longer and she knew it. Because she still maintained her own relations with tradespeople, she was rated 2 on anomie, alienation, and isolation. But her style was so weakly held it was given a rating of 3.

Dependent-Persistent (*Top*) No cases.

Dependent-Persistent (*Middle*) No cases.

Dependent-Persistent (*Bottom*)

97. *The Peddler—Male, Age 61.* "The Peddler" appeared in the senior author's original study under the title "The Isolate." This is how he was described at that time:

> This fifty-nine-year-old man lives entirely alone. He is a self-employed salesman of small objects—in short, a peddler. He is one of the cases intensively interviewed by a senior staff member, and her description of him is particularly apt: "He is also quite alone in the world, the most isolated, except for highly specific work contacts, of any of the intensively interviewed panel members. His mother died twenty years ago, his father four years ago. He has no brothers or sisters, and he never married, leaving him, when his father died, with only one significant relative, a lady cousin—who, however, died between the first and second waves of our study. He has no close friends and seemed to be on friendly, interactive terms with only one person outside of work—a neighbor, who, however, has now moved away. It appears, indeed, that Mr. S's only diffuse interactions (and even these are relatively nonobligatory) are with the interviewers from our study. We have, I think, roughly tripled his life space."
>
> He does not like living in Kansas City, especially because of the traffic, and frequently mentions that, while crossing the street, his father was killed by a hit-and-run driver. He grew up in a smaller city nearby and regrets that the family moved from there to Kansas City where his father and he owned and operated a number of small grocery stores until they were forced out by the chain stores. He is an alert and intelligent person with a remarkable memory and can give the exact addresses of all the places that his father and he worked. He says that all he does is work. He has no time for television. He does listen to the radio, but the programs are getting worse. On the second interview, however, he says a male cousin had given him a television set. He didn't think he would like it, but it does cheer him up and pass the time. This same male cousin takes him out to dinner on Christmas and other holidays. He recognizes that he has not measured up to what he should have been in life, but has no profound regrets and is in no sense bitter.

When asked, at one point, what was the best thing that had recently happened to him, he said that it was being in the hospital when he had a prostate operation. For a time he got a great deal of attention and was gleefully all alone in a room, being waited on hand and foot.

His health is fair, and his financial position is somewhat shaky. He clearly enjoys anyone's taking the trouble to do something for him (as when he was waited on in the hospital). He is mildly religious and goes to church occasionally, but does so less and less. This is not a disengagement process, for he was never very much engaged. The people closest to him in his network simply dropped off by death or moved away.

He has the highest possible alienation score and a high F score. His personality type is passive-mastery. He has been classified dependent-precarious and given a rank of twenty in this series; in other words, he is the least successful ager. It is probable that within a relatively brief time he will be a public charge in one way or another, perhaps in an institution, and he will probably enjoy this situation.

At the time that was written, the senior author did not have access to a seventh and later interview with this subject, which changed the ratings somewhat. Instead of becoming more precarious, he reversed the process by reaching out to establish a degree of friendship with some nearby relatives with whom he had not previously been in contact. Therefore, he could no longer be classed as the most unsuccessful ager, and his ratings were as follows: He was classed as dependent-persistent at the very bottom, and was given ratings of 3 in anomie, alienation, and isolation, but a 2 in coping because he was still in control of some crises. His style was clearly a pure example of Living Alone.

98. *Good Old Days—Male, Age 78*. A retired businessman, this bachelor lived with his sisters in an old boarding house. Despite his sisters, he was pathetically alone. As a child he had been his mother's pet and she had never let him go. The rest of his life he pursued this same type of love but it always eluded him. He was fully disengaged and dependent. He lived and talked in a world that existed, if ever, some sixty years ago. This was one of the few examples in which a style of Living Alone was associated with close dependence on other people. He was rated dependent-persistent, at the bottom, and was rated 3 on alienation and anomie, and 2 on isolation and coping.

He probably craved a style of Couplehood, but having failed to achieve it, fell into the style of Living Alone and depending on others as a poor substitute.

Dependent-Precarious (Top)

99. *Ugly Aging—Female, Age 76.* This respondent had never married. She was retired at the end of the study. Nursing had been her life's work, but she was an isolate and had been one most of her life. This was reflected in her feelings that the study was an invasion of her privacy.

For a time she had lived with her mother, brother, and his family, but now she lived alone, her chief contact being with a young couple to whom she rented rooms. She despised the couple, yet depended on them for much of her care as her health worsened. She also leaned on an older folks' social group to supply many of her other needs. This group was also a target for her vitriolic tongue. The evidence is that by the final interview this woman would be classed as dependent-precarious at the top. She was in the style of Living Alone, but because of an underlying life style of Minimal Involvement, she was given a style rating of 2. She was rated 2 on anomie and coping, and 3 on alienation and isolation.

100. *Cats and Filth—Female, Age 75.*

Dependent-Precarious (Middle)

101. *Don't Want No Friends—Male, Age 77.*

Dependent-Precarious (Bottom) No cases.

COUPLEHOOD

Autonomous-Persistent (Top)

102. *Enjoying Retirement—Male, Age 74.* He was retired from the hotel business and lived with his second wife, who was also retired. He seemed to be the kind of man who needed Couplehood for his optimum social system. He said, "A man's wife makes or breaks him in a sense of security and well-being." His words were more often prefaced by "we" than "I," especially in discussing the day's activities. He got a lot, but he gave a lot, and could act on his own when he

needed to. His mother's death had been quite difficult for him, as theirs had been a couplehood relation also.

His style was Couplehood 1, and he was autonomous-persistent, at the top, with ratings of 1 on all other categories.

103. *Two Halves Make a Whole—Male, Age 59.* "Grow old along with me—the best is yet to be" seemed the motto for this virtuous lower-middle-class maintenance worker and his wife. Couple-centered, and autonomous-persistent, the respondent had many close friends who cherished his warm associations with them. Some had known him since boyhood on the farm. But most important to him was his wife, and since there had never been children, their unity came from a deep couple-centered love that should survive aging as well as it had the many other problems that had come their way. He was rated 1 on everything and was at the top of the autonomous-persistent group.

104. *Mellowing With Age—Male, Age 75.* This respondent was a nice old gentleman, devoted to his rather shrewish wife, by whom he had no children. He had been married once before for a brief time to a similar person. He had always enjoyed gardening and reading, although he had little more than a grade school education. He liked Couplehood, and he characterized himself by saying he lived on faith. His style rating was Couplehood 1, and he was rated 1 on all other action energy usages.

105. *Isolated Couplehood in Misery—Male, Age 79.*

106. *From Brewer to Baker—Male, Age 77.* This retired brewer had aged quietly and with little change. His beloved wife died shortly after his retirement so he kept house for himself and an adopted niece. He found he enjoyed cooking and, except for an occasional threat of ill health, he found a real satisfaction in his life with his niece. At the top of his success category, he rated 2 on isolation and 1 on all other ratings.

107. *Couplehood on Through Widowhood—Female, Age 74.* This respondent had been widowed just a few months prior to the beginning of the study. She elected to continue to live alone in their seven-room house. She and her husband had lived there many years, and she knew many neighbors with whom she visited frequently. She had no relatives in Kansas City but corresponded and occasionally saw relatives elsewhere. Her husband had been a semiskilled worker and she, herself, had worked off and on for about twenty years of her life. At the first interview she described her husband as having had a good disposition, "a home guy," and said they spent a lot of time together.

In a later interview she described him again as "down to earth, a hard worker and honest." He enjoyed people very much. He drank somewhat and she had not liked that, but she hastened to add that he was not a drunk and said, "I sure do miss him." She found everything a little harder to do. She was bothered by children running through the yard, making noise, and doing damage in the garden—a frequent source of bother to many of the older people in this panel. In a still later interview she was described as grieving for her husband. She made several visits to her old hometown in a nearby state. Thus, we have an example of a widow who persists in Couplehood with thoughts of her husband, and relates to a small group of friends, with some Familism in the background. The style can persist even when the partner is gone. There is no doubt about her success category and rank, and all of her modes of use of action energy have been rated 1.

108. *Couplehood Though Alone—Male, Age 74.*

Autonomous-Persistent (Middle)

109. *Am I Aging?—Female, Age 56.* This woman was clinging closely to her husband, but doing a good job with her interpersonal relationships. Their grown and married daughter came often to visit, and the respondent enjoyed keeping the grandchildren. She had once worked as a secretary in a business firm, but it was just something she drifted into to keep from being idle. Some problems of missing work tended to give her difficulty in coping after her retirement. This caused her to be rated 2 on coping. Otherwise she was rated 1 on all other ratings, including style. Her style was Couplehood, and she was autonomous-persistent, in the middle.

110. *Reluctant Babysitter—Male, Age 73.* This old gentleman retired to a life of rather easy living with his wife. He sometimes had to cope with sitting with his grandchildren. But, in general, he found life not too bad as he disengaged. He was rated 1 on everything but coping, which was rated 2.

111. *Two in a Trailer—Male, Age 55.* Sometimes a couple with no children can be so close they override the desire for children and build a happy, mature relationship based on the needs of each other.

Such a couple was this telephone worker foreman and his wife, who took on second lives as trailer-court owners and operators. They showed by their independence and mutual give and take how autonomous-persistent behavior and the Couplehood style of life can be quite compatible. Each was secure in the other and made independent decisions, but the other one was the reason for attempting to age as gracefully as possible. He was rated 1 on alienation, isolation, and coping, but 2 on style because of strong underlying style of Living Fully. He was also rated 2 on anomie.

112. *Beyond Couplehood—Female, Age 65.* This lady had been widowed for four years at the beginning of the study. Her husband had been in the field of physical education and they had gone to Florida each winter. She had lived in Kansas City all her life and liked it very much. After her husband's death, she continued to live in a small home on a lake in country surroundings in a suburb of Kansas City where she and her husband had lived for many years. The house was too big for her, but her husband was buried nearby and she had many memories of him. She occasionally thought of moving but did not do so during the entire five years of the study, nor was there any indication that she would. She was working at the beginning of the study and commuted into Kansas City each day. She worked for a small company with a rather familistic atmosphere. At one point she indicated, "I have just quit all activity since my husband died." Yet she did belong to a church group and played piano and organ for Sunday school and church. She had a few relatives who visited her fairly regularly. She kept thinking about retiring but had not done so by the end of the study.

This is an interesting case of the style of Couplehood which persisted through her memories, rather than being transposed to another person. At the same time, she had a strong underpinning of Familism. She got into familistic-like situations at church and at work. Her actual family was close but she did not go to live with them, even though they wanted her to do that. Her balance of action energy was quite clearly autonomous, and she could go on that way for a long time. She had no problems with disengagement and was on the verge of a successful retirement. There were some signs of anomie, and a strong sense of loneliness, overcome by watching a lot of television. Her style rating was 2, which, in her case, made it easier for the style to persist than if it had been of a quality to be rated 1. However, she was rated 1 on alienation, isolation, and coping.

113. *November Song—Male, Age 68.* This man's life had been dominated by the World of Work for many years. He had had two sons, one of whom was killed in the Second World War. The other son, who was a pilot in the War, had done very well, and he was very proud of him. After twenty-nine years of marriage, his first wife had divorced him, and this had been quite a blow. Then late in life he remarried. He and his second wife ran a small business together. But

they talked frequently about buying a trailer and going to Canada and Florida. They did manage to spend fairly long vacations together. As the study progressed, he and his wife were working toward partial retirement. He thought of the best years of his life as being since the age of fifty-three, when he had found peace and happiness with his second wife. By the end of the study he and his wife were operating the business from their home. They were very happy about this because they had more time together and for trips. His wife enjoyed fishing with him.

This respondent represents a case who was able rather successfully to make a shift in style. Throughout most of his adult life it had been the World of Work, but he then achieved Couplehood late in life. If anything should happen to his second wife he could probably make another shift in style to Living Alone and fishing, with some relatively low level of involvement with his family. He was rated 1 on anomie, alienation, isolation, and coping, and 2 on style.

114. *Successful Widowhood—Female, Age 74.*

115. *The Retired Working Girl—Female, Age 75.* Having worked all her life, this woman found retirement a somewhat anxious time. She was single but lived with her brother. If he was not around, her closest contact was a niece who lived nearby. She spent most of her time at civic and patriotic groups. She was placed in the middle of the autonomous-persistent group and was rated 1 on all but style.

116. *A Long Retirement—Male, Age 81.*

117. *Enjoying an Old-Age Home—Female, Age 81.* This respondent had been widowed during the First World War and again around 1950. She had no children. She was Catholic and living in a Catholic home. However, she was in no sense "institutionalized." She was quite spry for her age, had an alert mind, and was able to have a room on the fourth floor of the home. She had lived for seventy-three years in Kansas City and loved it. She commented on the need for a home for old married people. She had begun to feel old about seven years previously, when her second husband died. She was quite concerned about living alone and had moved into the home.

From general information we have on her life history it seems clear that she had achieved the style of Couplehood in two marriages, most clearly for the second. After the death of her second husband, she was able to diffuse out her Couplehood to a number of friendships. An old-age home seems an ideal place in which the style of Couplehood can persist in this more diffuse way. She was rated 1 on all of her characteristic uses of action energy, except for clarity of style. The rating of 2 on that variable may reflect the fact that she was somewhat reluctant to talk about her past, rather than the true clearness of style. Her ability to maintain a Couplehood style in the old-age home, on a 2 level, may well indicate that earlier she would have been rated 1 and had a very strong tendency to Couplehood.

Autonomous-Persistent (*Bottom*)

118. *Goodbye Miss Chips—Female, Age 61.*

119. *The Henpecked Husband—Male, Age 55.* This respondent had been a retail salesman since the age of fifteen, and had risen to be district manager. His wife, two years younger, or forty-eight at the beginning of the study, was a secretary. She was present through most of the interviews and made frequent comments. They lived in a pleasant home in which he had built a recreation room with a well-stocked bar, and at the beginning of the study he was found laying bricks in the patio.

His mode of life is best glimpsed by various comments he made throughout the study. When asked what his wife did, he said she was a secretary, but he had no idea about her work; his wife commented, "Oh, my aching back," especially when he did not even know where she worked. He said he did not like taking out the garbage. On the second round of interviews he said he was all right but had had a virus; his wife said things had been awful—that her brother had stayed with them through the winter and had died of cancer. He was not sure whether he had any cousins or not, although he knew that his father had had a lot of brothers and half-brothers. He liked his neighbors and knew them more or less casually. The most important thing in life was "just living." When asked about the preferred age of friends, he said the same age or younger, and his wife added, "especially the women."

He said he would "sort of like to try" retirement to see how things would go. When asked whether he would decide on retirement, or someone else would, he said, "someone else"—namely, his wife. On the fourth round of interviewing he said he had been fine and there had been nothing unpleasant, but his wife said that Flopsy, the dog, had had ten teeth pulled. Respondent was lonely in the mornings because his wife went to work earlier. When asked about the best time in his life, he said it was when he was in school, but his wife said it was when he was in the Army. He claimed he had never really had bad times. He had never been out of a job. He seldom got angry, but would "blow his top" when his car would not start. And he commented that his wife often pouted for days. In response to one of the story questions, he said that whether or not Jones would take the job would depend on his wife. However, Mrs. Birch would marry. If he had his life to live over he would still go into selling, perhaps a different field where he could make more money so he could think of retirement. Even so, he had done fairly well in the stock market. Toward the end of the study he had given up his job and gone on the road, but his wife did not like it so he took over managing another store. He always came straight home from work. He had to because "we have obligations to our dog."

He and his wife argued at some length in response to a question about where they would most like to live. When asked at what point in his life he would like to start living it over, he said he would like to go back and live his whole life over and that if he had known earlier what he knew now he would not be working at age fifty-six. He claimed he had a temper and his wife claimed he did not, and they argued this at great length until he finally gave up in defeat. The wife then commented, "We fight like we always did." His wife commented that he had never cared what anybody thought of him. He liked to wear casual clothes, but he did not get to wear them at work where he was the boss. On changes in spending with age, he said he bought more gin and bourbon than he used to.

He has been placed in the autonomous-persistent category, toward the bottom, because, although he was dominated by his wife, he was not dependent on her in our sense. He just managed to keep his system in balance, and it was the degree of autonomy, rather than the persistence, that pulled him toward the bottom of this category. He could probably go on in this way for years. Retirement was not a problem. In fact, he would have liked to retire in his mid-fifties. Disengagement would be no problem for him, because of his low level of involvement. He was rated 3 on clarity and saliency of style. It approached but did not reach Easing Through Life With Minimal Involvement. He had no very pronounced style but he did have a style, and it was Couplehood. All decisions were made with reference to his wife, probably most of them by her. He rather enjoyed being henpecked. This case well illustrates the point that a relationship need not be "good," according to usual standards, to be Couplehood, to be in balance, and to be persistent.

120. *Aging Busman's Holiday—Male, Age 62.* This man found much more security in the Teamsters' Union than in any church he had found. Religion had not helped him any, but the Teamsters' had,

and he gave credit where he felt credit was due. He liked his job, his family, and his friends at the firehouse, but most of all he was glad he had married his wife. She and his health were the most important things he could think of. He and his working wife shared almost all tasks, and both enjoyed visiting their two grown daughters and the four grandchildren.

Disengagement set in during the course of the study when he reached retirement age. But he took retirement gracefully. Every day he drove his wife to work. She had easy access to public transportation but he liked the driving and being with her. He would let her off and then go play cards with some cronies until it was time to get his wife again. On the weekends they visited the children a great deal. All in all, he felt, the last years were the happiest of his life.

His style of life was Couplehood, with a strong underpinning of Familism. Consequently, the style was a little less clear and was rated 2. He was autonomous-persistent at the bottom—very close to being dependent-persistent. At the time of the ratings, he was in balance, but changes in their life pattern could have made his autonomy precarious. Because of his genial contentment and well-being with himself, family, and friends, he was rated 1 in alienation, isolation, anomie, and coping.

121. *No Style to Speak of—Male, Age 69.* This interesting tradesman had a major physical disability which affected his speech. During the years of the interviews he seemed to have hit the lowest point of his life, and it was accompanied by heavy drinking, general alienation, and anomie. He had undoubtedly been a man who had held the style of Living Fully. The crippling disability, growing age, and the subsequent disengagement process were drastic for him.

Then he shifted his style to a kind of Couplehood, began to reach out to help others, and at the same time he also began to cope with his disability by trying to live with it more acceptingly. Consequently, he ended up as autonomous-persistent, toward the bottom, with a style rating of 3. Because he was still struggling with his style change and expressed many values of disappointment with the world and his wife's relatives' treatment of her, in particular, he was rated 2 on anomie and isolation and a 1 on alienation and coping. These might have been rated 2 except for the real changes in each of these areas that were evidenced over the period of the study.

122. *Take Care of Yourself—Male, Age 76.* This man rather resisted the study. He had been a professional man. He had been married three times. The first two marriages ended in divorce early in his

life, and his third marriage had lasted since 1930. He was born and raised in Kansas City and was "pleased to call it home." He had missed work since retirement at seventy, largely because work kept his mind occupied. He had once attended the Jewish services, but now, if he ever went, he went to his wife's church. Age brought a time to relax even though he was not as spry as he used to be, and he found his happiness in just puttering around the house with his wife.

His life space had been greatly reduced since he was in his forties, and he even said he wished he saw less of his neighbors. They seemed pleased to visit him, however. He neither looked nor acted his age and attributed it to "taking care of himself." Although clearly disengaged at most levels, he was aging rather successfully. He was rated autonomous-persistent, at the bottom, and given a 2 for anomie and alienation, but a 1 for isolation and coping. His Couplehood style rated a 3, as he had some faint underlying style of World of Work, which had probably been his chief style of life in his more physically active years, although Couplehood had always been present.

123. *Wife—Female, Age 75.* This case was touched on briefly in the section on Couplehood. As the dominant member of this pair (see "Husband," page 277), she supported and held the balance of exchange of action energies. Her age and failing physical abilities curbed her autonomy a bit; nevertheless she was rated autonomous-persistent, at the bottom, in a style of Couplehood 1. She also rated 1 in the other ratings, due to her social contacts and activities outside of the home.

124. *Doc—Male, Age 90.* This ex-pharmacist progressed from helping his wife around the house to full care of her as she degenerated into a prolonged terminal illness. She was very dear to him, and he disengaged from all other activities to devote himself to her. His style was beginning to be influenced by a style of Living Alone. Finances were a great worry for him, but his own physical and mental health were remarkably sound. He was at the bottom of the autonomous-persistent group and was rated 1 for anomie, alienation, and coping. Isolation and style were rated 2.

Autonomous-Precarious (Top)

125. *The Duke and the Duchess—Female, Age 58.*

Autonomous-Precarious (Middle) No cases.

Autonomous-Precarious (Bottom) No cases.

Dependent-Persistent (Top)

126. *Hostile Disengagement—Female, Age 73*. At the beginning
of the study, at age sixty-seven, this respondent led a rather dreary
life, and the rest of the interview years strengthened the picture of
a lonely, hostile, ailing old woman who disengaged with reluctance
and became increasingly dependent on her semiskilled laboring husband. She had never had any children and had spent her life first
yielding to her mother's wishes and still later to her husband's. She
read a lot and had some social contacts, but religion was not important. The only really important feature of life outside of her husband was her health. She depended on her husband for financial and
emotional support as well as expecting him to carry a large part of the
household chores when she did not feel well.

She was given a rating of Couplehood 3 because the Couplehood
style, as such, did not appear strong. She was rather lacking in style
generally. She was placed in the dependent-persistent category, at the
top, and was rated 2 on alienation, anomie, isolation, and coping.

Dependent-Persistent (Middle)

127. *The Dreamy Home Companion—Female, Age 57*. This was
one of the original studies in the first article by Richard H. Williams
in *Processes of Aging* (see Appendix One, Notes). He described her
as follows:

> This . . . woman, a high school graduate, assists her hus-
> band, who is a professional man. They have no children. Her ISC
> is fifty-two, which puts her toward the bottom of the upper-middle
> class.
>
> She is very much wrapped up in her life as it is. She belongs
> to a "Unity" church and is very active in the Unity movement.
> She was hostess for a Sunday school junior department, but she
> loves to stay home and indicates that, as one gets older, there is
> not so much need for social life. She has one sister and two
> aunts in Kansas City and some cousins on the West Coast. She
> feels close to some nieces, but they do not live in Kansas City.
> She rarely sees her mother. Her parents were divorced, and she
> was raised by her grandmother. She does not visit with the neigh-
> bors, but she interacts freely and frequently with the many people
> who come into her husband's office. She is vaguely bothered by the
> idea of retirement. There is indication that her husband had a

psychiatric illness at one time, an area of her life about which she does not want to talk.

She is not particularly concerned with health and is in good financial position. It seems fairly clear that she gives more to her marriage than she gets from it. On special occasions she is happy to help others.

Her final ratings after the seventh round of interviews were changed somewhat. She was styled as Couplehood 1 and classed dependent-persistent, in the middle, because of her clear dependence on her husband for major action energy exchange. She received ratings of 1 on anomie, alienation, and isolation.

128. *Baby Sister—Female, Age 61.* This case was touched on briefly in the section under Couplehood. Because of obvious dependence on her sister, she was rated dependent-persistent, in the middle. Her style was only 2 because she had a style of Living Alone. She did not have the deep affectional ties with her sister or family that would have characterized pure Couplehood. She was also rated 2 in anomie, alienation, isolation, and coping.

129. *True Blue Dependent—Male, Age 59.* The life of a cabbie seemed to suit this man. His wife worked as a clerk, and her steady hand was evidently the controlling force in his life. He had no really close friends or relatives. Despite his protests to the contrary, most of his social contacts came through his wife. All his life he had had no real goals. Nevertheless, the latter years were not unhappy ones. If he had his life to live over, though, he felt he would have gotten more education and had some children.

As the years of the interviews went by, he became increasingly more dependent on his wife—especially when he retired and she did not. He described her as "true blue" and noted that they did more and more things together.

His style was weak Couplehood, with an underpinning of Easing Through Life With Minimal Involvement. He seemed to find it more comfortable to hold the style of Couplehood and be dependent than to adopt the clear style of minimal involvement and be autonomous. He had too much action energy to be dependent and minimally involved.

He had once been autonomous-persistent, then precarious, but was judged dependent-persistent at the time of the close of the study. Because of his minimal relations with family and friends and his growing involvement with his wife, he was rated 2 on anomie, alienation, isolation, and coping.

Dependent-Persistent (Bottom)

130. *Trapped in Couplehood—Female, Age 63.*

131. *Husband—Male, Age 79.* This case was touched on briefly in the section on Couplehood. As the dependent member of the pair (see "Wife," page 274), he was on the receiving end of most of the action energy exchange. He relied heavily on his wife to keep him functioning and provide a contact with the outside world. He was classed as dependent-persistent, toward the bottom, with a rating of Couplehood 1. He was rated 2 on all the other categories.

Dependent-Precarious (Top)

132. *Rejected and Hurt—Male, Age 69.*
133. *Anxious Mother—Female, Age 58.*
134. *The Frustrated Inventor—Male, Age 61.*

Dependent-Precarious (Middle) No cases.

Dependent-Precarious (Bottom) No cases.

EASING THROUGH LIFE WITH MINIMAL INVOLVEMENT

Autonomous-Persistent (Top)

135. *Taking It Easy—Male, Age 58.* A college professor who grew up on a midwest farm, he had just taken life as it came from the beginning. A pleasant family man and a good neighbor, he was active in his church and proud of his three married daughters but not involved in their lives. Life was pleasant but dull, and, as he grew older, it seemed easier to worry over finding a place to park rather than to worry what was happening to him as he aged. He simply began to disengage without awareness or concern. He was in the top of the autonomous-persistent group and was rated 1 on everything except for a 2 on isolation.

136. *The Crony—Male, Age 70.*

Autonomous-Persistent (Middle)

137. *Life Goes On—Male, Age 61.* At the beginning of the study this respondent was living with his wife, age forty, and together they took care of the building in which they lived. He also supervised thirty-five buildings of eight hundred units for a real estate company. He

had had three sons by his second marriage. He worked about twelve hours a day, including Saturdays, and Sundays he worked around the building in which they lived. On the second round of interviewing, his life looked very similar. He was obviously very fond of a parakeet. He had no time for anything but work. When asked to mention the closest person in his life he had a little difficulty but finally mentioned one of his sons, "I guess," who lived in another midwestern city some distance away. He had been to see him recently, for the first time in four years. The other sons he saw every few months. His wife "buddied around" with a few neighbors, but he did not have time to do that. The most important thing in life for him was his health.

By the third round of interviewing he had made two moves. His wife was managing an apartment-hotel and he had taken a full-time job as a delivery man on a truck. He had simply gotten tired of looking after so many buildings. He mentioned a very few friends whom he saw occasionally. He had grown up in a foster home; after he was grown and had three sons of his own, he looked up his father. His father's response was, "Can't you keep those brats quiet?" The respondent did by taking them away and never seeing his father again. The most important things in his life which he mentioned were always things that one tends to do alone. On the fourth round of interviews he had moved again, and his wife was no longer managing a hotel. Everything was just routine. When not working, he read, watched television, and rested. The worst thing in life was still having to work. The best time of his life was when he had no worries and was free to do as he pleased. When asked what he would do if he had only six months to live, he said he would do just as he was doing then—not much of anything.

In the fifth round of interviews he complained he was getting a bit tired of watching television and said he had not been to a picture show in five years. On Sundays he got up about noon and just stayed around the house. In response to the story question about Jones, he said he did not know what Jones would do and that it would depend on how badly Jones needed the money. He would not like to be young now the way the world is today. The world was too crowded and in too much of a rush. During that round we also learned that he had first been married at the age of nineteen and divorced at nineteen, married again at twenty and divorced at thirty-six. The third marriage was at thirty-eight to "one of those redheads with too much temper," and this marriage had lasted about a year. His fourth marriage at forty-three was still intact.

In the sixth round of interviewing, we learned that he had considered his life's work to have been a very special type of construction work which he got into quite accidentally. He would have liked to be a civil engineer but never quite got there. He commented on his foster home—that it had been a good one but that he had never been very closely identified with it. He had run off once or twice. His foster mother never scolded him. His foster father had been a college professor who wanted him to go through college, but he had just fooled around and did not do it.

In the last round of interviewing, he was beginning to have trouble with his vision. His wife was not very well. However, he was cheerful and amiable. He was still working nine and one-half hours a day six days a week at the age of sixty-one, and at fairly heavy work. He did not watch television any longer. He commented that "Sunday seems like the week long." When asked about his favorite things, he could not think of any and asked his wife, who said, "TV, I guess." He then added, "Me and an old guy across the hall play pool occasionally." He also said of himself, "All I buy is work clothes. I never dress up." When his children were growing up he was working in the specialized construction business and had not been in one place long enough to know anybody. Sometimes he had been away from home for three or four weeks at a time. He had no hobbies, except "loafing, I guess." And his main purpose in life was to be healthy.

This man, who grew up in a foster home, never achieved any true identification. He achieved the style Easing Through Life With Minimal Involvement very early in life, but even it was not achieved very clearly. There was a very shadowy Couplehood in the background which was more important in the first two interviews, when he and his wife shared in work, but it had certainly faded by the end of the study. He was in fair balance with his social system but at a very low level of involvement. Disengagement was no problem for him. Retirement might be, but he would probably ease off work and perhaps manage an apartment house again. He was rated 2 on anomie, alienation, and isolation, and 3 on style. However, he was rated 1 on coping. It is possible to be somewhat anomic, alienated, and isolated and yet cope very well, if one's style is one of Minimal Involvement.

Autonomous-Persistent (Bottom)

    138. *Keep on Living—Male, Age 87.*

Autonomous-Precarious (Top)

    139. *Then She Married—Female, Age 57.*

Autonomous-Precarious (Middle) No cases.

Autonomous-Precarious (Bottom) No cases.

Dependent-Persistent (Top)

140. *Keeping Alive—Male, Age 55.* His mother and older sister kept this man functioning. Unmarried and an unskilled factory worker at forty-nine, at the beginning of the study, he got by in life with as little effort and energy as possible. He made no bones about it. He said, "I'd rather loaf around than work." It was too much trouble for him to make friends. When he came home in the evenings he would do a little yard work and then just lie around and listen to the radio. It was his best time of day.

Weekends he would read or go for rides—to no place in particular. He liked Sunday night least of all because it meant that Monday morning and work were almost upon him again. His only friend he described as "a big fat slob that I get together with once in a while." He did not know his neighbors very well.

The most important thing to him was just keeping alive. Nothing else really mattered.

His style was very definitely one of Minimal Involvement. He was dependent-persistent at the top and was rated 2 on anomie, 3 on alienation and isolation, and 2 on coping.

141. *Nearly Styleless—Male, Age 70.*

Dependent-Persistent (Middle)

142. *Ain't Got Nothing—Male, Age 64.* Some people in Kansas City were born on the wrong side of the tracks and were never able to cross over. They aged early, and life held little promise for them. This man, a common laborer with only a couple of grades of education, was in this class. He had been married three times and at the first interview lived with his third wife in a run-down house near the railroad tracks. His wife worked, and so did he. His relations with his grown children by former marriages were occasional and unsatisfactory.

If he had his life to live over, he said, he would get more education and not drink as much. He certainly did not look forward to retirement, although he did not particularly like his work either. He even wished he had a close friend, but he did not trust anyone's loyalty. He depended on a succession of wives and girlfriends for what little emotional satisfaction he got.

The rest of the interviews were similar. This was a style of Minimal Involvement, but this man was not a happy-go-lucky type who eased along without worrying. He was a weary plodder who declared, "Mostly I feel beat before I start. I just ain't got nothing."

He was classed as dependent-persistent, in the middle, because of the nature of his relationship with his wives and girlfriends. His style was Easing Through Life With Minimal Involvement 2, and he was rated 3 on alienation, anomie, and coping; he was given a 2 on isolation because his dependent nature always led him to relate to some woman in close physical proximity.

Dependent-Persistent (Bottom)

143. *I'm Sick—Male, Age 72.* A weak style of Easing Through Life With Minimal Involvement and a still weaker style of World of Work were about the clearest findings from this man's rather confused life history. An unskilled laborer, he had variously reported one, two, and three marriages and different numbers of children to the interviewers. He was a hypochondriac and played up his real and imagined illnesses to keep his family under control. He had few friends and was generally unpleasant in any exchange of action energy. In addition to rating him 3 in style, for the style was not too clear, he was classed as dependent-persistent at the bottom, and rated 3 in anomie and alienation and 2 in isolation and coping.

Dependent-Precarious (Top)

144. *A Life That Was Not Lived—Male, Age 60.*
145. *Disengaging, Lonely, and Afraid—Male, Age 62.*

Dependent-Precarious (Middle)

146. *Living With the Children—Male, Age 81.*

Dependent-Precarious (Bottom) No cases.

LIVING FULLY

Autonomous-Persistent (Top)

147. *Middle-Class Virtues—Male, Age 57.* This man was a mature, well-rounded, intelligent, likeable person. He loved his family, his work in a government profession, and his few close friends. In-

dependent, yet interdependent with his loved ones, he had planned his life well and faced aging with no serious qualms. His only child, a son, had married and established an independent life, suggesting that the father had been a good provider for the child's needs as well as for his own.

He was considered in style to be Living Fully and was rated autonomous-persistent, at the top. His degree of style was only 2 because his interests were more limited to his immediate family than many others who were classed as Living Fully. He was otherwise given 1 ratings in all categories.

148. *Like Charlie Weaver—Male, Age 74.*

149. *The Iron Fist in the Velvet Glove—Female, Age 72.* Born to money, this upper-class widow had kept skillful control of her late husband's fortune and was dedicated to preserving it for their two married daughters and the grandchildren, who were her pride and joy.

She enjoyed her social, civic, and financial roles to the hilt. Descriptions of her usually included such adjectives as friendly, gracious, charming, delightful, and the like. She was all of these, and more.

But the "more" was that she was a tyrant to her offspring, controlling them with calculated kindness and keeping them ensnared in complex emotional relationships by using the web of money. She was not aging at all and showed no disengagement. She was rated at the top of the autonomous-persistent group and had a rating of 1 throughout.

150. *The Competent One—Female, Age 72.*

151. *Ministering to the Town—Male, Age 72.*

152. *Forced Disengagement—Female, Age 67.*

153. *Responsible Aging—Female, Age 63.*

154. *Dimes Ain't Everything—Female, Age 81.* This was one of the outstandingly successful agers. Hers was a rural background, although she had been living in Kansas City for fifty years. At age seventy-eight, at the first interview, she lived with her daughter, was retired from laundry work, and was glad of it. She was in excellent health and lived fully in her slowly decreasing life space. Despite the increasing physical strain, she enjoyed frequent travel overseas with her daughter (whose job involved travel and who paid her mother's way on these trips). She loved babysitting with her grandchildren, and she continued to do most of the housekeeping to maintain balanced relations with her daughter.

Her life's work had been her home and children, and although she became blue when she thought of her long-dead husband and recently dead son, life was still worth living and she liked much about her age. Before the study was over, she was in her eighties, still traveling, keeping house, reading extensively, and giving fully of herself to her daughter and niece. The way she summed up the pursuits of her life gave rise to the name we gave her. She felt that when you look for the real meaning of life, "dimes ain't everything." She was easily rated autonomous-persistent, at the top. She was also in the clear style of Living Fully, with a strong supportive style of Familism. Her ratings on all the other areas were also 1 and made her one of the most successful agers in the panel.

155. *Joyful Day in Successful Disengagement—Female, Age 76.* This woman was widowed at sixty-three. She missed her husband but enjoyed the day for whatever it brought; for her, it was always full of beauty. She attended church, Sunday school, and had several friends. She enjoyed bringing pleasure to others. She had a stroke in 1959 from which she recovered fairly well, was able to reduce her obligations and activities, and was still enjoying life. She just did not have bad moods. When asked about irritating things, she replied, "You ask the funniest questions. [Laugh] Honey, I just wouldn't know. Life is just mighty pleasant, day to day." She became virtually blind before the end of the study, and was again able to disengage as needed, and maintain her joy in living as fully as possible. She also illustrates the relativity of disengagement; some people never achieve the level of engagement this woman had when she was one-half to three-quarters disengaged. At the top of her success category, her ratings were all 1.

156. *Resisting Senility—Male, Age 92.* This retired minister was first seen in June 1957. He lived alone in a house in which he and his wife had lived for many years; his wife was then in a nursing home. The interviewer found him in the front yard talking with his daughter, who was visiting from an eastern state. The interviewer noticed no handicaps, a quick gait, and said that the respondent could pass for twenty-five years younger. He was very active in the ministry until the late seventies or early eighties. When he was in his sixties he traveled a great deal, preached three sermons a day, and came back to his suburb of Kansas City to preach in his own church. At eighty-seven he still preached at a few funerals. He had not felt old until he reached the age of seventy-five. His second wife had been in a rest home for many years. His daughter, who was his wife's stepdaughter, went out to see her every day. He described his first wife, the mother of his children, as an "angel." He had been the only child of wealthy parents. He said

he felt worst in the morning and best from about 3 P.M. to 10 P.M., after a nap. He had the reputation of being a very liberal minister. He had a very wide network of friends. His father had been a breeder of fast horses in Kentucky, and he had kept some in the suburb of Kansas City. He commented that some of the ladies of the church did not think a preacher should have fast horses.

In February 1959 he complained of a little nose and throat trouble but no serious illness. He talked of his second wife as being mentally and physically destroyed in the nursing home. He still mentioned lots of friends. He was rather irked at being as inactive as he had to be at his age. He described himself as having always been an energetic redhead and wished he had more to do. He felt somewhat lonely. His great interest in life was to be friends with lots of people, to be physically active, and to enjoy material rewards and mental activities.

In June 1959 the situation was about the same. He went to visit his second wife every Sunday afternoon. In response to the story question about Jones, he said that Jones would do as he pleased.

In January 1960, in response to a question about what he considered his life's work, he, of course, said that he had been a minister, but hastened to add that the interviewer should not put down any denomination because he was very liberal and considered himself a minister to all mankind. He said he was still satisfied at age ninety because he could still read. He never wanted to be a burden on anyone.

He was seen by the clinical psychologist in July 1960, who wrote only a brief note and indicated that he considered the respondent "quite senile." The respondent still mentioned his second wife being in a nursing home, but the clinical psychologist had checked and found that the wife had died a year ago. The respondent had not remembered about the appointment and was quite hostile. He could not remember anything about the previous interviews. The psychologist also noticed an old paralyzed dog living with the respondent.

In June 1961, an observer interviewed the respondent's son, who was a high-leved businessman in Kansas City. The son said his father had aged tremendously in the last year. However, his father still adamantly lived by himself. He said his father's memory was gone and that he did not want visitors. He had become a recluse, waiting to die. The son thought the death of the respondent's wife had affected him. The observer saw the respondent in July 1961 and found that he was still caring for himself and going to the store once or twice a week. He did his own cooking and cleaning, that is, what little of it was done.

In January 1962, the interviewer found him paying his paper boy. He wanted to reminisce about his days at various universities he had attended. He had a spry walk. He was quite alert at times and somewhat rambling at others. He gave the exact date of his wife's death. He said his son did not want him to go out. He had a cleaning lady once in a while, and he mentioned several means of income. He was still reading and listening to the radio, which had been broken in the summer of 1960 when the clinical psychologist had seen him. He said the family visited him on Sunday evening. He enjoyed reading more than anything else. Of himself, he said, "I am slipping, and am less able to get around and think straight, but I still see well and read well." The previous year he had helped to preach two funerals but felt that he was "not up to it" now. It was only after four o'clock in the afternoon when he felt like doing anything. His son called him nearly every day. He still saw friends occasionally and got mail from all over the United States. He said he had always tried to be fair to everybody. He described himself as feeling old and helpless. He said as a young man he always had his suits tailor-made and had the reputation of being very well dressed. He remembered his first wife well and how old she was when she died. The interviewer rated him 95 per cent on morale.

This man apparently became "senile" at age ninety, but was still going strong and showed no outward signs of senility at ninety-two. He was living as fully as physically possible at the time of the last interview. We do not have enough evidence to know what his clinical condition actually was. It is known that senility sometimes goes in waves. His action system was remarkably persistent. He has been rated 1 on all of the uses of action energy.

157. *No Aging—Female, Age 85.*

158. *When the Saints—Female, Age 86.* This widowed woman had had a full life of pioneering, raising her family, and participating in her church, the Latter Day Saints. She approached the closing of her life with calm, mature acceptance. She did as much as she could for her children but accepted her increasing disability with grace. She was at the top of the autonomous-persistent group and was rated 2 in style because of her growing limitations. She was 2 in anomie and 1 in all other ratings.

Autonomous-Persistent (Middle)

159. *Slow and Easy—Male, Age 63.*

160. *A Tangled Web—Female, Age 56.* This divorced woman had

been born in Europe and lived as a resident manager of an apartment hotel owned by her family. She had been married once but did not care to be again. Nevertheless, she led a full life and enjoyed the contacts she made through her work. She was in the middle of the autonomous-persistent group. Her style was 3, with World of Work underlying. She rated 2 in anomie and alienation and 1 in isolation and coping.

161. *My Lives Have Fallen in Pleasant Places—Female, Age 77.* This woman had divorced her husband forty years ago, after fifteen years of marriage and two children. The rest of her life was spent as an aggressively successful businesswoman, good citizen, and church leader. She found retirement to the role of grandmother a bit irksome but enjoyed the family's closeness, and was branching out into activities in her new setting. Because her style of life was Living Fully—a bridging style into the World of Work and Familism, which were both underpinning styles weakly held, she had sufficient action energy to try to make a new life for herself when she moved, on retirement, to live in a new city with her daughter and family.

Unfortunately, she was accustomed to being an acknowledged leader and the role of interfering newcomer was hard for her to accept when she realized that was how many of her new acquaintances viewed her. This threatened her system noticeably and accounts for the rating of 3 on style and a 2 on anomie. Nevertheless, she was judged 1 on alienation, isolation, and coping. The latter was justified by her recognition of her situation and her attempts to handle it maturely—even by changing style to a more pure Familism, if necessary.

162. *Well Integrated—Female, Age 80.* This woman was widowed in 1943. She lived in a hotel run by her daughter and son-in-law, and worked as a desk clerk there. She belonged to two clubs at the beginning of the study, and six at the end. She went out as she could, watched some television, did a good deal of reading, and worked crossword puzzles. She got along well with the daughter (who was not an easy person) and son-in-law. She had a heart attack about midway in the study but recovered and adjusted well to it. She gave things up as necessary; for example, she gave up concerts due to loss of hearing, and wore a hearing aid. She was in the middle of her success category and rated 1 in all but style. This was a 2 because of her increasing limitations.

Autonomous-Persistent (Bottom)

163. *Thoroughly Disengaged—Female, Age 91.*

Autonomous-Precarious (Top)

164. *Disengaging Under Protest—Female, Age 75.*

Autonomous-Precarious (Middle)

165. *Don't Want to Age—Female, Age 62.*

166. *Pollyanna—Female, Age 62.* For most of their thirty-year marriage, this telephone operator and her husband had maintained separate apartments in separate cities during the work week, because of the job advantages. The marriage had been marked by many battles, and she deeply resented his refusal to have children, but publicly she claimed to be his happy, devoted slave. At fifty-seven she retired and moved in with her husband. She was beset with anxieties over her sex life and compensated by overeating that started her putting on weight at an alarming rate.

Now that she had time on her hands, she was on the go constantly with civic, social, and religious activities. Her constant proclamations about how happy she was were beginning to sound false, and her facade was moving toward eventual collapse. Her style was 2 with an underlying style of Couplehood. She was in the middle of the autonomous-precarious group and rated 1 on isolation, 3 on anomie, and 2 on alienation and coping.

167. *No Nonsense—Female, Age 77.*

Autonomous-Precarious (Bottom) No cases.

Dependent-Persistent (Top, Middle, Bottom) No cases.

Dependent-Precarious (Top)

168. *Doctor's Widow—Female, Age 78.*

Dependent-Precarious (Middle, Bottom) No cases.

INDEX

❦

INDEX OF CASE HISTORIES

❧